A National Football League Book

NFL Properties, Inc., Creative Services Division, 10880 Wilshire Boulevard, Los Angeles, California 90024

First Printing, July 1985

Printed in the United States of America

PHOTOGRAPHY

Tom Albert 207; Bob Allen 197; Bill Amatucci 87; David Boss 97, 227; Jim Chaffin 77; Thomas J. Croke 37; Timothy Culek 57; Jay Dickman 147; Miguel Elliot 217; Malcolm Emmons 177; Nate Fine 187; Nancy Hogue 67, 267; Ed. Mahan 167; Vic Milton 237, 257; Bill Mount 127; George Robarge 277; Ron Ross 17, 27; Manny Rubio 247; Mark Sherengo 117; Robert L. Smith 7; Corky Trewin 137; Jim Turner 47, 157; Hank Young 107.

Trades, retirements, and veterans' rosters are accurate as of June 10, 1985.

CONTENTS

1985 NFL SCHEDULE

(All times local. CBS and NBC television doubleheader games to be announced.)

1985 REGULAR SEASON
FIRST WEEK
Sunday, September 8 (NBC-TV doubleheader)
1. Denver at L.A. Rams 1:00
2. Detroit at Atlanta 1:00
3. Green Bay at New England 1:00
4. Indianapolis at Pittsburgh 1:00
5. Kansas City 12:00
6. Miami at Houston 12:00
7. N.Y. Jets at L.A. Raiders 1:00
8. Philadelphia at N.Y. Giants 1:00
9. St. Louis at Cleveland 1:00
10. San Diego at Buffalo 4:00
11. San Francisco at Minnesota 12:00
12. Seattle at Cincinnati 1:00
13. Tampa Bay at Chicago 12:00
Monday, September 9
14. Washington at Dallas . . . . (ABC) 8:00
SECOND WEEK
Thursday, September 12
15. L.A. Raiders at Kansas City . . . (ABC) 7:00
Sunday, September 15 (CBS-TV doubleheader)
16. Atlanta at San Francisco 1:00
17. Buffalo at N.Y. Jets 1:00
18. Cincinnati at St. Louis 12:00
19. Dallas at Detroit 1:00
20. Houston at Washington 1:00
21. Indianapolis at Miami 1:00
22. L.A. Rams at Philadelphia 1:00
23. Minnesota at Tampa Bay 4:00
24. New England at Chicago 12:00
25. New Orleans at Denver 2:00
26. N.Y. Giants at Green Bay 3:00
27. Seattle at San Diego 1:00
Monday, September 16
28. Pittsburgh at Cleveland . . . . . (ABC) 9:00
THIRD WEEK
Thursday, September 19
29. Chicago at Minnesota . . . . . . (ABC) 7:00
Sunday, September 22 (CBS-TV doubleheader)
30. Cleveland at Dallas 12:00
31. Denver at Atlanta 1:00
32. Detroit at Indianapolis 12:00
33. Houston at Pittsburgh 1:00
34. Kansas City at Miami 4:00
35. New England at Buffalo 1:00
36. N.Y. Jets vs. Green Bay at Milw. 3:00
37. Philadelphia at Washington 1:00
38. St. Louis at N.Y. Giants 1:00
39. San Diego at Cincinnati 1:00
40. San Francisco at L.A. Raiders 1:00
41. Tampa Bay at New Orleans 12:00
Monday, September 23
42. L.A. Rams at Seattle . . . . (ABC) 6:00

FOURTH WEEK
Sunday, September 29 (NBC-TV doubleheader)
43. Atlanta at Los Angles Rams 1:00
44. Cleveland at San Diego 1:00
45. Dallas at Houston 12:00
46. Green Bay at St. Louis 12:00
47. Indianapolis at N.Y. Jets 4:00
48. L.A. Raiders at New England 1:00
49. Miami at Denver 2:00
50. Minnesota at Buffalo 1:00
51. New Orleans at San Francisco 1:00
52. N.Y. Giants at Philadelphia 1:00
53. Seattle at Kansas City 12:00
54. Tampa Bay at Detroit 1:00
55. Washington at Chicago 12:00
Monday, September 30
56. Cincinnati at Pittsburgh . . . . . (ABC) 9:00
FIFTH WEEK
Sunday, October 6 (NBC-TV doubleheader)
57. Buffalo at Indianapolis 12:00
58. Chicago at Tampa Bay 1:00
59. Dallas at N.Y. Giants . . . . (ABC) 9:00
60. Detroit at Green Bay 12:00
61. Houston at Denver 2:00
62. Kansas City at L.A. Raiders 1:00
63. Minnesota at L.A. Rams 1:00
64. New England at Cleveland 1:00
65. New York Jets at Cincinnati 4:00
66. Philadelphia at New Orleans 12:00
67. Pittsburgh at Miami 1:00
68. San Diego at Seattle 1:00
69. San Francisco at Atlanta 1:00
Monday, October 7
70. St. Louis at Washington . . . . . (ABC) 9:00
SIXTH WEEK
Sunday, October 13 (CBS-TV doubleheader)
71. Atlanta at Seattle 1:00
72. Buffalo at New England 1:00
73. Chicago at San Francisco 1:00
74. Cleveland at Houston 12:00
75. Denver at Indianapolis 12:00
76. Detroit at Washington 1:00
77. Kansas City at San Diego 1:00
78. L.A. Rams at Tampa Bay 1:00
79. Minnesota vs. Green Bay at Milw. . . . 12:00
80. New Orleans at L.A. Raiders 1:00
81. N.Y. Giants at Cincinnati 1:00
82. Philadelphia at St. Louis 12:00
83. Pittsburgh at Dallas 12:00
Monday, October 14
84. Miami at N.Y. Jets . . . . (ABC) 9:00
SEVENTH WEEK
Sunday, October 20 (NBC-TV doubleheader)
85. Cincinnati at Houston 12:00

1985 NFL SCHEDULE

86.	Dallas at Philadelphia	1:00
87.	Indianapolis at Buffalo	1:00
88.	L.A. Raiders at Cleveland	1:00
89.	L.A. Rams at Kansas City	12:00
90.	New Orleans at Atlanta	1:00
91.	N.Y. Jets at New England	4:00
92.	St. Louis at Pittsburgh	1:00
93.	San Diego at Minnesota	12:00
94.	San Francisco at Detroit	1:00
95.	Seattle at Denver	2:00
96.	Tampa Bay at Miami	4:00
97.	Washington at N.Y. Giants	1:00

Monday, October 21

98.	Green Bay at Chicago	(ABC)	8:00

EIGHTH WEEK

Sunday, October 27 (CBS-TV doubleheader)

99.	Atlanta at Dallas	12:00
100.	Buffalo at Philadelphia	1:00
101.	Denver at Kansas City	12:00
102.	Green Bay at Indianapolis	1:00
103.	Houston at St. Louis	12:00
104.	Miami at Detroit	1:00
105.	Minnesota at Chicago	12:00
106.	New England at Tampa Bay	1:00
107.	N.Y. Giants at New Orleans	3:00
108.	Pittsburgh at Cincinnati	4:00
109.	San Francisco at L.A. Rams	1:00
110.	Seattle at N.Y. Jets	1:00
111.	Washington at Cleveland	1:00

Monday, October 28

112.	San Diego at L.A. Raiders	(ABC)	6:00

NINTH WEEK

Sunday, November 3 (NBC-TV doubleheader)

113.	Chicago at Green Bay	12:00
114.	Cincinnati at Buffalo	1:00
115.	Cleveland at Pittsburgh	1:00
116.	Denver at San Diego	1:00
117.	Detroit at Minnesota	12:00
118.	Kansas City at Houston	12:00
119.	L.A. Raiders at Seattle	1:00
120.	Miami at New England	1:00
121.	New Orleans at L.A. Rams	1:00
122.	N.Y. Jets at Indianapolis	4:00
123.	Philadelphia at San Francisco	1:00
124.	Tampa Bay at N.Y. Giants	1:00
125.	Washington at Atlanta	1:00

Monday, November 4

126.	Dallas at St. Louis	(ABC)	8:00

TENTH WEEK

Sunday, November 10 (CBS-TV doubleheader)

127.	Atlanta at Philadelphia	1:00
128.	Cleveland at Cincinnati	1:00
129.	Dallas at Washington	4:00
130.	Detroit at Chicago	12:00
131.	Green Bay at Minnesota	12:00
132.	Houston at Buffalo	1:00
133.	Indianapolis at New England	1:00
134.	L.A. Raiders at San Diego	1:00
135.	L.A. Rams at N.Y. Giants	1:00
136.	N.Y. Jets at Miami	4:00

137.	Pittsburgh at Kansas City	12:00
138.	St. Louis at Tampa Bay	1:00
139.	Seattle at New Orleans	12:00

Monday, November 11

140.	San Francisco at Denver	(ABC)	7:00

ELEVENTH WEEK

Sunday, November 17 (NBC-TV doubleheader)

141.	Buffalo at Cleveland	1:00
142.	Chicago at Dallas	12:00
143.	Cincinnati at L.A. Rams	1:00
144.	Kansas City at San Francisco	1:00
145.	L.A. Rams at Atlanta	1:00
146.	Miami at Indianapolis	1:00
147.	Minnesota at Detroit	4:00
148.	New England at Seattle	1:00
149.	New Orleans vs. Green Bay at Milw.	12:00
150.	Pittsburgh at Houston	12:00
151.	St. Louis at Philadelphia	1:00
152.	San Diego at Denver	2:00
153.	Tampa Bay at N.Y. Jets	1:00

Monday, November 18

154.	N.Y. Giants at Washington	(ABC)	9:00

TWELFTH WEEK

Sunday, November 24 (CBS-TV doubleheader)

155.	Atlanta at Chicago	12:00
156.	Cincinnati at Cleveland	1:00
157.	Denver at L.A. Raiders	1:00
158.	Detroit at Tampa Bay	1:00
159.	Green Bay at L.A. Rams	1:00
160.	Indianapolis at Kansas City	3:00
161.	Miami at Buffalo	1:00
162.	New England at N.Y. Jets	1:00
163.	New Orleans at Minnesota	12:00
164.	N.Y. Giants at St. Louis	3:00
165.	Philadelphia at Dallas	3:00
166.	San Diego at Houston	12:00
167.	Washington at Pittsburgh	1:00

Monday, November 25

168.	Seattle at San Francisco	(ABC)	6:00

THIRTEENTH WEEK

Thursday, November 28 (Thanksgiving Day)

169.	N.Y. Jets at Detroit	(NBC)	12:30
170.	St. Louis at Dallas	(CBS)	3:00

Sunday, December 1 (CBS-TV doubleheader)

171.	Buffalo at San Diego	1:00
172.	Cleveland at N.Y. Giants	1:00
173.	Denver at Pittsburgh	1:00
174.	Houston at Cincinnati	1:00
175.	Kansas City at Seattle	1:00
176.	L.A. Raiders at Atlanta	4:00
177.	L.A. Rams at New Orleans	12:00
178.	Minnesota at Philadelphia	1:00
179.	New England at Indianapolis	1:00
180.	San Francisco at Washington	4:00
181.	Tampa Bay at Green Bay	12:00

Monday, December 2

182.	Chicago at Miami	(ABC)	9:00

FOURTEENTH WEEK

Sunday, December 8 (NBC-TV doubleheader)

183.	Atlanta at Kansas City	12:00

184.	Cleveland at Seattle		1:00
185.	Dallas at Cincinnati		1:00
186.	Detroit at New England		1:00
187.	Indianapolis at Chicago		12:00
188.	L.A. Raiders at Denver		2:00
189.	Miami at Green Bay		12:00
190.	New Orleans at St. Louis		12:00
191.	N.Y. Giants at Houston		3:00
192.	N.Y. Jets at Buffalo		1:00
193.	Pittsburgh at San Diego	(ABC)	6:00
194.	Tampa Bay at Minnesota		3:00
195.	Washington at Philadelphia		1:00

Monday, December 9

| 196. | L.A. Rams at San Francisco | (ABC) | 6:00 |

FIFTEENTH WEEK
Saturday, December 14

| 197. | Chicago at N.Y. Jets | (CBS) | 12:30 |
| 198. | Kansas City at Denver | (NBC) | 2:00 |

Sunday, December 15 (NBC-TV doubleheader)

199.	Buffalo at Pittsburgh		1:00
200.	Cincinnati at Washington		1:00
201.	Green Bay at Detroit		1:00
202.	Houston at Cleveland		1:00
203.	Indianapolis at Tampa Bay		1:00
204.	Minnesota at Atlanta		1:00
205.	N.Y. Giants at Dallas		12:00
206.	Philadelphia at San Diego		1:00
207.	St. Louis at L.A. Rams		1:00
208.	San Francisco at New Orleans		12:00
209.	Seattle at L.A. Raiders		1:00

Monday, December 16

| 210. | New England at Miami | (ABC) | 9:00 |

SIXTEENTH WEEK
Friday, December 20

| 211. | Denver at Seattle | (ABC) | 5:00 |

Saturday, December 21

| 212. | Pittsburgh at N.Y. Giants | (NBC) | 12:00 |
| 213. | Washington at St. Louis | (CBS) | 3:00 |

Sunday, December 22 (CBS-TV doubleheader)

214.	Atlanta at New Orleans		12:00
215.	Buffalo at Miami		1:00
216.	Chicago at Detroit		1:00
217.	Cincinnati at New England		1:00
218.	Cleveland at N.Y. Jets		1:00
219.	Dallas at San Francisco		1:00
220.	Green Bay at Tampa Bay		1:00
221.	Houston at Indianapolis		4:00
222.	Philadelphia at Minnesota		12:00
223.	San Diego at Kansas City		12:00

Monday, December 23

| 224. | L.A. Raiders at L.A. Rams | (ABC) | 6:00 |

POSTSEASON GAMES

Saturday, December 29 . . . . . . AFC and NFC First
Round Playoffs (NBC and CBS)
Saturday, January 4 . . . . . AFC and NFC Divisional
Playoffs (NBC and ABC)
Sunday, January 5 . . . . . . AFC and NFC Divisional
Playoffs (NBC and CBS)
Sunday, January 12 . AFC and NFC Championship
Games (NBC and CBS)
Sunday, January 26 . . . Super Bowl XX at Louisiana
Superdome, New Orleans, Louisiana (NBC)
Sunday, February 2 . . . . AFC-NFC Pro Bowl
Honolulu, Hawaii (ABC)

Nationally Televised Games

(All games carried on NBC Network Radio.)

Regular Season

Monday, September 9 . . . . . Washington at Dallas
(night, ABC)
Thursday, September 12 . . . . L.A. Raiders at
Kansas City (night, ABC)
Monday, September 16 . . . . Pittsburgh at Cleveland
(night, ABC)
Thursday, September 19 . . . . Chicago at Minnesota
(night, ABC)
Monday, September 23 . . . . . . L.A. Rams at Seattle
(night, ABC)
Monday, September 30 . . . Cincinnati at Pittsburgh
(night, ABC)
Sunday, October 6 . . . . Dallas at N.Y. Giants
(night, ABC)
Monday, October 7 . . . . . . St. Louis at Washington
(night, ABC)
Monday, October 14 . . . . Miami at N.Y. Jets
(night, ABC)
Monday, October 21 . . . . Green Bay at Chicago
(night, ABC)
Monday, October 28 . . . . San Diego at L.A. Raiders
(night, ABC)
Monday, November 4 . . . . Dallas at St. Louis
(night, ABC)
Monday, November 11. . . . San Francisco at Denver
(night, ABC)
Monday, November 18 . . N.Y. Giants at Washington
(night, ABC)
Monday, November 25. . . . Seattle at San Francisco
(night, ABC)
Thursday, November 28. . . (Thanksgiving) N.Y. Jets
at Detroit (day, NBC)
St. Louis at Dallas (day, CBS)
Monday, December 2. . . . . Chicago at Miami
(night, ABC)
Sunday, December 8 . . . . . Pittsburgh at San Diego
(night, ABC)
Monday, December 9 . . L.A. Rams at San Francisco
(night, ABC)
Saturday, December 14 . . . . . . Chicago at N.Y. Jets
(day, CBS)
Kansas City at Denver (day, NBC)
Monday, December 16 . . . . . New England at Miami
(night, ABC)
Friday, December 20 Denver at Seattle (night, ABC)
Saturday, December 21 . . . Pittsburgh at N.Y. Giants
(day, NBC)
Washington at St. Louis (day, CBS)
Monday, December 23 . . . . L.A. Raiders at
L.A. Rams (night, ABC)

AMERICAN FOOTBALL CONFERENCE
EAST: Ron Borges
CENTRAL: Dale Robertson
WEST: Rick Gosselin

BUFFALO BILLS

The Bills were 8-8 in 1983, and under the impression that things were beginning to turn around in Buffalo. Then came 1984.

"I never thought anything like this could happen," fullback Booker Moore said.

For the Bills to have started any slower last fall they would have had to stay locked up in their training camp. Buffalo lost its first 11 games before upsetting the Dallas Cowboys, but not even that win could do much to salve the wounds of their twenty-fifth anniversary year.

Buffalo finished 2-14, the most losses in the club's history. One of the good things to come out of the season was that the team was awarded the number-one pick in this spring's college draft.

Even that has been a double-edged sword for the Bills the past few years. One need only recall 1979 when they had the top pick and selected Ohio State's All-America linebacker Tom Cousineau, who declined the invitation and headed for Canada. Two years later they made Moore their top choice and he was hit with a debilitating illness that cost him an entire season.

Running back Greg Bell was AFC's rookie of the year.

Kay Stephenson

Then there was 1983, when the Bills thought they had solved their growing quarterback problem by drafting Miami's Jim Kelly. Kelly was within five minutes of signing when his agent, Greg Lustig, was told that he had a phone call waiting. Lustig went into another office and when he came back out, Kelly was on his way to the USFL.

Since each of these unhappy occurrences came in an odd-numbered year one can see why Bills fans were not all that elated about having suffered through the oddest of seasons only to be handed the draft's top choice in 1985.

But things seem to be changing for the better. Buffalo announced it was after consensus All-America defensive end Bruce Smith and, immediately, Smith's agent began talking about the USFL. But this time Bills' owner Ralph Wilson would have none of that, and the Bills moved up at least one grade in the pass-rushing department by signing the Virginia Tech All-America to a four-year contract.

The Bills managed to turn around one jinx. Now, if they can do something similar to their record....

OFFENSE

Looking at the Bills' offense in 1984 was simple because all you had to do was watch rookie running back Greg Bell. He was a surprising number-one choice a year ago after an oft-injured career at Notre Dame. Basically, he had spent much of his career in the trainer's room because of an assortment of injuries—a broken leg, ankle sprains, and tendinitis.

But Bell arrived in Buffalo intent on proving he belonged in the NFL, and, after rushing for 1,100 yards and seven touchdowns while finishing second in receptions with 34, he proved his point. He played in the 1985 Pro Bowl as an alternate.

Those figures become more amazing when one realizes he gained just 77 yards on the ground in the season's first four games. Once he got going, Bell gained 1,023 in the final 12 games.

"Obviously, we were very happy with Greg, but we know we have to get more people involved in the running game," coach Kay Stephenson said.

Stephenson probably would get no quarrel from Bell on that point. He carried 262 times; the team's next-leading rusher handled the ball just 49 times. But even with the absence of a supporting cast around Bell, the running game hardly was the cause of Buffalo's offensive problems.

The Bills ended the year twenty-seventh in the NFL in total offense and twenty-fifth in points scored with 250. But the cause of such woes was a passing game that dissolved when Jerry Butler was injured, Frank Lewis retired, and 12-year veteran quarterback Joe Ferguson was benched for the first time in his career because of nagging injuries and a fall-off in performance.

So, the Bills ended their association with Ferguson, trading him to the Detroit Lions on draft day for future draft choices.

Buffalo quarterbacks were sacked 60 times. Only four teams allowed more. Not good news for Joe Dufek, who moves into the number-one spot.

Dufek threw 150 passes last year, completing 74 for 829 yards and 4 touchdowns. He also threw eight interceptions. Matt Kofler (33 of 93 for 432 yards, 2 touchdowns, 5 interceptions), moves up to number two.

"We're trying to get done as much as we possibly can as quickly as we can," Stephenson says. "But we're going to need every minute before the first kickoff to do it. We're going to have a lot of fresh thinking. In our situation it was impossible to stand still."

Steve Freeman

Jim Haslett

Eugene Marve

The Bills will be hoping Butler's battered knee will stand up well enough to get him back to the form he showed three years ago. If he cannot come back, Buffalo must find someone else.

That someone could turn out to be fleet Mitchell Brookins, a fourth-round draft choice a year ago who caught 18 passes for 318 yards, a 17.7-yard average. Brookins has the kind of speed Butler used to have, and he combined neatly with Byron Franklin, whose 69 receptions came within one of the club record. There's also Preston Dennard, the former Rams receiver.

Franklin is a possession receiver who averaged 12.5 yards per catch. If he can be complemented by both Butler and Brookins, the Bills' passing game would improve markedly.

Tight end Tony Hunter, like Bell, a short-yardage receiver, was third on the club in receptions with 33.

If the Bills' line can't protect the quarterback better than it did last year, these questions of who's catching and who's throwing will be moot.

In that regard, Stephenson hired Hall of Fame center Jim Ringo to handle the Bills' line. Ringo was Buffalo's head coach (1976-1977) during the waning days of O. J. Simpson and the Electric Company, the group that produced the first 2,000-yard rushing season in NFL history. (Simpson's 2,003 in 1973). Ringo's goal is to cut the sack total in half. He is willing to make changes wherever necessary.

Right now the player in the greatest danger is center Will Grant, who will be pressed hard by Tim Vogler.

Guards Jim Ritcher and Jon Borchardt, and tackles Ken Jones and Joe Devlin are not likely to be challenged, unless Justin Cross is given a second shot at one of the tackle positions.

If Dufek can get a passing game going, and Bell can duplicate his rookie season, the Bills could cause some problems.

DEFENSE

Buffalo's pass rush produced just 26 sacks, which was next-to-last in the league, and allowed nearly twice as many points as the offense scored (454 to 250).

But there is talk of changes for the better, with the ad-

Three Years at a Glance

Averages NFL Rank	OFFENSE			DEFENSE		
	1984	1983	1982	1984	1983	1982
Points	**15.6**	**17.7**	**16.7**	**28.4**	**21.9**	**17.1**
Rank	25T	23	19	27	18	6
Yards	**271.3**	**301.4**	**325.2**	**348.9**	**363.1**	**259.3**
Rank	27	25	11	23	24	2
Rushing Yards	**102.7**	**108.5**	**152.3**	**131.6**	**156.4**	**114.9**
Rank	26	24	1	19	24	16
Passing Yards	**168.6**	**192.9**	**172.9**	**217.3**	**206.6**	**144.4**
Rank	25	18	20	19	18	2
Sacks	**3.8**	**2.3**	**1.3**	**1.6**	**2.0**	**1.3**
Rank	23T	8T	3T	27	24T	27
Turnovers	**2.8**	**2.5**	**2.9**	**2.3**	**1.9**	**2.3**
Rank	28	17	23T	11	24T	17T
Punt Returns	**9.0**	**5.5**	**4.6**	**11.5**	**9.6**	**3.0**
Rank	9	28	28	27	21	1
Kickoff Returns	**18.7**	**21.3**	**22.0**	**21.8**	**17.9**	**17.8**
Rank	23	4	3	25	4	4
Penalty Yards	**62.3**	**68.4**	**64.7**	**45.9**	**81.1**	**43.9**
Rank	23	28	26	23	1	23

	W-L Total	Home	Road	Playoffs
1982	4-5	4-1	0-4	None
1983	8-8	3-5	5-3	None
1984	2-14	2-6	0-8	None

dition of Smith and defensive coordinator Hank Bullough giving this unit cause for renewed optimism.

"All the players are looking forward to this year," linebacker Jim Haslett said. "We know we're a better team than we showed. With the addition of Bruce Smith, I think our seven guys up front can be as good as any in the NFL. And with the scheme we have on defense now I think we can be one of the best defenses."

Haslett is a positive thinker, and with Smith, nose tackle Fred Smerlas, and defensive end Ben Williams, Buffalo does have the foundation for a solid pass rush.

"Smith is the kind of player who can come right in and have an impact," Stephenson said. "He's a unique athlete for his position because of his hand and foot speed. They don't come along often with the ability he has to move his feet and hands."

Smerlas remains a dominant nose tackle, and Williams is one of the most underrated pass rushers in the game. Add Haslett, Eugene Marve, and Darryl Talley, and Buffalo has three of the four linebackers it needs to form that seven-man front Haslett is talking about.

Bullough probably will turn his eye first to the secondary, where left cornerback remains a problem and safety is weak at best.

Charlie Romes is the most stable player in the secondary but there is great uncertainty at the other cornerback position. Rookie Rodney Bellinger had his moments, but he is one of those small, fast, sometimes overzealous types who can hurt more than he helps if he isn't careful. But even with his weaknesses, Bellinger is the best available man for the job, unless first-round choice Derrick Burroughs can come on.

Veteran Steve Freeman is likely to return at strong safety, while Donald Wilson will be trying to knock out a few more receivers this season from the free-safety spot if he can knock back the challenge of oft-injured veteran Rod Kush first.

Wilson was the surprise of 1984. Signed as a free agent out of North Carolina State, he started 11 games, was the fourth-leading tackler with 93, and averaged 16.9 yards per kickoff return and nine yards per punt return.

Jim Richter   *Fred Smerlas*   *Donald Wilson*

Bullough is cautious about an instant turnaround.

"My whole thing is to help build a good, solid foundation," Bullough said. "I'm not a quick-shot guy. I'm not a quick-fix guy. I'm just a guy who likes to see progress.

"We are going to have to replace some people, but in this profession you're not trying to replace—for example—a Fred Smerlas. We have to replace the guys at the bottom, the back-up player, and let the new ones work their way to the top."

SPECIAL TEAMS

Buffalo went through two kickers last season, a sign that no placekicker has any sure footing at the moment. Unless someone unexpected emerges, it appears likely that Chuck Nelson will win the position.

Nelson came in at the expense of Joe Danelo, who wore out his welcome by hitting only one of his seven field-goal attempts from 40 yards or longer. Nelson ended up converting three of his five kicks (including two of three beyond 40 yards). Rookie punter John Kidd started quickly, but the fire went out late in the year. He averaged 42 yards gross on 88 kicks. Still, Kidd's average was the best by a Bills punter since 1976, which is enough to earn a second chance.

Buffalo had two of the best return men in football, perhaps in part because with 12 rookies on the team there was no dearth of enthusiasm on special teams. Wilson was the only player to return a punt all season, bringing back 33 for a 9-yard average.

Wilson and Van Williams split the kick-return duties, with Williams taking 39 back for 820 yards, an average of 21 yards a crack. Wilson handled 34 kicks for a 16.9-yard average.

VETERAN ROSTER

No.	Name	Pos.	Ht.	Wt.	NFL Exp.	Birthdate	College	Games in 1984
75	Acker, Bill	NT	6-3	255	6	11/7/56	Texas	15
50	Azelby, Joe	LB	6-1	225	2	3/5/62	Harvard	14
84	Barnett, Buster	TE	6-5	235	5	11/24/58	Jackson State	16
43	Bayless, Martin	S	6-2	195	2	10/11/62	Bowling Green	13
28	Bell, Greg	RB	5-10	210	2	8/1/62	Notre Dame	16
36	Bellinger, Rodney	CB	5-8	181	2	6/4/62	Miami	10
73	Borchardt, Jon	G	6-5	255	7	8/13/57	Montana State	16
86	Brammer, Mark	TE	6-3	235	6	5/3/58	Michigan State	12
81	Brookins, Mitchell	WR	5-11	196	2	12/10/60	Illinois	16
80	Butler, Jerry	WR	6-0	178	6	10/12/57	Clemson	0
30	Carpenter, Brian	CB	5-10	170	4	11/27/60	Michigan	13
63	Cross, Justin	T	6-6	265	4	4/29/59	Western State, Colo.	7
59	David, Stan	LB	6-3	210	2	2/17/62	Texas Tech	16
89	Dawkins, Julius	WR	6-1	196	3	1/4/61	Pittsburgh	16
83	Dennard, Preston	WR	6-1	183	8	11/28/55	New Mexico	16
70	Devlin, Joe	T	6-5	250	9	2/23/54	Iowa	16
19	Dufek, Joe	QB	6-4	215	3	8/23/61	Yale	5
85	Franklin, Byron	WR	6-1	185	4	9/4/58	Auburn	16
22	Freeman, Steve	S	5-11	185	11	5/8/53	Mississippi State	15
53	Grant, Will	C	6-3	255	8	3/7/54	Kentucky	16
55	Haslett, Jim	LB	6-3	232	7	12/9/56	Indiana, Pa.	15
25	Hill, Rod	CB	6-0	188	3	3/14/59	Kentucky State	2
87	Hunter, Tony	TE	6-4	237	3	5/22/60	Notre Dame	11
91	Johnson, Ken	DE	6-5	253	7	3/25/55	Knoxville College	16
48	Johnson, Lawrence	CB	5-11	204	6	9/11/57	Wisconsin	10
72	Jones, Ken	T	6-5	260	10	12/1/52	Arkansas State	16
52	Keating, Chris	LB	6-2	233	7	10/12/57	Maine	16
4	Kidd, John	P	6-3	201	2	8/22/61	Northwestern	16
10	Kofler, Matt	QB	6-3	192	4	8/30/59	San Diego State	16
42	Kush, Rod	S	6-0	188	6	1/31/53	Nebraska-Omaha	16
61	Lynch, Tom	G	6-5	250	9	5/24/55	Boston College	16
54	Marve, Eugene	LB	6-2	230	4	8/14/60	Saginaw Valley State	16
95	McNanie, Sean	DE	6-5	252	2	9/9/61	San Diego State	15
34	Moore, Booker	FB	5-11	224	4	6/23/59	Penn State	15
88	Mosley, Mike	WR	6-1	186	4	6/30/58	Texas A&M	4
41	Neal, Speedy	FB	6-2	254	2	8/26/62	Miami	12
13	Nelson, Chuck	K	5-11	175	3	2/23/60	Washington	7
38	Nixon, Jeff	S	6-3	190	5	10/13/56	Richmond	0
49	Norris, Ulysses	TE	6-4	232	7	1/15/57	Georgia	14
58	Potter, Steve	LB	6-3	235	5	11/6/57	Virginia	10
79	Prater, Dean	DE	6-4	245	4	9/28/58	Oklahoma State	13
40	Riddick, Robb	RB	6-0	195	4	4/26/57	Millersville State	16
51	Ritcher, Jim	G	6-3	251	6	5/21/58	North Carolina State	14
26	Romes, Charles	CB	6-1	190	9	12/16/54	North Carolina Central	16
57	Sanford, Lucius	LB	6-2	216	8	2/14/56	Georgia Tech	8
76	Smerlas, Fred	NT	6-3	270	7	4/8/57	Boston College	16
56	Talley, Darryl	LB	6-4	235	3	7/10/60	West Virginia	16
	Taylor, Roger	T	6-6	275	2	1/5/58	Oklahoma State	0
65	Vogler, Tim	C	6-3	245	7	10/2/56	Ohio State	16
60	Wenglikowski, Al	LB	6-1	220	2	8/3/60	Pittsburgh	5
27	White, Craig	WR	6-1	194	2	10/8/61	Missouri	14
77	Williams, Ben	DE	6-3	260	10	9/1/54	Mississippi	15
23	Williams, Van	RB	6-0	208	3	3/15/59	Carson-Newman	16
21	Wilson, Donald	S	6-2	190	2	7/21/61	North Carolina State	16

Coaching Staff

Kay Stephenson, head coach; **Art Asselta,** tight ends; **Hank Bullough,** assistant head coach, defensive coordinator; **Kay Dalton,** quarterbacks; **Monte Kiffin,** linebackers; **Bob Leahy,** receivers; **Dick Moseley,** defensive backs; **Elijah Pitts,** running backs; **Jim Ringo,** offensive coordinator, offensive line; **Jim Speros,** strength and conditioning; **Ardel Wiegandt,** defensive line.

1985 Schedule

Preseason

Aug. 9	at Detroit	8:00
Aug. 17	at Miami	8:00
Aug. 24	CLEVELAND	6:00
Aug. 31	at Chicago	6:00

Regular Season

Sept. 8	SAN DIEGO	4:00
Sept. 15	at New York Jets	1:00
Sept. 22	NEW ENGLAND	1:00
Sept. 29	MINNESOTA	1:00
Oct. 6	at Indianapolis	12:00
Oct. 13	at New England	1:00
Oct. 20	INDIANAPOLIS	1:00
Oct. 27	at Philadelphia	1:00
Nov. 3	CINCINNATI	1:00
Nov. 10	HOUSTON	1:00
Nov. 17	at Cleveland	1:00
Nov. 24	MIAMI	1:00
Dec. 1	at San Diego	1:00
Dec. 8	N.Y. JETS	1:00
Dec. 15	at Pittsburgh	1:00
Dec. 22	at Miami	1:00

1984 Results

Sept. 2	NEW ENGLAND	17-21
Sept. 9	at St. Louis	7-37
Sept. 17	MIAMI (Mon.)	17-21
Sept. 23	N.Y. JETS	26-28
Sept. 30	at Indianapolis	17-31
Oct. 7	PHILADELPHIA	17-27
Oct. 14	at Seattle	28-31
Oct. 21	DENVER	7-37
Oct. 28	at Miami	7-38
Nov. 4	CLEVELAND	10-13
Nov. 11	at New England	10-38
Nov. 18	DALLAS	14-3
Nov. 25	at Washington	14-41
Dec. 2	INDIANAPOLIS	21-15
Dec. 8	at N.Y. Jets (Sat.)	17-21
Dec. 16	at Cincinnati	21-52

1985 Draft Choices

1. Bruce Smith—1, DE, Virginia Tech
1. Derrick Burroughs—14, DB, Memphis State, from Green Bay
2. Mark Traynowicz—29, T, Nebraska
2. Chris Burkett—42, WR, Jackson State, from Green Bay
3. Frank Reich—57, QB, Maryland
3. Hal Garner—63, LB, Utah State, from Cleveland
4. Andre Reed—86, WR, Kutztown, Pa.
4. Dale Hellestrae—112, T, Southern Methodist, from San Francisco
5. Choice to L.A. Rams
5. Jimmy Teal—130, WR, Texas A&M, from Dallas
6. Mike Hamby—141, DT, Utah State
7. Ron Pitts—169, DB, UCLA
8. Jacque Robinson—197, RB, Washington
9. Glenn Jones—225, DB, Norfolk State
10. Chris Babyar—253, G, Illinois
11. James Seawright—282, LB, South Carolina
12. Choice to Washington
12. Paul Woodside—333, K, West Virginia, from Seattle

INDIANAPOLIS COLTS

The move of the Colts in 1984 left a great gnashing of teeth in Baltimore, their old home, and an outburst of hossanahs in Indianapolis, their new home.

The cheers remained in the Colts' new home, the Hoosier Dome, through the first five games of the season as the Colts won two and lost three games—games in which they scored 30 or more points three times.

Then the Colts finished with a thud—seven losses in the last eight games. Coach Frank Kush quit with one game to play.

As they have been for at least four years now, the problems for the Colts remain offensive. If one has any doubt, examine the statistics. The Colts were last in the league in points scored, last in total yards, and last in passing yards.

But the Colts made a move to rectify that situation by replacing Kush with St. Louis Cardinals offensive coordinator Rod Dowhower, a man who is considered a master of the passing game.

Dowhower studied as an assistant to Don Coryell at San Diego State, Dick Vermeil at UCLA, and Bill Walsh at Stanford.

Last year, Kush rotated his quarterbacks more frequently than some baseball managers rotate their pitching staffs, starting Mike Pagel in nine games, Mark Herrmann in two, and Art Schlichter in five.

If nothing else, Dowhower has made it clear that he will return things to normalcy in this area, with Schlichter and Pagel the candidates to win the starting job. Herrmann was traded to San Diego during the offseason.

"I want Pagel and Schlichter to know that they both

Linebacker Johnie Cooks is a key man in the Colts' defense.

Rod Dowhower

will have a shot at the job and that there is no number one at this point," Dowhower said. "It all depends on how hard they want to work, how they adapt to my plans, and how they take directions. In terms of my philosophy, the players are the focal point. I look at myself as a teacher."

OFFENSE

Dowhower helped build the NFC's leading passing game in St. Louis, where the Cardinals led the conference with an average of 266.1 yards per game. The Colts, meanwhile, have been mired at the bottom of the NFL passing list for two years, which is one of the reasons Dowhower is in Indianapolis.

Dowhower favors throwing to his backs, which should be good news not only to running backs Randy McMillan and Curtis Dickey, but to Schlichter, who seems more adept at the short passing game than the long one.

Accuracy, however, remains a problem for Schlichter, who finished the season completing just 44.3 percent of his 140 attempts for only 702 yards. He threw just three touchdown passes while giving up seven interceptions.

Such numbers are not the kind Dowhower is looking for, but when he looks at Pagel he won't see much difference.

Pagel, who has been the Colts' starter for the past three years, finished with 114 completions in 212 attempts, a 53.8 average. But those throws produced only 1,426 yards and eight touchdowns. Unfortunately, they also produced eight interceptions.

None of those facts will change Dowhower's approach to offensive football.

"I've been with systems where we throw the ball a lot, and that's the type of offense I want here," he said. "I'm prone to the forward pass. I've been brought up that way. They understand how I feel about the job."

What would make Dowhower feel better would be to get more production from his best receiver, Ray Butler, who caught 43 passes last year for 664 yards and six touchdowns.

Butler has the speed to stretch a defense and the hands to catch a football, but injuries and the ineptitude of the Colts' passing game in recent years have hurt him. What Dowhower is hoping is that he can find the key to unlock the Roy Green he hopes is inside Ray Butler.

Joining Butler will be Tracy Porter, who showed potential last season, making 39 catches and averaging 15 yards per reception, and possession receiver Matt Bouza (22 for 270) and tight end Tim Sherwin.

Dowhower's passing game also is likely to get high mileage from his running backs, and he has two potential superstars there in McMillan and Dickey.

McMillan was beaten and battered for most of the second half of 1984, but still led the club in rushing with 705 yards. That was down nearly 100 yards from 1983, so he can do much more in the right situation.

What Dowhower likes most about the powerful running back, however, is that four years ago he caught 50 passes to lead the club, something that may happen again this year even though his numbers fell to just 19 receptions last season.

Dickey also is a tale of two players. In 1983, it seemed he finally had harnessed his sprinter's speed and his mercurial emotions. He rushed for 1,122 yards and averaged 20 yards per catch on his 24 receptions. But he was knocked out in the sixth game of the year against the Washington Redskins. After that, Dickey was ineffective, which explains his falling to just 523 yards rush-

Ray Butler

Nesby Glasgow

Chris Hinton

ing and 14 receptions after averaging 26 catches a year in his first four seasons.

For Dowhower to get all of these players untracked, however, will take continued improvement from an offensive line that is anchored by third-year guard Chris Hinton, who went to the AFC-NFC Pro Bowl in his rookie season. The only problem is that the anchor went down with the ship in the game against the Redskins when Hinton tore up his knee and was lost for the rest of the season.

Hinton is expected to be back in full health. He is joined by one of the conference's best centers in Ray Donaldson and a future star in second-year guard Ron Solt. Tackles Jim Mills and Karl Baldischwiler, who will attempt to come back from a neck injury, round out a group that appears to have potential if no one is injured.

DEFENSE

Depending on what part of the season you believe, the Colts are either young and growing on defense or young and groaning on defense. Early in the year, with defensive end Donnell Thompson on the sidelines in a contract dispute, the Colts were pushed from one end of the field to the other, ranking twenty-seventh in the NFL after 10 weeks.

Through the first 11 games, Indianapolis allowed an average of 382 yards and produced just 15 sacks, but over the final six games, with Thompson in top playing shape and the defense settled down, they held opponents to just 293 yards a game and produced 28 sacks.

Perhaps the best testimony concerning their overall improvement, however, can be given by safety Nesby Glasgow, who for the first time in three years did *not* lead the team in tackles.

Dowhower would like to believe the unit he will be sending out this season is the one that finished up in 1984, and, barring injury, that would seem to be the case, especially if Dowhower's offense produces. One of the Colts' major defensive weaknesses was the fact it often was on the field so long it weakened.

But they are young, talented, very hungry, and solid in all three areas.

Three Years at a Glance

Averages NFL Rank	OFFENSE			DEFENSE		
	1984	1983	1982	1984	1983	1982
Points	**14.9**	**16.5**	**12.6**	**25.9**	**22.1**	**26.2**
Rank	28	26	28	25	19	26
Yards	**258.3**	**313.6**	**275.9**	**348.6**	**352.5**	**366.2**
Rank	28	21	27	22	23	26
Rushing Yards	**126.6**	**168.4**	**116.0**	**125.4**	**132.4**	**163.7**
Rank	12	2	14	17	17	28
Passing Yards	**131.7**	**145.2**	**159.9**	**223.1**	**220.1**	**202.6**
Rank	28	28	24	22	21	15
Sacks	**3.6**	**2.9**	**2.2**	**2.6**	**2.6**	**1.2**
Rank	22	17T	9T	19T	16T	28
Turnovers	**2.4**	**2.1**	**2.3**	**1.9**	**2.3**	**1.2**
Rank	18T	6T	11T	20T	17T	28
Punt Returns	**7.3**	**6.7**	**5.6**	**9.7**	**11.7**	**8.7**
Rank	19	25	25	20	28	18
Kickoff Returns	**19.3**	**19.3**	**17.9**	**20.2**	**18.7**	**21.5**
Rank	17	15	26	15	9	21
Penalty Yards	**49.9**	**61.6**	**48.1**	**50.8**	**41.6**	**51.8**
Rank	10	22	12	17	28	11

	W-L Total	Home	Road	Playoffs
1982	0-8-1	0-3-1	0-5	None
1983	7-9	3-5	4-4	None
1984	4-12	2-6	2-6	None

Along the line there is Thompson, who can rush the passer with the best of them when he feels inspired, at one defensive end, and Blaise Winter at the other, with Leo Wisniewski at nose tackle. Wisniewski finished fourth on the club in tackles and second in sacks with a remarkable 7½ from the nose position.

The linebackers are led by Barry Krauss, the team's leading tackler last season, and Cliff Odom, who was second. But the two players with perhaps the most potential for stardom are Johnie Cooks and Vernon Maxwell, each of whom spent more than his share of the time in Kush's doghouse the last few years.

Cooks, however, re-asserted himself last season by making 11½ sacks. Incredibly, 10 of them came in the final six games. If there are any questions about Cooks's ability one should consult the game film of the Colts' 1984 contest against the Los Angeles Raiders, against whom he registered 4½ sacks.

Maxwell, like Cooks, has speed and strength, but at times during his NFL career has been his own worst enemy. If Dowhower and his new staff of assistants can harness Maxwell, he could raise the level of this defense considerably.

In the secondary, rookie cornerback Eugene Daniel led the team with six interceptions and should improve. The same can be said for Preston Davis, a rookie from Baylor who was pressed into service just four days after he signed a contract last September 18. Davis started the final eight games at left corner and may become a fixture.

Although Glasgow was not as busy as he has been the past few seasons, he still finished third on the club in tackles. Glasgow and the Colts both would be better off if those tackles were being made closer to the line of scrimmage, but the presence of him and Mark Kafentzis still is reassuring for a young unit that does not yet know how good it could be.

"Everybody's fitting into slots," Krauss said. "The people were gaining confidence every week last year. Slowly you build character on the defense and it gets consistent. I think there's a good feeling developing here."

Randy McMillan   *Rohn Stark*   *Donnell Thompson*

That feeling could develop further if Dowhower's offense can take some of the heat off this defense. Last season that was not the case, however, and they felt the pressure as the weeks passed.

By season's end, the defense had been on the field almost 100 minutes longer than the offense. If that number can be reversed, Indianapolis would be a dramatically improved team.

SPECIAL TEAMS

This recently has been a solid area of strength for the Colts, and that did not change last season, even though placekicker Raul Allegre was not quite as imposing as he had been when he converted 85.7 percent of his kicks as a rookie.

Allegre made 11 of 18 last year, although three of his misses came on kicks of farther than 50 yards (two were blocked). While Allegre struggled, punter Rohn Stark continued to bomb his kicks, tying Miami's Reggie Roby for second in the NFL with a 44.7-yard punting average. He also finished third in the league with a 37.2 net punting average and he tied Kansas City's Jim Arnold for first in most attempts with 98.

Perhaps because he had plenty of practice (the Colts allowed 414 points, a 25.8-per-game average), Larry Anderson was third in the NFL in kickoff returns with a 23.9-yard average (22 for 525 yards).

Anderson was less productive on punt returns, averaging just 6.7 yards on 27 returns.

One way to measure the success of Dowhower's offense this season will be to look at the number of punts Stark has to unleash and the number of kick returns Anderson has to make.

VETERAN ROSTER

No.	Name	Pos.	Ht.	Wt.	NFL Exp.	Birthdate	College	Games in 1984
2	Allegre, Raul	K	5-10	165	3	6/15/59	Texas	12
30	Anderson, Larry	S	5-11	194	8	9/25/56	Louisiana Tech	12
61	Bailey, Don	C	6-4	257	2	3/24/61	Miami	10
	Baldischwiler, Karl	T	6-5	260	8	1/19/56	Oklahoma	0
97	Beach, Pat	TE	6-4	243	3	12/28/59	Washington State	0
48	Bell, Mark	TE	6-5	246	6	8/30/57	Colorado State	16
5	Biasucci, Dean	K	6-0	188	2	7/25/62	Western Carolina	15
85	Bouza, Matt	WR	6-3	209	4	4/8/59	California	16
52	Bracelin, Greg	LB	6-1	216	6	4/16/57	California	16
45	Burroughs, James	CB	6-1	187	4	1/21/58	Michigan State	6
80	Butler, Ray	WR	6-3	197	6	6/28/56	Southern California	16
72	Call, Kevin	T	6-7	289	2	11/13/61	Colorado State	15
98	Cooks, Johnie	LB	6-4	243	4	11/23/58	Mississippi State	16
38	Daniel, Eugene	CB	5-11	179	2	5/4/61	Louisiana State	15
27	Davis, Preston	CB	5-11	180	2	3/10/62	Baylor	12
33	Dickey, Curtis	RB	6-0	222	6	11/27/56	Texas A&M	10
53	Donaldson, Ray	C	6-4	273	6	5/17/58	Georgia	16
65	Gardner, Ellis	T-G	6-5	250	3	9/16/61	Georgia Tech	9
25	Glasgow, Nesby	S	5-10	180	7	4/15/57	Washington	16
58	Hathaway, Steve	LB	6-4	238	2	4/26/62	West Virginia	6
88	Henry, Bernard	WR	6-1	180	4	4/9/60	Arizona State	14
75	Hinton, Chris	G	6-4	283	3	7/31/61	Northwestern	6
57	Humiston, Mike	LB	6-3	240	5	1/8/59	Weber State	16
51	Jones, Ricky	LB	6-2	230	8	3/9/55	Tuskegee Institute	0
29	Kafentzis, Mark	S	5-10	200	4	6/30/58	Hawaii	16
63	Kirchner, Mark	T	6-3	261	3	10/19/59	Baylor	11
55	Krauss, Barry	LB	6-3	249	7	3/17/57	Alabama	16
56	Maxwell, Vernon	LB	6-2	238	3	10/25/61	Arizona State	16
32	McMillan, Randy	FB	6-0	212	5	12/17/58	Pittsburgh	16
43	Middleton, Frank	RB	5-11	201	2	10/28/60	Florida A&M	16
76	Mills, Jim	T	6-9	281	3	9/23/61	Hawaii	14
23	Moore, Alvin	RB	6-0	198	3	5/30/59	Arizona State	13
84	Oatis, Victor	WR	6-0	184	2	1/6/59	Northwestern Louisiana	0
93	Odom, Cliff	LB	6-2	235	5	9/15/58	Texas-Arlington	16
90	Padjen, Gary	LB	6-2	241	4	7/2/58	Arizona State	16
18	Pagel, Mike	QB	6-2	205	4	9/13/60	Arizona State	11
78	Parker, Steve	DE	6-3	262	3	9/21/59	Eastern Illinois	9
71	Petersen, Ted	T	6-5	253	9	2/7/55	Eastern Illinois	9
87	Porter, Tracy	WR	6-2	202	5	6/1/59	Louisiana State	16
21	Radachowsky, George	CB-S	5-11	178	2	9/7/62	Boston College	16
35	Randle, Tate	CB	6-0	196	4	8/15/59	Texas Tech	16
10	Schlichter, Art	QB	6-3	210	3	4/25/60	Ohio State	9
95	Scott, Chris	DE	6-5	253	2	12/11/61	Purdue	14
83	Sherwin, Tim	TE	6-6	245	5	5/4/58	Boston College	16
91	Smith, Byron	DE	6-5	264	2	12/21/62	California	3
86	Smith, Phil	WR	6-3	188	3	4/28/61	San Diego State	16
66	Solt, Ron	G	6-3	275	2	5/19/62	Maryland	16
3	Stark, Rohn	P	6-3	203	4	6/4/59	Florida State	16
99	Thompson, Donnell	DE	6-5	263	5	10/27/58	North Carolina	10
64	Utt, Ben	G	6-5	280	4	6/13/59	Georgia Tech	16
94	Virkus, Scott	DE	6-5	248	3	9/7/59	San Francisco C.C.	6
92	White, Brad	NT	6-2	260	5	8/18/58	Tennessee	15
39	Williams, Newton	FB	5-10	219	3	5/19/59	Arizona State	0
40	Williams, Vaughn	CB-S	6-2	193	2	12/14/61	Stanford	10
96	Winter, Blaise	DE	6-3	262	2	1/31/62	Syracuse	16
69	Wisniewski, Leo	NT	6-1	259	4	11/6/59	Penn State	14
34	Wonsley, George	RB	6-0	212	2	11/23/60	Mississippi State	14
81	Young, Dave	TE	6-5	243	4	2/9/59	Purdue	13

Coaching Staff

Rod Dowhower, head coach; **John Becker,** quarterbacks; **George Catavolos,** secondary; **George Hill,** defensive coordinator; **Tom Lovat,** assistant head coach, offensive line; **Billie Matthews,** offensive coordinator, running backs; **Chip Myers,** receivers; **Keith Rowen,** special teams, assistant offensive line; **Steve Sidwell,** defensive line; **Rick Venturi,** linebackers; **Tom Zupancic,** strength.

1985 Schedule

Preseason

Aug. 10	SEATTLE	7:30
Aug. 17	at Chicago	6:00
Aug. 24	at Denver	7:00
Aug. 30	CINCINNATI	7:30

Regular Season

Sept. 8	at Pittsburgh	1:00
Sept. 15	at Miami	1:00
Sept. 22	DETROIT	12:00
Sept. 29	at N.Y. Jets	4:00
Oct. 6	BUFFALO	12:00
Oct. 13	DENVER	12:00
Oct. 20	at Buffalo	1:00
Oct. 27	GREEN BAY	1:00
Nov. 3	N.Y. JETS	4:00
Nov. 10	at New England	1:00
Nov. 17	MIAMI	1:00
Nov. 24	at Kansas City	3:00
Dec. 1	NEW ENGLAND	1:00
Dec. 8	at Chicago	12:00
Dec. 15	at Tampa Bay	1:00
Dec. 22	HOUSTON	4:00

1984 Results

Sept. 2	N.Y. JETS	14-23
Sept. 9	at Houston	35-21
Sept. 16	ST. LOUIS	33-34
Sept. 23	at Miami	7-44
Sept. 30	BUFFALO	31-17
Oct. 7	WASHINGTON	7-35
Oct. 14	at Philadelphia	7-16
Oct. 21	PITTSBURGH	17-16
Oct. 28	at Dallas	3-22
Nov. 4	SAN DIEGO	10-38
Nov. 11	at N.Y. Jets	9-5
Nov. 18	NEW ENGLAND	17-50
Nov. 25	at L.A. Raiders	7-21
Dec. 2	at Buffalo	15-21
Dec. 9	MIAMI	17-35
Dec. 16	at New England	10-16

1985 Draft Choices

1. Duane Bickett—5, LB, Southern California
2. Don Anderson—32, DB, Purdue
3. Anthony Young—61, DB, Temple
4. Willie Broughton—88, DE, Miami
5. Roger Caron—117, T, Harvard
6. Choice to Dallas
7. James Harbour—173, WR, Mississippi
8. Ricky Nichols—200, WR, East Carolina
9. Mark Boyer—229, TE, Southern California
10. Andre Pinesett—256, DT, Cal State-Fullerton
11. Choice to L.A. Rams
12. Dave Burnette—312, T, Central Arkansas

MIAMI DOLPHINS

The Miami Dolphins are the Beast from the AFC East, a team that has punched out its AFC East opponents more often than Muhammad Ali hit George Chuvalo.

The Dolphins have won or tied in their division 12 of the past 14 years. But last season, Miami's dominance was remarkable even by its own standards.

The 14-2 Dolphins not only won the division in a walk (by five games over second-place New England), they did not lose a game to an AFC East opponent, a feat not performed since they did it in 1972.

Victories are victories, of course, but Miami consistently seemed to take winning even further last year. Against divisional opponents, for example, the Dolphins won eight games by an average margin of 19½ points, a fact that has caused the rest of the AFC East to fire coaches, shuffle players, and generally seek some way to get out of Miami's vise.

The only problem is there is no shelter from the passing arm of Dan Marino, a young man who in two years has not only rewritten the NFL's passing records, but also has rewritten the way the Dolphins do business.

"In preparing for Miami, you become obsessed with trying to deal with Marino's passing," San Francisco 49ers' coach Bill Walsh said.

"That's the overwhelming factor. When we played him in the Super Bowl, we were playing the greatest forward passer of all time, as I understand it."

Miami used to grind it out, running to two world championships and that remarkable 17-0 season in 1972. Back then, power runners Larry Csonka and Jim Kiick, with an assist from speedster Mercury Morris, carried the load.

Mark Clayton caught a record 18 touchdown passes.

Don Shula

Quarterback Bob Griese and wide receiver Paul Warfield were fearsome competitors and talented players, but they were merely adjuncts to the offense. Mostly, Miami simply ran over opponents that stood in its way.

Marino has changed all that, and his coach has changed with him.

The Dolphins no longer grind you down. Now they bomb you out, a change that makes it clear just how good a coach Don Shula really is.

"Shula has really adjusted as a coach," said guard Ed Newman, one of the few remaining Dolphins from Miami's first set of glory years back in the mid-1970s.

"In those early years it was ball control—Csonka, Csonka, Csonka, run, run, run. Then he gets Marino and his eyes light up.

"Now it's pass, pass, pass. The big play. No more grinding it out. You have to give credit to him for fitting what he does to the players he has to work with, rather than the other way around." Of course, the rules changes helped, too.

While others marvel at how Shula could alter his strategic philosophy, Shula knows the obvious—that what he really believes in is winning and that does not always come the way you might expect.

"I'm flexible," Shula said. "I try to gear what we do to work with the personnel we have. Right now, we have great personnel to throw the ball so that's what we've done."

OFFENSE

Shula has assembled a passing attack so potent that it made Miami the leading scoring team in the NFL last season with an average of 32.1 points per game.

It also made the Dolphins the overall leader in yardage with an average of 433.5 per game. They were sixteenth in rushing with an average of 119.9 yards per game, so you probably have a clue how they moved the ball the rest of the time—the Marino Corps.

Miami averaged 313.6 passing yards a game and scored every 16 plays because Marino simply destroyed defenses with his accuracy, receivers Mark Duper and Mark Clayton destroyed secondaries with their speed, and an offensive line led by center Dwight Stephenson destroyed nearly every pass rush it faced.

Working in concert they destroyed almost everything in their path until they reached the Super Bowl and the San Francisco 49ers.

Marino threw for 5,084 yards by completing 64.2 percent of his passes. Of those completions, a record 48 went for touchdowns, bringing his two-year NFL total to 68 touchdowns and 7,294 yards.

"He may have the best arm of any quarterback who ever played the game when it comes to throwing the ball deep with velocity and accuracy," said Patriots' player personnel director Dick Steinberg.

That hardly is good news for Miami's opponents, especially when you realize he is throwing it to two of the classiest receivers in the game.

Duper and Clayton approached horizons unknown to most receivers in 1984. Clayton led Miami with 73 receptions for 1,389 yards and a record 18 touchdowns. Duper countered with 71 catches for 1,306 yards, and eight scores.

Those totals don't even begin to reflect running back Tony Nathan's 61 catches or the 43 veteran Nat Moore caught (six for touchdowns) or the combined total of 74 hauled in by Miami's three tight ends, Dan Johnson, Joe Rose, and Bruce Hardy.

None of this would have been possible, however, without the presence of an offensive line that allowed Marino to be sacked just 13 times all season.

Doug Betters

Mark Duper

Dan Marino

Despite throwing more than any other quarterback (564 times), Marino was sacked fewer times than any other quarterback, a testimony to his quick release but also to the blocking of Stephenson, Newman, Roy Foster, Jon Giesler, Eric Laakso, and those three tight ends.

"Defenses are so hungry to sack him just once you'd think he was golden or something," Foster said. "It's as if they feel if they can just touch him, then they can go home and tell their wives and family about it. He's the most wanted man in the NFL."

The Dolphins should have an improved running game this year. Fullback Andra Franklin injured his ankle in the second game of the season and was out for the year and no one really picked up the slack. Franklin will be back this year, however.

Woody Bennett, a career journeyman, led the team in rushing in 1984 with 606 yards. There are two other bright spots in Miami's running game—1984 rookie surprise Joe Carter and fullback Pete Johnson, who will get a full season in Miami under his belt.

Actually, it is what was under Johnson's belt when he arrived in Miami from San Diego last fall that caused him problems. Although he rushed for 12 touchdowns, his pants were outfitted with an expandable waistline, something Shula wants changed this year.

If Johnson can control his weight, he still is young enough to go back to being the powerful inside runner he was with the Cincinnati Bengals.

And Carter, who rushed for five yards a carry in 100 attempts, flashed potential as a productive and explosive back if he continues to improve.

Carter, Franklin, Johnson, Bennett, and Nathan (the latter primarily a pass receiver) could total a strong backfield if things go right.

DEFENSE

Miami's defense had an unusual season in 1984 by allowing many yards (338.8) but few points (18.6 per game). That is a tricky formula to keep brewing.

What Shula would like to see is some new sting from the Killer B's, but to get it he will need a return to good health for A.J. Duhe, Bob Baumhower, Mike Charles, and Kim Bokamper.

Three Years at a Glance

Averages NFL Rank	OFFENSE			DEFENSE		
	1984	1983	1982	1984	1983	1982
Points	32.1	24.3	22.0	18.6	15.6	14.6
Rank	1	7	10	7	1	2
Yards	433.5	324.7	295.3	338.8	314.9	256.9
Rank	1	16	19	19	7	1
Rushing Yards	119.9	134.4	149.3	134.7	127.3	142.8
Rank	16	13	3	22	13	24
Passing Yards	313.6	190.3	146.0	204.1	187.6	114.1
Rank	1	19	27	14	8	1
Sacks	0.9	1.4	1.2	2.6	3.1	3.2
Rank	1	1T	1T	19T	9	12
Turnovers	1.8	1.7	2.6	2.3	2.7	3.0
Rank	3T	2	14T	12T	10	3T
Punt Returns	9.4	10.6	8.8	8.1	7.2	5.5
Rank	7	7	8	11	6	6
Kickoff Returns	18.2	23.1	21.1	20.7	19.0	21.3
Rank	28	1	7	17	12	19
Penalty Yards	32.9	35.4	26.7	48.3	52.3	51.2
Rank	1	1	1	20	11T	12

	W-L Total	Home	Road	Playoffs
1982	7-2	4-0	3-2	3-1, Lost SuperBowl XVII
1983	12-4	7-1	5-3	0-1, Lost Divisional Playoff Game
1984	14-2	7-1	7-1	2-1, Lost Super Bowl XIX

As injuries began to mount in the middle of the year, so did the points scored by the Dolphins' opponents. From games 10 through 15, they were giving up an average of 25 points per Sunday, although there was little harmful effect because Marino was scoring even faster. Still, they sustained their only two losses, to San Diego and the Los Angeles Raiders, during that time.

A key could be Charles, a defensive end and tackle who showed flashes of what could come this season if his knee and his discipline hold up.

Defensive end Doug Betters (14 sacks) would become an even more dangerous pass rusher than he already is if Charles lives up to his potential. Bokamper is expected to be back at full strength at defensive end, and Shula hopes that nose tackle Bob Baumhower returns to the level of play of two years ago after playing all year with an assortment of nagging injuries.

The linebackers also have more potential than they showed in 1984, even though number-one draft choice Jackie Shipp ran aground. Shula has not lost all hope in him, but even if he can't perform, there still is leading tackler Mark Brown, Charles Bowser (nine sacks), Bob Brudzinski, surprising Jay Brophy, Duhe, and Earnest Rhone.

That may not be the most fearsome group ever assembled in the NFL, but they are solid enough to keep the Dolphins at the top.

The secondary, which is led by cornerback Don McNeal, is in a similar position.

McNeal is a solid performer who doesn't get much work because people know enough to stay away from him. He teams with cornerback William Judson and safeties Lyle and Glenn Blackwood.

Glenn Blackwood led the team with six interceptions last year while brother Lyle was tied for third with 62 solo tackles. Lyle would just as soon not have to face quite as many open-field tackles, but, if he has to, then he has to because even if he misses there's a guy named Marino ready to get the points back in a hurry.

SPECIAL TEAMS

Placekicker Uwe von Schamann is facing the most pivotal year of his career. After five seasons of consistent

Don McNeal

Ed Newman

Joe Rose

kicking, von Schamann went haywire last season, converting just 9 of 19 field-goal attempts.

He missed all seven kicks from beyond 40 yards and ultimately caused Shula to alter his strategy in several games because of von Schamann's failures. Prior to last year, von Schamann had made 70 percent of his kicks, which made his fall more surprising.

Shula stuck with him through thin and thinner and von Schamann enters 1985 as the favorite to hold on to his job. But both know Shula cannot and will not wait and wonder in 1985 the way he did in 1984.

For the first time since he arrived as a rookie and unseated former all-pro Garo Yepremian six years ago, von Schamann comes to training camp having to prove he still belongs with the Dolphins.

That is hardly the case with punter Reggie Roby. An AFC Pro Bowl selection, Roby was named to most all-pro teams as a result of his 44.7-yard average on 51 kicks. Of those punts, 15 landed inside the 20 and another 10 were touchbacks, so half his punts could not be returned.

Roby is considerably more than a distance man, however. He is noted for the hang time of his punts.

Because of Roby's ability to keep the ball in flight, Miami has become one of the best coverage teams in football, but the Dolphins also haven't done badly on the other end of the kicking game.

For the fourth year Fulton Walker is expected to handle the bulk of the return chores. Last year he brought back 21 punts for an average of 8 yards per attempt. That hardly was distinctive, but his 21.3-yard return average on 29 kickoffs was.

VETERAN ROSTER

No.	Name	Pos.	Ht.	Wt.	NFL Exp.	Birthdate	College	Games in 1984
70	Barnett, Bill	DE	6-4	260	6	5/10/56	Nebraska	16
73	Baumhower, Bob	NT	6-5	265	9	8/4/55	Alabama	15
34	Bennett, Woody	FB	6-2	225	7	3/24/55	Miami	16
78	Benson, Charles	DE	6-3	267	3	11/21/60	Baylor	16
75	Betters, Doug	DE	6-7	265	8	6/11/56	Nevada-Reno	16
47	Blackwood, Glenn	S	6-0	190	7	2/23/57	Texas	16
42	Blackwood, Lyle	S	6-1	190	13	5/24/51	Texas Christian	16
58	Bokamper, Kim	DE	6-6	255	9	9/25/54	San Jose State	11
56	Bowser, Charles	LB	6-3	235	4	10/2/59	Duke	15
53	Brophy, Jay	LB	6-3	233	2	7/27/60	Miami	11
43	Brown, Bud	S	6-0	194	2	4/19/61	Southern Mississippi	16
51	Brown, Mark	LB	6-2	225	3	7/18/61	Purdue	16
59	Brudzinski, Bob	LB	6-4	223	9	1/1/55	Ohio State	16
23	Carter, Joe	RB	5-11	198	2	6/23/62	Alabama	13
71	Charles, Mike	NT	6-4	285	3	9/23/62	Syracuse	10
76	Clark, Steve	G	6-4	255	4	8/2/60	Utah	12
83	Clayton, Mark	WR	5-9	175	3	4/8/61	Louisville	15
77	Duhe, A. J.	LB	6-4	235	9	11/27/55	Louisiana State	12
85	Duper, Mark	WR	5-9	187	4	1/25/59	N.W. State, La.	16
61	Foster, Roy	G	6-4	275	4	5/24/60	Southern California	16
37	Franklin, Andra	FB	5-10	225	4	8/22/59	Nebraska	2
79	Giesler, Jon	T	6-5	260	7	12/23/56	Michigan	16
74	Green, Cleveland	T	6-3	262	7	9/11/57	Southern	16
84	Hardy, Bruce	TE	6-5	232	8	6/1/56	Arizona State	16
88	Heflin, Vince	WR	6-0	185	4	7/7/59	Central State, Ohio	16
90	Hester, Ron	LB	6-2	222	2	5/26/59	Florida State	0
31	Hill, Eddie	RB	6-2	210	7	5/13/57	Memphis State	16
11	Jensen, Jim	WR	6-4	215	5	11/14/58	Boston University	16
87	Johnson, Dan	TE	6-3	240	3	5/17/60	Iowa State	16
46	Johnson, Pete	FB	6-0	250	9	3/22/54	Ohio State	16
49	Judson, William	CB	6-1	190	4	3/26/59	South Carolina State	16
40	Kozlowski, Mike	S	6-1	198	6	2/24/56	Colorado	16
68	Laakso, Eric	T	6-4	260	8	11/29/56	Tulane	4
38	Landry, Ron	FB	6-2	225	1	7/8/62	McNeese State	0
44	Lankford, Paul	CB	6-2	184	4	6/15/58	Penn State	16
72	Lee, Ronnie	G	6-4	265	7	12/24/56	Baylor	16
13	Marino, Dan	QB	6-4	214	3	9/15/61	Pittsburgh	16
28	McNeal, Don	CB	5-11	192	5	5/6/58	Alabama	11
89	Moore, Nat	WR	5-9	188	12	9/19/51	Florida	16
22	Nathan, Tony	RB	6-0	206	7	12/14/56	Alabama	16
64	Newman, Ed	G	6-2	255	13	6/4/51	Duke	16
55	Rhone, Earnie	LB	6-2	224	10	8/20/53	Henderson, Ark.	15
4	Roby, Reggie	P	6-2	243	3	7/30/61	Iowa	16
80	Rose, Joe	TE	6-3	230	6	6/24/57	California	9
50	Shipp, Jackie	LB	6-2	236	2	3/19/62	Oklahoma	16
52	Shiver, Sanders	LB	6-2	235	10	2/14/55	Carson-Newman	14
45	Sowell, Robert	CB	5-11	175	3	6/23/61	Howard	16
57	Stephenson, Dwight	C	6-2	255	6	11/20/57	Alabama	16
10	Strock, Don	QB	6-5	220	12	11/27/50	Virginia Tech	16
54	Thomas, Rodell	LB	6-2	225	5	8/2/58	Alabama State	14
60	Toews, Jeff	G-C	6-3	255	7	11/4/57	Washington	16
32	Vigorito, Tom	RB	5-10	190	3	10/23/59	Virginia	0
5	von Schamann, Uwe	K	6-1	185	7	4/23/56	Oklahoma	16
41	Walker, Fulton	CB	5-11	196	5	4/30/58	West Virginia	12

Coaching Staff

Don Shula, head coach; **Tom Keane,** special teams; **Bob Matheson,** linebackers; **Mel Phillips,** defensive backs; **John Sandusky,** offense, offensive line; **Mike Scarry,** defensive line; **David Shula,** receivers, quarterbacks; **Chuck Studley,** defense; **Carl Taseff,** offensive backfield; **Junior Wade,** strength and conditioning.

1985 Schedule

Preseason

Aug. 10	MINNESOTA	8:00
Aug. 17	BUFFALO	8:00
Aug. 24	at L.A. Raiders	6:00
Aug. 30	at Atlanta	8:00

Regular Season

Sept. 8	at Houston	12:00
Sept. 15	INDIANAPOLIS	1:00
Sept. 22	KANSAS CITY	4:00
Sept. 29	at Denver	2:00
Oct. 6	PITTSBURGH	1:00
Oct. 14	at N.Y. Jets (Mon.)	9:00
Oct. 20	TAMPA BAY	4:00
Oct. 27	at Detroit	1:00
Nov. 3	at New England	1:00
Nov. 10	N.Y. JETS	4:00
Nov. 17	at Indianapolis	1:00
Nov. 24	at Buffalo	1:00
Dec. 2	CHICAGO (Mon.)	9:00
Dec. 8	at Green Bay	12:00
Dec. 16	NEW ENGLAND (Mon.)	9:00
Dec. 22	BUFFALO	1:00

1984 Results

Sept. 2	at Washington	35-17
Sept. 9	NEW ENGLAND	28-7
Sept. 17	at Buffalo (Mon.)	21-17
Sept. 23	INDIANAPOLIS	44-7
Sept. 30	at St. Louis	36-28
Oct. 7	at Pittsburgh	31-7
Oct. 14	HOUSTON	28-10
Oct. 21	at New England	44-24
Oct. 28	BUFFALO	38-7
Nov. 4	at N.Y. Jets	31-17
Nov. 11	PHILADELPHIA	24-23
Nov. 16	San Diego*	28-34
Nov. 26	N.Y. JETS (Mon.)	28-17
Dec. 2	L.A. RAIDERS	34-45
Dec. 9	at Indianapolis	35-17
Dec. 17	DALLAS (Mon.)	28-21
Dec. 29	SEATTLE	31-10
Jan. 6	PITTSBURGH	45-28
Jan. 20	San Francisco	16-38

1985 Draft Choices

1. Lorenzo Hampton—27, RB, Florida
2. Choice to San Diego
3. George Little—65, DT, Iowa, from Philadelphia
3. Alex Moyer—83, LB, Northwestern
4. Mike Smith—91, DB, Texas-El Paso, from Cleveland
4. Jeff Dellenbach—111, T, Wisconsin
5. Choice to Denver
6. George Shorthose—145, WR, Missouri, from Atlanta
6. Ron Davenport—167, RB, Louisville
7. Fuad Reveiz—195, K, Tennessee
8. Dan Sharp—223, TE, Texas Christian
9. Adam Hinds—251, DB, Oklahoma State
10. Mike Pendleton—279, DB, Indiana
11. Mike Jones—307, RB, Tulane
12. Ray Noble—335, DB, California

NEW ENGLAND PATRIOTS

Like most mysteries, it is difficult to explain exactly how the New England Patriots managed to self-destruct last season, or, more importantly, how that collapse will affect them this year.

Before the 1984 season began, they insisted the mutinies that had plagued them since the arrival of coach Ron Meyer in 1982 were behind them. Presumably, everything was in place to make a run at the Miami Dolphins, the big fish in the AFC East's pond. This would be the best year for the Patriots since 1776.

Then the season began and the roof fell in. Meyer was fired, and the Patriots missed the playoffs. Why? It seemed the talent was there. The team opened 5-3 with the only losses coming to two of the league's strongest teams, Miami (twice) and Washington.

Three weeks into the season, Meyer found a new young quarterback to replace Steve Grogan: Tony Eason, who had new mobility and a ballistic arm.

After releasing Meyer, the team finally said it had a coach it could play for—Raymond Berry. Then it lost three of its last four games with a wild-card playoff spot on the line.

But the beauty of sports is that there always is a new year and another chance just around the corner. It is like the coming of spring after a long, dark winter. This year spring comes to New England with Berry in charge from the start and the Patriots' split-back and I-formations out of moth balls.

"Our players are aware of the standard of effort needed on every play if we're to become a winner," Berry said. "Losing those games showed us exactly where we are in this league. Obviously, we were not good

John Hannah still rates as one of the NFL's best guards.

Raymond Berry

enough to be a playoff team.

"But I believe the talent is here. We have a lot of good things in place. I don't believe we're very far away from the playoffs."

OFFENSE

One thing the Patriots always have been able to do, is move the football. That shouldn't change, even though the face of their offense will.

"With all the talented running backs we have, I don't see any reason to use just one of them at a time," Berry said, explaining his decision to junk Meyer's one-back offense.

In truth, however, formations hardly appeared to be New England's problem because even with all of last season's turmoil it finished tenth in the NFL in scoring (up from twenty-fourth a year earlier) and sixteenth in total passing (up from twenty-fifth).

Yet if one thing was made plain it was the need to get the ball into the hands of running back Craig James, who arrived in New England last summer after two injury-plagued seasons in the USFL.

James, the former college running mate of Eric Dickerson at SMU, spent the first half of the season on the bench, but got his chance after Meyer was fired. James finished with enough of a rush to post a club-leading 790 yards and a 4.9-yard-per-carry average.

Those numbers were enough to return former Pro Bowl running back Tony Collins to the bench, a situation Berry plans to avoid this year.

Collins, who gained just 550 yards after rushing for 1,049 yards in 1983, will join James in a tandem.

But when the split backs are replaced by the I-formation, it seems likely James and Collins will alternate behind the blocking of Mosi Tatupu (553 yards).

Even with Collins back on the field more often this season, it seems apparent that the future lies with James, who rushed for more than 100 yards three times and averaged more than 4.5 yards a carry in all but two games.

The Patriots, like everyone else, enjoy dealing from

strength whenever possible and that clearly is the case at quarterback, where Eason made it obvious there will be no quarterback controversy in New England this summer.

Taking over for Grogan with his team trailing Seattle 23-0 on September 16, Eason began work throwing on the run and hitting medium-range passes he favors.

The result was the greatest comeback in New England's history, a 38-23 victory that turned into a coming-out party for a new Patriots leader after 10 seasons under Grogan.

Eason finished his second year in the league as the NFL's third-rated passer, trailing only Miami's Dan Marino and San Francisco's Joe Montana, with a 93.4 rating. But where Marino is a knockout puncher who does his damage with one looping pass, Eason's game is precision.

He delivers his middle-range passes with speed and accuracy and a scrambling style that forces defenses to move to his beat. This was never more evident than in the three late-season losses when Eason was pinned in the pocket and assaulted from all sides. Sacked 22 times, he became just another quarterback.

Yet whenever he was free to move, Eason took his team with him. Twice he passed for more than 300 yards, finishing with 3,228 yards, 23 touchdowns and only 8 interceptions (a rate of just 1.9 percent).

Because of this, it was no surprise when Berry announced this spring, "Tony Eason is our quarterback. That doesn't mean we don't believe Steve can do the job, but a team needs to know who will be its leader."

Ray Clayborn

Tony Eason

Irving Fryar

Along the line, which is the NFL's biggest, age is beginning to show. Center Pete Brock, 31, remains one of the best in the AFC, but his wobbly knees no longer allow him to play 16 games. Whenever he has been out New England has lost consistently.

Next to Brock stands Pro Bowl fixture John Hannah, who has been called the greatest lineman in football history. Hannah is approaching 35, and has had neck and back problems. He remains one of the game's most solid performers.

Counterbalancing this is the continued improvement of guard Ron Wooten and young tackles Darryl Haley and Brian Holloway, another Pro Bowler. But even as that threesome matures, Brock and Hannah continue to age and there are no immediate replacements.

The receivers also have holes in their resumes, although they also have an abundance of talent and a track team's speed.

First, there is the mysterious Stanley Morgan, a player possessing awesome physical tools and a tendency to misuse them.

Last season Morgan had only 38 receptions, although his average of 18.7 yards per catch gives a hint of his capabilities. But Morgan never has caught 60 passes in a season during his eight-year career.

"Stanley has not played as well as he could the past couple of years, but he will have his greatest season," predicted Berry, who once was Morgan's mentor when he coached New England's receivers four years ago.

If he does, that should free Irving Fryar to do considerably more damage than he did with his 11 receptions. Fryar, the NFL's number-one draft pick in 1984, suffered an assortment of rib and shoulder injuries that slowed his progress.

Behind them sit capable veterans Cedric Jones (19 for 244), Stephen Starring (46 for 657), and Clarence Weathers (eight catches and two touchdowns despite missing most of the year with a broken foot).

One of Berry's pleasant dilemmas will be to find a way to utilize both Derrick Ramsey and Lin Dawson at tight end. Dawson is a powerful blocker who would help the running game immensely, while Ramsey is a

Three Years at a Glance

Averages NFL Rank	OFFENSE			DEFENSE		
	1984	1983	1982	1984	1983	1982
Points	**22.6**	**17.1**	**15.9**	**22.0**	**18.1**	**17.4**
Rank	10	24	21	18	3	7
Yards	**328.9**	**331.9**	**292.6**	**318.8**	**348.5**	**312.0**
Rank	14	13	21	9	20	13
Rushing Yards	**127.0**	**162.8**	**149.7**	**117.9**	**142.6**	**143.2**
Rank	11	5	2	12	21	25
Passing Yards	**201.9**	**169.1**	**142.9**	**200.9**	**205.9**	**168.8**
Rank	16	25	28	12	17	5
Sacks	**4.1**	**2.8**	**1.7**	**3.4**	**2.4**	**2.2**
Rank	27	14T	5T	7T	19	17T
Turnovers	**1.8**	**2.4**	**1.9**	**1.6**	**2.3**	**2.6**
Rank	6	11T	5T	23T	17T	12T
Punt Returns	**9.0**	**9.1**	**8.7**	**9.8**	**8.2**	**7.3**
Rank	10	10	10	21	14	11
Kickoff Returns	**19.8**	**20.3**	**23.1**	**18.8**	**19.7**	**19.2**
Rank	12	11	1	6	16	10
Penalty Yards	**42.1**	**50.9**	**45.8**	**48.3**	**42.1**	**32.2**
Rank	4	13	9	19	27	28

	W-L Total	Home	Road	Playoffs
1982	5-4	3-1	2-3	0-1, Lost First Round Game
1983	8-8	5-3	3-5	None
1984	9-7	5-3	4-4	None

receiver in the mold of Ozzie Newsome. Ramsey set a club record with 66 receptions in his first full season.

DEFENSE

The Patriots have been searching for a pass-rushing lineman longer than Ponce de Leon searched for the Fountain of Youth and they have had just about as much luck finding one.

That remains one of the two missing links in an otherwise sound defense. The other is a cornerback to team with Raymond Clayborn. The problem is obvious, considering the unit moved from twentieth in the NFL to ninth in total defense, yet it fell from third in points allowed (289) to eighteenth (352).

Defensive end Kenneth Sims had his most productive year, finishing fifth on the club in tackles and second in quarterback pressures with 21, but he was not strongly supported by anyone except linebacker Andre Tippett.

The Patriots enter the season with undersized nose tackle Dennis Owens and tiny but tenacious defensive end Toby Williams as the up-front starters with Sims. Behind them sit overweight, injury-plagued former number-one choice Lester Williams, aging Julius Adams, and Doug Rogers.

A Patriot plus is one of the most solid linebacking corps in the game with Tippett (18½ sacks and a Pro Bowl selection) leading the charge. Joining him on the AFC Pro Bowl squad last year was veteran inside linebacker Steve Nelson, the voice of wisdom among a group of lethal juveniles that includes Don Blackmon, Clayton Weishuhn (coming off knee surgery), Larry McGrew, and Johnny Rembert.

In the secondary, which was once populated by five number-one draft choices, times have grown tough.

For the past two seasons, Clayborn has played his position as well as anyone in the game, although it seems few have taken the time to notice. The other corner spot is filled by either Ronnie Lippett or Ernest Gibson. Gibson was a rookie who, like most, had his ups and downs. Lippett was a greater disappointment. After a surprisingly sound rookie season when he replaced Mike Haynes (who was traded to the Los Angeles Raid-

Steve Nelson

Derrick Ramsey

Mosi Tatupu

ers midway through the 1983 season), Lippett fell apart last year. Attacked constantly because teams did not want to quarrel with Clayborn, Lippett finally had to be replaced by Gibson.

Neither seem to be the future, however, and at the moment the Patriots are staking their hopes on Rod Mc-Swain, a raw talent acquired from Atlanta with just one year of college experience at corner.

Veterans Roland James, Ricky Sanford, and Fred Marion will return at safety, with James a fixture on the strongside. Sanford and Marion will resume their annual summer battle at free safety.

"I think this is a young defense that has worked hard to try and make itself better," Nelson said. "I think we learned last year what the stretch is all about."

SPECIAL TEAMS

One of the bright spots of the '84 season was Tony Franklin. The Patriots had suffered through a season with the poorest field-goal kicking in the NFL a year earlier. But Franklin came in, beat out seven challengers after being acquired in a trade with the Eagles, and produced 109 points, the highest total of his six-year career. He connected on 78.6 percent of his kicks (22 of 28) and combined nicely with Rich Camarillo, the 1983 Pro Bowl punter who came back from a preseason knee operation to finish the final seven games averaging 42.1.

Punt returns were equally as spectacular, with Fryar averaging 9.6 per return (fourth-best in the AFC) and constantly threatening to break loose. But the same could not be said for kickoff returns until rookie Jon Williams was replaced by Collins, who averaged 21.8 yards per carry in 25 attempts.

VETERAN ROSTER

No.	Name	Pos.	Ht.	Wt.	NFL Exp.	Birthdate	College	Games in 1984
85	Adams, Julius	DE	6-3	265	14	4/26/48	Texas Southern	16
55	Blackmon, Don	LB	6-2	230	5	3/14/58	Tulsa	16
58	Brock, Pete	C	6-3	225	10	7/14/54	Colorado	12
3	Camarillo, Rich	P	5-11	191	5	11/29/59	Washington	7
26	Clayborn, Ray	CB	6-0	186	9	1/2/55	Texas	16
33	Collins, Tony	RB-KR	5-11	212	5	5/27/50	East Carolina	16
87	Dawson, Lin	TE	6-3	240	5	6/24/59	North Carolina State	16
47	Dombroski, Paul	S	6-0	185	6	8/8/56	Linfield College	14
11	Eason, Tony	QB	6-4	212	3	10/8/59	Illinois	16
56	Fairchild, Paul	G	6-2	235	2	8/14/61	Kansas	7
1	Franklin, Tony	K	5-8	182	7	11/18/56	Texas A&M	16
80	Fryar, Irving	WR-KR	6-0	200	2	9/28/62	Nebraska	14
43	Gibson, Ernest	CB	5-10	185	2	10/3/61	Furman	15
59	Golden, Tim	LB	6-1	220	4	11/15/59	Florida	15
14	Grogan, Steve	QB	6-4	210	11	7/24/53	Kansas State	3
68	Haley, Darryl	T	6-4	275	4	2/16/61	Utah	16
73	Hannah, John	G	6-3	265	13	4/4/51	Alabama	15
40	Hawthorne, Greg	WR-RB	6-3	225	7	9/5/56	Baylor	14
70	Henson, Luther	NT	6-0	275	4	3/25/9	Ohio State	9
76	Holloway, Brian	T	6-7	285	5	7/25/59	Stanford	16
51	Ingram, Brian	LB	6-4	235	4	10/31/59	Tennessee	12
32	James, Craig	RB	6-0	215	2	1/2/61	Southern Methodist	15
38	James, Roland	S	6-2	191	6	2/18/58	Tennessee	15
83	Jones, Cedric	WR	6-0	184	4	6/1/60	Duke	14
19	Kerrigan, Mike	QB	6-3	205	3	4/27/60	Northwestern	1
22	Lee, Keith	S	5-11	193	5	12/22/57	Colorado State	15
42	Lippett, Ronnie	CB	5-11	180	3	12/10/60	Miami	16
31	Marion, Fred	S	6-2	191	4	8/2/59	Miami	16
50	McGrew, Larry	LB	6-5	233	5	7/23/57	Southern California	16
23	McSwain, Rod	CB	6-1	198	2	1/28/62	Clemson	15
67	Moore, Steve	T	6-4	285	3	10/1/60	Tennessee State	16
86	Morgan, Stanley	WR	5-11	181	9	2/17/55	Tennessee	13
75	Morriss, Guy	C	6-4	270	13	5/13/51	Texas Christian	16
57	Nelson, Steve	LB	6-2	230	12	4/26/51	North Dakota State	16
98	Owens, Dennis	NT	6-1	258	4	2/24/60	North Carolina State	16
88	Ramsey, Derrick	TE	6-5	235	8	12/23/56	Kentucky	16
52	Rembert, Johnny	LB	6-3	234	3	1/19/61	Clemson	7
95	Reynolds, Ed	LB	6-5	230	3	9/23/61	Virginia	16
41	Robinson, Bo	RB	6-2	235	7	5/27/56	West Texas State	16
65	Rogers, Doug	DE	6-5	270	4	6/23/60	Stanford	12
25	Sanford, Rick	S	6-1	192	7	1/9/57	South Carolina	16
77	Sims, Ken	DE	6-5	271	4	10/31/59	Texas	16
81	Starring, Stephen	WR-KR	5-10	172	3	7/30/61	McNeese State	16
30	Tatupu, Mosi	RB	6-0	227	8	4/26/55	Southern California	16
56	Tippett, Andre	LB	6-3	241	4	12/27/59	Iowa	16
82	Weathers, Clarence	WR	5-9	170	3	1/10/62	Delaware State	9
24	Weathers, Robert	RB	6-2	222	4	9/13/60	Arizona State	2
53	Weishuhn, Clayton	LB	6-2	221	3	10/9/59	Angelo State	1
54	Williams, Ed	LB	6-4	244	2	8/9/61	Texas	14
44	Williams, Jon	RB-KR	5-9	205	2	6/1/61	Penn State	9
72	Williams, Lester	NT	6-3	272	4	1/19/59	Miami	7
90	Williams, Toby	DE	6-3	265	3	11/19/59	Nebraska	16
61	Wooten, Ron	G	6-4	273	4	6/28/59	North Carolina	16

Coaching Staff

Raymond Berry, head coach; **Dean Brittenham,** strength and conditioning; **Jim Carr,** defensive backs; **Bobby Grier,** offensive backs; **Rod Humenuik,** assistant head coach-offense, offensive line; **Harold Jackson,** assistant receivers coach; **Ed Khayat,** defensive line; **Rod Rust,** defensive coordinator; **Dante Scarnecchia,** special teams; **Don Shinnick,** linebackers; **Les Steckel,** quarterbacks-receivers.

1985 Schedule

Preseason

Aug. 10	NEW ORLEANS	3:30
Aug. 17	at Kansas City	7:30
Aug. 23	at Washington	8:00
Aug. 31	at L.A. Rams	7:00

Regular Season

Sept. 8	GREEN BAY	1:00
Sept. 15	at Chicago	12:00
Sept. 22	at Buffalo	1:00
Sept. 29	L.A. RAIDERS	1:00
Oct. 6	at Cleveland	1:00
Oct. 13	BUFFALO	1:00
Oct. 20	N.Y. JETS	4:00
Oct. 27	at Tampa Bay	1:00
Nov. 3	MIAMI	1:00
Nov. 10	INDIANAPOLIS	1:00
Nov. 17	at Seattle	1:00
Nov. 24	at N.Y. Jets	1:00
Dec. 1	at Indianapolis	1:00
Dec. 8	DETROIT	1:00
Dec. 16	at Miami (Mon.)	9:00
Dec. 22	CINCINNATI	1:00

1984 Results

Sept. 2	at Buffalo	21-17
Sept. 9	at Miami	7-28
Sept. 16	SEATTLE	38-23
Sept. 23	WASHINGTON	10-26
Sept. 30	at N.Y. Jets	28-21
Oct. 7	at Cleveland	17-16
Oct. 14	CINCINNATI	20-14
Oct. 21	MIAMI	24-44
Oct. 28	N.Y. JETS	30-20
Nov. 4	at Denver	19-26
Nov. 11	BUFFALO	38-10
Nov. 18	at Indianapolis	50-17
Nov. 22	at Dallas (Thanks.)	17-20
Dec. 2	ST. LOUIS	10-33
Dec. 9	at Philadelphia	17-27
Dec. 16	INDIANAPOLIS	16-10

1985 Draft Choices

1. Choice to San Francisco
1. Trevor Matich—28. C. Brigham Young. from San Francisco
2. Garin Veris—48. DE. Stanford
2. Jim Bowman—52. DB. Central Michigan. from Los Angeles Raiders
2. Ben Thomas—56. DE. Auburn. from San Francisco
3. Choice to San Francisco
3. Audrey McMillian—84. DB. Houston. from San Francisco
4. Tom Toth—102. T. Western Michigan
4. Gerard Phelan—108. WR. Boston College. from L.A. Raiders
5. Choice to Cincinnati
6. Choice to Philadelphia
7. Choice to L.A. Raiders
8. Choice to Atlanta
8. Milford Hodge—224. DT. Washington State. from San Francisco
9. Choice to Pittsburgh
10. Choice to Denver
11. Paul Lewis—295. RB. Boston U.
12. Tony Mumford—328. RB. Penn State

NEW YORK JETS

The New York Jets took off like the Concorde last season with a 6-2 start, but it would take an FAA investigation to deduce exactly what happened after that.

While it is true they had not played the toughest competition in those giddy early weeks, it is just as true that the Jets hardly were the team they turned into over the second half of the season, in which they lost seven of eight games. Perhaps all that is necessary to know about the kind of year the Jets suffered is to realize they lost seven-year starting cornerback Bobby Jackson in the season's fifth week with a pulled hamstring—while stretching in the locker room before the game.

To his credit, coach Joe Walton ignored the hospital ward-full of injuries that plagued his team and instead chose the candid road to explain what happened.

"I didn't think we were that good even when we were six and two," Walton said. "We were playing hard and together but we weren't playing that well."

Apparently, the Jets stopped flying somewhere after they blew a 20-3 lead to the New England Patriots in the ninth game of the season, losing 30-20. This was followed by an emotionally crushing 31-17 loss to the Miami Dolphins.

"It's sad to say, but I think we became front runners," quarterback Pat Ryan said. "We had a tendency to slide when things didn't go our way."

Their problems began in earnest when Ryan was injured at midseason and was replaced by inexperienced Ken O'Brien. During that 6-2 start New York had scored 201 points with Ryan running the offense. Over the second half of the season, with O'Brien doing most of the playing because of Ryan's mounting injuries,

Defensive end Mark Gastineau led NFL in sacks with 22.

Joe Walton

that total slid to 131. With the wreckage of Jets' Flight 1984 still smoldering, Walton came up with a plan for survival. He swept away more than half his coaching staff and all of his past defensive strategies.

Assistant head coach and defensive coordinator Joe Gardi resigned and was replaced by Bud Carson, who immediately announced he would replace the Jets' 4-3 defense with the 3-4.

Walton then fired defensive assistants Ralph Baker and Billy Baird. For all intents and purposes, Walton had remained the Jets' offensive coordinator even after replacing Walt Michaels as head coach in 1983, but this year he has decided to hand that job to Rich Kotite, who had been his receivers coach.

In an attempt to improve his quarterback situation in one way, Walton hired veteran assistant Zeke Bratkowski as quarterback coach and tutor.

OFFENSE

Despite the promotion of Kotite, it is not expected that the Jets will alter their approach a great deal this season because their strength remains the running of Freeman McNeil, whenever he is healthy enough to do so, and the fleet feet of wide receivers Wesley Walker and Johnny (Lam) Jones.

"We'll basically be doing what we've been doing," Kotite said. "Multiple formations, ability to go with one or two backs and one, two or three tight ends.

"Joe and I believe that gives the defenses problems. And one of the things we've always done best is run on third down against Nickel defenses, so we don't want to lose that advantage."

The thing the Jets did best last year was hand the ball off to McNeil, who rushed for a club-record 1,070 yards despite missing four games and suffering with badly battered ribs much of the season.

McNeil was rewarded for his work by being named to the AFC Pro Bowl team's starting lineup for the second consecutive season, and there is no reason to believe he won't do that again if he stays healthy.

What might help him in that quest for health would be the emergence of a running partner to assume some of the pressure.

Johnny Hector, who surprisingly gained 531 yards after rushing for just 85 yards the previous year, gave McNeil the majority of his support last season, but look for Marion Barber, Bruce Harper, and the surprise of last training camp, sixth-round pick Tony Paige (who led the club with eight touchdowns despite carrying just 35 times), to get more work.

As long as McNeil is in the backfield, however, the Jets' running game is sound. But the same cannot be said about their passing attack, which fluctuated last year more than the price of gold.

Ryan became the starter in training camp after Richard Todd was traded and O'Brien had spent most of the preseason testifying in a New York courtroom in an assault trial with teammate Mark Gastineau.

After having thrown just 86 passes in six years with the Jets, Ryan was as rusty as expected when the season opened. But, with each passing week, he seemed to grow a bit more assured until he was injured at the midway point. For the year, Ryan threw for 1,939 yards and 14 touchdowns. He also threw 14 interceptions.

O'Brien, meanwhile, was 1-4 in games he started, although he completed 57.1 percent of his passes for 1,402 yards. But he threw more interceptions than touchdowns (7 to 6) and often seemed shaky.

"In the preseason, our situation there was unsettled, then settled when Pat Ryan played well, then unsettled when Pat got those concussions and rib injury and Ken

Joe Fields

Bobby Humphery

Johnny Jones

O'Brien wasn't ready to take over," Walton said. "But when the season ended, I felt we had found two quarterbacks we can start and win with."

If Walker and Jones can return to form, whoever is playing quarterback will find his job easier.

Jones was lost for nearly half the season with injuries, and Walker missed the presence of another deep threat. As a result, Walker finished with just 41 catches for 623 yards and an average of 15.2 yards per catch, although he did manage to score seven times.

But Jones gave a signal at the end of the year that he might yet be ready to turn into the threat the Jets always hoped he would be when he turned on his world-class speed and hauled in 32 passes.

Tight end Mickey Shuler emerged last season as the club's leading receiver. Shuler had 68 receptions for 782 yards and six touchdowns, the best figures of his seven-year career.

Squarely in the middle of all these offensive questions stands the Jets' line, a group Walton says was "the most consistent unit for us."

Although Powell seemed to slip a bit from his former pre-eminent position as an all-pro tackle, Dan Alexander, Joe Fields, Stan Waldemore, Reggie McElroy, and the improvment of Jim Sweeney at guard late in the year all bode well for 1985.

"I'm very happy with what I've seen of this line.…We were number-one in rushing [in the AFC] last year, but I'd like to see us do a better job of protecting the quarterback," said new line coach Bill Austin, who replaces Jim Ringo this year.

DEFENSE

There seems to be no room for debate on the greatness of defensive end Mark Gastineau. But not even Davy Crockett could save the Alamo alone, and no one man will be enough to save the Jets' defense. Hence the decision to bring in a new coach with a new approach.

"I felt our defense needed a change and a challenge," Walton said. "We have the people to fit this system [the 3-4]. It will give us more diversity."

Walton would like nothing more diverse from Gastineau than a continuation of his Pro Bowl MVP form.

Three Years at a Glance

Averages NFL Rank	OFFENSE			DEFENSE		
	1984	1983	1982	1984	1983	1982
Points Rank	**20.8** 15	**19.6** 19	**27.2** 3	**22.8** 20	**20.7** 10	**18.4** 9
Yards Rank	**321.8** 16	**343.3** 11	**357.6** 4	**347.9** 21	**331.3** 13	**292.1** 6
Rushing Yards Rank	**136.8** 5	**129.3** 17	**146.3** 4	**129.0** 18	**148.6** 23	**109.2** 11
Passing Yards Rank	**184.9** 21	**214.1** 10	**211.2** 7	**218.9** 20	**182.7** 7	**182.9** 9
Sacks Rank	**3.3** 18	**2.7** 12T	**2.6** 12T	**2.8** 15T	**3.0** 10	**2.2** 17T
Turnovers Rank	**2.1** 10T	**2.9** 20T	**2.0** 7	**2.1** 16T	**2.3** 17T	**2.9** 5T
Punt Returns Rank	**9.3** 8	**11.1** 3T	**8.0** 15	**6.5** 7	**7.8** 13	**9.0** 19
Kickoff Returns Rank	**23.0** 1	**20.8** 5	**20.2** 14	**21.5** 22	**21.3** 24	**21.2** 18
Penalty Yards Rank	**48.7** 9	**66.2** 27	**59.2** 23	**45.2** 24T	**49.0** 19	**38.3** 25

	W-L Total	Home	Road	Playoffs
1982	6-3	3-1	3-2	2-1, Lost AFC Championship Game
1983	7-9	2-6	5-3	None
1984	7-9	3-5	4-4	None

Once again Gastineau led the NFL in sacks with 22, but he always has rushed out of the 4-3, an advantage few other defensive ends have these days.

But Carson insists that rather than hurting his best player's game, the switch to the 3-4 could give him even more leeway to rush the passer as he pleases.

Gastineau appeared to make the transition easily enough in the Pro Bowl, where he moved from side to side and produced four sacks out of the 3-4, made seven tackles, and dumped Eric Dickerson for a safety.

It is likely that defensive tackle-end Joe Klecko will be asked to move inside to nose tackle in Carson's new defense, where his overwhelming upper body strength quickly could make him one of the best in the AFC.

Klecko's problem, though, has been injuries. He severely injured his knee several years ago and last season was hampered by hamstring and elbow problems.

It would appear that Ron Faurot, who started nine games as a rookie at defensive end last season will man the other end position, with Marty Lyons and Barry Bennett fighting it out for the designated pass-rushing slot at tackle when the Jets switch to the 4-3.

Linebacking is essential in a 3-4 alignment, and the Jets' linebackers are known for their relative lack of speed. That is one of the reasons Gardi seldom blitzed out of the 4-3, fearing that his players simply lacked the speed to get to the quarterback before disaster struck.

Carson, however, always has favored the blitz and intends to find some way to move Bob Crable, Lance Mehl (who is coming off an off-year), Kyle Clifton, Bobby Bell, Greg Buttle, and John Woodring to the ball with greater speed.

"My philosophy is to be very aggressive, to force mistakes," Carson said. "I believe you can teach people to blitz. You have to coach it at full speed in training camp. But you can teach it."

Carson also plans to teach man-to-man coverage in his secondary. Judging by last season, that seems less of a problem than keeping that secondary intact.

By the time the year was out, Walton had lost Russell Carter, Johnny Lynn, free safety Darrol Ray, Nickel back Harry Hamilton, and, of course, Jackson. No sec-

Freeman McNeil   *Ken Schroy*   *Mickey Shuler*

ondary could have survived that assault.

Carson is counting on a wholesale return to good health by his secondary, and the emergence of pressure, man-to-man pass coverage not unlike the defenses used by the San Francisco 49ers in 1984 and the Los Angeles Raiders in 1983.

"Basically, I'm a man-to-man coach," Carson said. "Multiple techniques will allow us a little flexibility, but I like an aggressive style of secondary play."

That would seem to be right up Carter's alley. He was impressive as a rookie once he overcame injuries and became a starter; he led the club with four interceptions.

Veteran safeties Ray and Ken Schroy should rejoice at the arrival of Carson, because it will give them the chance to unload on someone without the strict discipline of zone defenses to restrict them.

SPECIAL TEAMS

Placekicker Pat Leahy seemed to sink along with his teammates last season, making 17 of 24 after converting 15 of his first 18 field-goal attempts. Punter Chuck Ramsey did not cover himself with glory either, averaging a gross of just 39.7 yards a punt.

But while Walton may not have gotten much of a kick out of the kicking half of his special teams, he certainly got a boost from return man Bobby Humphery.

Humphrey led the NFL in kick returns with an average of 30.7 yards. That included a 97-yard touchdown run and a number of near breakaways.

Punt returner Kirk Springs was not quite as threatening as Humphrey, but he did manage an 8.8-yard average on 28 returns.

VETERAN ROSTER

No.	Name	Pos.	Ht.	Wt.	NFL Exp.	Birthdate	College	Games in 1984
60	Alexander, Dan	G	6-4	260	9	6/17/55	Louisiana State	16
35	Augustyniak, Mike	FB	5-11	226	4	7/17/56	Purdue	0
17	Avellini, Bob	QB	6-2	209	11	8/28/53	Maryland	4
95	Baldwin, Tom	DT	6-4	270	2	5/13/61	Tulsa	16
63	Banker, Ted	G-C	6-2	255	2	2/17/61	Southeast Missouri	4
31	Barber, Marion	FB	6-2	224	4	12/6/59	Minnesota	14
58	Bell, Bobby	LB	6-3	217	2	2/7/62	Missouri	15
78	Bennett, Barry	DT	6-4	260	8	12/10/55	Concordia	15
64	Bingham, Guy	C-G-T	6-3	255	6	2/25/58	Montana	16
23	Bligen, Dennis	RB	5-11	215	2	3/3/62	St. John's	1
83	Bruckner, Nick	WR	5-11	185	3	5/19/61	Syracuse	16
46	Burgess, Fernanza	S	6-1	210	2	3/6/60	Morris Brown	14
51	Buttle, Greg	LB	6-3	232	10	6/20/54	Penn State	14
27	Carter, Russell	CB-S	6-2	195	2	2/10/62	Southern Methodist	11
59	Clifton, Kyle	LB	6-4	233	2	8/23/62	Texas Christian	16
50	Crable, Bob	LB	6-3	234	4	9/22/59	Notre Dame	5
88	Davidson, Chy	WR	5-11	175	2	5/9/59	Rhode Island	3
22	Dennis, Mike	S-CB	5-10	195	6	6/6/58	Wyoming	6
86	Dennison, Glenn	TE	6-3	225	2	11/17/61	Miami	16
52	Eliopulos, Jim	LB	6-2	229	3	4/18/59	Wyoming	11
74	Faurot, Ron	DE-LB	6-7	262	2	1/27/62	Arkansas	15
65	Fields, Joe	C	6-2	253	11	11/14/53	Widener	16
38	Floyd, George	S-CB	5-11	190	3	12/21/60	Eastern Kentucky	8
81	Gaffney, Derrick	WR	6-1	182	8	5/24/55	Florida	12
99	Gastineau, Mark	DE	6-5	265	7	11/20/56	East Central Oklahoma	16
94	Guilbeau, Rusty	LB	6-4	237	4	11/20/58	McNeese State	16
39	Hamilton, Harry	S	6-0	193	2	11/29/62	Penn State	8
42	Harper, Bruce	RB-KR	5-8	179	9	6/20/55	Kutztown State	4
34	Hector, Johnny	RB	5-11	197	3	11/26/60	Texas A&M	13
84	Humphery, Bobby	WR-KR	5-10	170	2	8/23/61	New Mexico State	16
40	Jackson, Bobby	CB	5-10	180	8	12/23/56	Florida State	3
	Jackson, Charles	LB	6-2	222	8	3/22/55	Washington	4
80	Jones, Johnny (Lam)	WR	5-11	180	6	4/4/58	Texas	8
	Judie, Ed	LB	6-2	235	3	7/6/59	Northern Arizona	2
73	Klecko, Joe	DT-DE	6-3	263	9	10/15/53	Temple	12
89	Klever, Rocky	TE	6-3	225	3	7/10/59	Montana	16
5	Leahy, Pat	K	6-0	193	12	3/19/51	St. Louis University	16
29	Lynn, Johnny	CB-S	6-0	198	6	12/19/56	UCLA	14
93	Lyons, Marty	DE-DT	6-5	269	7	1/15/57	Alabama	13
68	McElroy, Reggie	T	6-6	270	3	3/4/60	West Texas State	16
24	McNeil, Freeman	RB	5-11	212	5	4/22/59	UCLA	12
56	Mehl, Lance	LB	6-3	233	6	2/14/58	Penn State	16
25	Minter, Cedric	RB-KR	5-10	200	2	11/13/58	Boise State	8
20	Mullen, Davlin	CB-KR	6-1	177	3	2/17/60	Western Kentucky	15
7	O'Brien, Ken	QB	6-4	214	3	11/27/60	Cal-Davis	10
49	Paige, Tony	FB	5-10	230	2	10/14/62	Virginia Tech	16
79	Powell, Marvin	T	6-5	270	9	8/30/55	Southern California	16
15	Ramsey, Chuck	P	6-2	194	9	2/24/52	Wake Forest	16
28	Ray, Darrol	S	6-1	198	6	6/25/58	Oklahoma	15
10	Ryan, Pat	QB	6-3	210	8	9/16/55	Tennessee	16
48	Schroy, Ken	S	6-2	198	9	9/22/52	Maryland	12
82	Shuler, Mickey	TE	6-3	231	8	8/21/56	Penn State	16
87	Sohn, Kurt	WR	5-11	180	4	6/26/57	Fordham	5
21	Springs, Kirk	S-KR	6-0	192	5	8/10/58	Miami, Ohio	16
53	Sweeney, Jim	G-C	6-4	260	2	8/8/62	Pittsburgh	10
70	Waldemore, Stan	G-T	6-4	269	8	2/20/55	Nebraska	14
85	Walker, Wesley	WR	6-0	182	9	5/26/55	California	12
57	Woodring, John	LB	6-2	232	5	4/4/59	Brown	15

COACHING STAFF

Joe Walton, head coach; **Bill Austin,** offensive line; **Zeke Bratkowski,** quarterbacks; **Ray Callahan,** defensive line; **Bud Carson,** special assistant to head coach; **Bobby Hammond,** running backs; **Rich Kotite,** offensive coordinator, receivers; **Larry Pasquale,** special teams; **Dan Radakovich,** linebackers.

1985 Schedule

Preseason

Aug. 10	PHILADELPHIA	8:30
Aug. 17	at Cincinnati	7:00
Aug. 24	at N.Y. Giants	8:00
Aug. 31	at Green Bay	7:00

Regular Season

Sept. 8	at L.A. Raiders	1:00
Sept. 15	BUFFALO	1:00
Sept. 22	Green Bay at Milw.	3:00
Sept. 29	INDIANAPOLIS	4:00
Oct. 6	at Cincinnati	4:00
Oct. 14	MIAMI (Mon.)	9:00
Oct. 20	at New England	4:00
Oct. 27	SEATTLE	1:00
Nov. 3	at Indianapolis	4:00
Nov. 10	at Miami	4:00
Nov. 17	TAMPA BAY	1:00
Nov. 24	NEW ENGLAND	1:00
Nov. 28	at Detroit (Thanks.)	12:30
Dec. 8	at Buffalo	1:00
Dec. 14	CHICAGO (Sat.)	12:30
Dec. 22	CLEVELAND	1:00

1984 Results

Sept. 2	at Indianapolis	23-14
Sept. 6	PITTSBURGH (Thurs.)	17-23
Sept. 16	CINCINNATI	43-23
Sept. 23	at Buffalo	28-26
Sept. 30	NEW ENGLAND	21-28
Oct. 7	at Kansas City	17-16
Oct. 14	at Cleveland	24-20
Oct. 21	KANSAS CITY	28-7
Oct. 28	at New England	20-30
Nov. 4	MIAMI	17-31
Nov. 11	INDIANAPOLIS	5-9
Nov. 18	at Houston	20-31
Nov. 26	at Miami (Mon.)	17-28
Dec. 2	N.Y. GIANTS	10-20
Dec. 8	BUFFALO (Sat.)	21-17
Dec. 16	at Tampa Bay	21-41

1985 Draft Choices

1. Al Toon—10, WR, Wisconsin
2. Lester Lyles—40, DB, Virginia
3. Donnie Elder—67, DB, Memphis State
4. Doug Allen—94, WR, Arizona State
5. Troy Benson—120, LB, Pittsburgh, from Tampa Bay
5. Brian Luft—124, DT, Southern California
5. Tony Smith—134, WR, San Jose State, from Chicago
6. Jeff Deaton—151, G, Stanford
6. Rich Miano—166, DB, Hawaii, from Denver
7. Choice to Dallas through Kansas City
8. Matt Monger—208, LB, Oklahoma State
9. Mike Waters—235, RB, San Diego State
10. Kerry Glenn—262, DB, Minnesota
11. Brad White—292, DE, Texas Tech
12. Bill Wallace—319, WR, Pittsburgh

CINCINNATI BENGALS

For a couple hours last December, the Cincinnati Bengals looked as though they would be the rags-to-riches AFC Central champions. All that had to happen was for Pittsburgh to lose on the road to the defending Super Bowl champion Los Angeles Raiders, and the Bengals, who already had routed Buffalo 52-21, would be in the playoffs.

It didn't happen. But, if momentum counts, the Bengals are the team to beat in the division in 1985. They won their last four games and eight of their final 11, overcoming an 0-5 start brought on in part by the transition from tough-guy Forrest Gregg to easy-going Sam Wyche.

Wyche, a former Bengals quarterback who had played for Paul Brown in the late 1960s, was plucked from the Indiana University job when Gregg moved to Green Bay. Brown remembered him for his astute football mind.

San Francisco coach Bill Walsh, for whom Wyche served as quarterback coach the year the 49ers won Super Bowl XVI, has said: "Sam Wyche is the finest mind and teacher of football in the game today."

Brown's memory didn't deceive him, nor was Walsh's glowing assessment necessarily wrong. It just took awhile for the pieces to drop into place.

Two of the Bengals' three first-round draft choices failed to pan out, the Pete Johnson-for-James Brooks trade backfired, Isaac Curtis sagged to the lowest point of his 12-year career, and Wyche spent most of the season playing musical quarterbacks. Under the circumstances, Cincinnati's .500 record and near-championship was a minor miracle.

Wide receiver Cris Collinsworth made 64 catches in 1984.

Sam Wyche

"We played like champions at the finish," Wyche said, "but our front end wasn't good enough. We'll try to put two good halves together."

Once again, the Bengals will revolve around Ken Anderson, whose starting reign goes back to 1971, making him one of three quarterbacks with 14 years experience in the league (Jim Plunkett of the Raiders and Lynn Dickey of the Packers are the others). He is 36 and says he wants to play at least one more year. If he can stay healthy, which he didn't do in 1984, there's no reason why he won't last two or three more. Anderson passed for three touchdowns in the rout of Buffalo, lest anyone have thoughts during the offseason that he might be pressing his luck.

The best offseason news concerned Anderson's favorite target, Cris Collinsworth. This was the year that the popular Collinsworth was supposed to jump to the United States Football League's Tampa team. But he gained his release and will resume his career with the Bengals, for whom he has caught 247 passes and produced three 1,000-yard seasons.

OFFENSE

On one hand, Wyche finds himself with a quarterback problem. On the other hand, it is a nice problem. He has three good enough to start. All three did at one time or another in 1984. When Anderson got hurt, rookie Boomer Esiason replaced him. When Esiason got hurt, Turk Schonert was there. When Schonert faltered, Anderson was ready to return.

In his fourteenth—abbreviated—season, Anderson completed 64 percent of his passes for 2,107 yards and 10 touchdowns while appearing in 11 games. Fifth-year man Schonert had a 20-for-23 outing for 288 yards in a 35-14 burning of Atlanta, and completed 71.5 percent of his passes in the three games he started, two of which the Bengals won.

Young Esiason directed the Bengals' first victory, 13-3 over Houston, even running for a touchdown on a quarterback draw.

They all had one thing in common: They looked to Collinsworth. He played hurt late in the season, yet finished with 65 receptions for exactly 1,000 yards and 6 touchdowns. His total was 17 more than all other Bengal wide receivers combined.

Curtis is a huge question mark entering 1985. He caught just 12 passes in his twelfth season and only one over the final six games. This from a receiver who had averaged 37 for his career and was one of the game's most respected deep threats.

Steve Kreider is the likely successor to Curtis. He had 20 receptions in an injury-plagued year, falling off from 42 in 1983. When teamed with Collinsworth, the former Rhodes Scholar nominee from Lehigh gives Cincinnati one of the game's smartest, most sure-handed receiving combinations, although both lack sprinter's speed.

That's where Dave Verser comes in, if he ever does come in. Verser was drafted ahead of Collinsworth in 1981 but has yet to catch more than seven passes in a season and remains the Bengals' biggest offensive disappointment.

Running back James Brooks didn't live up to expectations. It was hoped his versatility in running and receiving would fit nicely into the balanced offense Wyche planned. Brooks's 33 receptions coming out of the backfield were respectable, but his 396 rushing yards fell far short of expectations.

Larry Kinnebrew picked up some of the slack. Free of Johnson's massive shadow, Kinnebrew ran for 623—averaging four yards per carry—and scored nine touchdowns. His job is secure, although he, like John-

Ken Anderson

Tim Krumrie

Mike Martin

son, battles a weight problem. Second-year man Stanford Jennings could join him in the starting backfield. Stanley Wilson is another candidate.

The Bengals' individual rushing numbers were deceiving. None stood out, but when you add them together, Cincinnati tied for sixth in the NFL standings.

Much of the credit belongs to a huge and physical offensive line that still has its best years ahead of it. Left tackle Anthony Muñoz, a Pro Bowl starter, remains the anchor, and seven-year man Mike Wilson on the right side is a sound, solid veteran. So is right guard Max Montoya. Center Dave Rimington, who is beginning just his third season, already has established himself.

The "baby of the bunch" is 300-pound left guard Brian Blados, who was supposed to watch from afar in 1984 but wound up as a starter after Mike Obrovac was injured during the preseason. Blados's bulk, it turned out, wasn't the liability some scouts feared.

Tight end M.L. Harris isn't a weak link as a run blocker, either; his 48 receptions for 759 yards were second to Collinsworth in both categories.

Bill Johnson, the team's former head coach (1976-78), returns as offensive coordinator, but his impact is expected to be more as a steadying influence for a young coaching staff than as a strategic innovator. After all, the Bengals had the NFL's fifth-best offense in 1984.

DEFENSE

It's a good thing Blados came through for the offense because the Bengals' two first-round defensive picks contributed almost nothing. One, linebacker Ricky Hunley, never even wore Cincinnati's uniform. After a protracted contract dispute caused him to miss much of the season, the Bengals traded him to Denver. End Pete Koch, whose primary responsibility as a Maryland senior was run defense, had to learn new skills in the pass-minded NFL. He spent his rookie season as Eddie Edwards's understudy. If Koch improves his leg strength coming off the line, he could play a much greater role.

Eight-year man Edwards turned in his third consecutive all-pro-type season, registering nine sacks and further establishing himself as one of the division's most versatile ends. Teammate Ross Browner (eight sacks)

Three Years at a Glance

Averages NFL Rank	OFFENSE			DEFENSE		
	1984	1983	1982	1984	1983	1982
Points Rank	**21.2** 13	**21.6** 16	**25.8** 4	**21.2** 16	**18.9** 6	**19.7** 14
Yards Rank	**342.5** 5	**330.4** 14	**365.3** 2	**328.7** 13	**270.4** 1	**321.4** 18
Rushing Yards Rank	**136.2** 6T	**131.5** 16	**105.4** 20	**116.8** 11	**93.7** 2T	**94.4** 3
Passing Yards Rank	**206.3** 13T	**198.9** 14	**259.9** 3	**211.9** 18	**176.8** 3	**227.0** 22
Sacks Rank	**2.8** 11T	**2.5** 10	**3.0** 19	**2.5** 21	**2.6** 16T	**2.4** 15T
Turnovers Rank	**2.4** 18T	**2.1** 6T	**1.8** 2T	**2.5** 8	**2.4** 13T	**2.2** 20T
Punt Returns Rank	**12.4** 1	**8.4** 13	**5.6** 24	**8.2** 12	**7.6** 11	**4.0** 4
Kickoff Returns Rank	**18.9** 22	**20.3** 8	**20.7** 10	**21.0** 19	**19.1** 13	**18.9** 9
Penalty Yards Rank	**43.3** 5	**52.3** 16	**52.8** 16	**46.4** 22	**54.4** 10	**61.2** 6

	W-L Total	Home	Road	Playoffs
1982	7-2	4-0	3-2	0-1, Lost First Round Game
1983	7-9	4-4	3-5	None
1984	8-8	5-3	3-5	None

isn't far behind, and nose tackle Tim Krumrie, a 1983 tenth-round draft choice who has greatly exceeded expectations, completes a formidable front three.

Krumrie had 57 solo tackles, second on the team and a remarkable statistic for a part-time starter who rarely found himself in a one-on-one situation. He has split time with Jerry Boyarsky the last two seasons, but that arrangement soon may end.

Still, overall the defense sagged from its its league-leading perch in 1983, dropping to thirteenth overall and eighteenth against the pass. The Bengals' linebackers had been the backbone of the team for a number of years, but the loss of Jim LeClair to the USFL, plus natural aging, is taking its toll.

Right-side backers Glen Cameron and Reggie Williams, entering their eleventh and tenth seasons, respectively, are long on experience and intelligence, but short on speed. Williams blitzed his way to nine sacks and led the team in tackles.

Losing Hunley, LeClair's designated replacement, was a major blow, although Ron Simpkins, a five-year veteran and a seventh-round draft choice in 1980, wound up filling the hole adequately. Fourth-year man Jeff Schuh shows promise.

Veteran back-ups Rick Razzano and Steve Maidlow can start in a pinch, and Leo Barker, a second-year man, should begin to make a move this year.

The defense played poorly at the start but well at the finish, which obviously had plenty to do with the Bengals' drastic turnaround. Cincinnati gave up an average of 30 points per game during its five season-opening losses but cut that to 17 over the last 11 games.

Left cornerback Louis Breeden is near the top of his class as a cover man with a nose for the ball. He intercepted four passes. That, of course, puts added weight on right corner Ray Horton, who also had the difficult task in 1984 of trying to follow in the footsteps of retired future Hall-of-Famer Ken Riley. Horton, who intercepted three passes as a second-year starter, figures to be much improved in 1985.

Fifth-year safeties Robert Jackson and Bobby Kemp, both are fearsome hitters whose futures should be

Pat McInally

Max Montoya

Anthony Muñoz

ahead of them. Kemp is called "The Enforcer"—because he does enforce with exceptionally hard hitting. Each had four interceptions.

Reserve cornerbacks John Simmons and Ray Griffin are dependable journeymen. Jimmy Turner and Jim Griffin, both third-year men, might be starting contenders elsewhere.

SPECIAL TEAMS

When Mike Martin broke his leg in 1983, his rookie season, there was some concern that his promising career as a punt-returner might be over. Not to worry. Martin bounced back better than ever in 1984. His per-return average of 15.7 yards—up from 9.3 a season earlier—was almost 2½ yards better than anyone else in the NFL with a minimum of 20 attempts.

Martin's 20.3-yard average on kickoff returns was less spectacular, but he and Jennings (20.5) complemented each other nicely as the deep backs. Brooks had a 20-yard average in limited kickoff-return duty.

The kicking game also is set. Pat McInally, entering his tenth year, remains the world's tallest punter—6 feet 6—and also one of the best. He averaged 42.3 yards per punt, slightly above his career norm, with a net of 35.3; he also put 19 punts inside opponent's 20-yard lines.

Placekicker Jim Breech surpassed 100 points (103) for the second time in his five seasons with the Bengals. He is deadly accurate from the chip-shot range, hitting 19 of 22 attempts from inside the 40 and all 37 of his extra-point attempts. He also was 3 for 4 in the 40- to 49-yard range, but beyond the 50, where he was 0 for 5, the Bengals are better off punting.

VETERAN ROSTER

No.	Name	Pos.	Ht.	Wt.	NFL Exp.	Birthdate	College	Games in 1984
40	Alexander, Charles	RB	6-1	226	7	7/28/57	Louisiana State	16
14	Anderson, Ken	QB	6-3	212	15	2/15/49	Augustana, Ill.	11
53	Barker, Leo	LB	6-1	221	2	11/7/59	New Mexico State	16
74	Blados, Brian	T	6-4	295	2	1/11/62	North Carolina	16
	Bird, Steve	WR	5-11	176	3	10/20/60	Western Kentucky	9
61	Boyarsky, Jerry	NT	6-3	290	5	5/15/59	Pittsburgh	15
3	Breech, Jim	K	5-6	161	7	4/11/56	California	16
34	Breeden, Louis	CB	5-11	185	8	10/26/53	North Carolina Central	16
21	Brooks, James	RB	5-10	182	5	12/28/58	Auburn	15
79	Browner, Ross	DE	6-3	261	8	3/22/54	Notre Dame	16
50	Cameron, Glenn	LB	6-2	228	11	2/21/53	Florida	16
11	Clark, Bryan	QB	6-2	196	3	7/27/60	Michigan State	3
76	Collins, Glen	DE	6-6	265	4	7/10/59	Mississippi State	16
80	Collinsworth, Cris	WR	6-5	192	5	1/27/59	Florida	15
85	Curtis, Isaac	WR	6-1	192	13	10/20/50	San Diego State	16
73	Edwards, Eddie	DE	6-5	256	9	4/25/54	Miami	16
7	Esiason, Boomer	QB	6-4	220	2	4/17/61	Maryland	10
33	Farley, John	RB	5-10	202	2	8/11/61	Cal State-Sacramento	13
58	Frazier, Guy	LB	6-2	221	5	7/20/59	Wyoming	16
22	Griffin, James	S	6-2	197	3	9/7/61	Middle Tennessee State	16
44	Griffin, Ray	CB	5-10	186	8	6/29/56	Ohio State	12
83	Harris, M.L.	TE	6-5	238	6	1/16/54	Kansas State	16
27	Hicks, Bryan	S	6-0	192	4	1/24/57	McNeese State	0
82	Holman, Rodney	TE	6-3	232	4	4/20/60	Tulane	16
20	Horton, Ray	CB	5-11	190	3	4/12/60	Washington	15
37	Jackson, Robert	S	5-10	186	4	10/10/58	Central Michigan	16
36	Jennings, Stanford	RB	6-1	205	2	3/12/62	Furman	15
26	Kemp, Bobby	S	6-0	191	5	5/29/59	Cal State-Fullerton	10
89	Kern, Don	TE	6-4	225	2	8/25/62	Arizona State	16
28	Kinnebrew, Larry	RB	6-1	252	3	6/11/59	Tennessee State	16
71	Koch, Pete	NT	6-6	265	2	1/23/62	Maryland	16
64	Kozerski, Bruce	C	6-4	275	2	4/2/62	Holy Cross	16
86	Kreider, Steve	WR	6-3	192	7	5/12/58	Lehigh	16
69	Krumrie, Tim	NT	6-2	262	3	5/20/60	Wisconsin	16
55	Maidlow, Steve	LB	6-2	234	3	6/6/60	Michigan State	16
88	Martin, Mike	WR	5-10	186	3	11/18/60	Illinois	15
87	McInally, Pat	P	6-6	212	10	5/7/53	Harvard	16
65	Montoya, Max	G	6-5	275	7	5/12/56	UCLA	16
78	Muñoz, Anthony	T	6-6	278	6	8/19/58	Southern California	16
68	Obrovac, Mike	G	6-6	275	4	10/11/55	Bowling Green	0
42	Pickering, Clay	WR	6-5	215	2	6/2/61	Maine	3
97	Pillman, Brian	LB	5-10	228	2	5/22/62	Miami, Ohio	6
51	Razzano, Rick	LB	5-11	227	6	11/15/55	Virginia Tech	10
75	Reimers, Bruce	T	6-7	280	2	9/18/60	Iowa State	15
52	Rimington, Dave	C	6-3	288	3	8/13/62	Nebraska	16
15	Schonert, Turk	QB	6-1	190	6	1/15/57	Stanford	8
59	Schuh, Jeff	LB	6-2	229	5	5/22/58	Minnesota	16
25	Simmons, John	CB	5-11	192	5	12/1/58	Southern Methodist	16
56	Simpkins, Ron	LB	6-1	235	5	4/2/58	Michigan	16
62	Smith, Gary	G	6-2	265	2	1/27/60	Virginia Tech	8
35	Turner, Jimmy	CB	6-0	187	3	6/15/59	UCLA	16
81	Verser, David	WR	6-1	202	5	3/1/58	Kansas	11
84	Williams, Gary	WR	6-2	215	2	9/4/59	Ohio State	8
57	Williams, Reggie	LB	6-0	228	10	9/19/54	Dartmouth	16
77	Wilson, Mike	T	6-5	271	8	5/28/55	Georgia	16
32	Wilson, Stanley	RB	5-10	210	2	8/23/61	Oklahoma	1

Coaching Staff

Sam Wyche, head coach; **Jim Anderson,** running backs; **Bruce Coslet,** wide receivers, passing game; **Bill Johnson,** tight ends; **Dick LeBeau,** defensive coordinator, defensive backs; **Jim McNally,** offensive line, running game; **Dick Selcer,** linebackers; **Bill Urbanik,** defensive line; **Kim Wood,** strength.

1985 Schedule

Preseason

Aug. 10	KANSAS CITY	7:00
Aug. 17	NEW YORK JETS	7:00
Aug. 23	at Detroit	8:00
Aug. 30	at Indianapolis	7:30

Regular Season

Sept. 8	SEATTLE	1:00
Sept. 15	at St. Louis	12:00
Sept. 22	SAN DIEGO	1:00
Sept. 30	at Pittsburgh (Mon.)	9:00
Oct. 6	N.Y. JETS	4:00
Oct. 13	N.Y. GIANTS	1:00
Oct. 20	at Houston	12:00
Oct. 27	PITTSBURGH	4:00
Nov. 3	at Buffalo	1:00
Nov. 10	CLEVELAND	1:00
Nov. 17	at L.A. Raiders	1:00
Nov. 24	at Cleveland	1:00
Dec. 1	HOUSTON	1:00
Dec. 8	DALLAS	1:00
Dec. 15	at Washington	1:00
Dec. 22	at New England	1:00

1984 Results

Sept. 2	at Denver	17-20
Sept. 9	KANSAS CITY	22-27
Sept. 16	at N.Y. Jets	23-43
Sept. 23	L.A. RAMS	14-24
Oct. 1	at Pittsburgh (Mon.)	17-38
Oct. 7	HOUSTON	13-3
Oct. 14	at New England	14-20
Oct. 21	CLEVELAND	12-9
Oct. 28	at Houston	31-13
Nov. 4	at San Francisco	17-23
Nov. 11	PITTSBURGH	22-20
Nov. 18	SEATTLE	6-26
Nov. 25	ATLANTA	35-14
Dec. 2	at Cleveland*	20-17
Dec. 9	at New Orleans	24-21
Dec. 16	BUFFALO	52-21

1985 Draft Choices

1. Eddie Brown—13, WR, Miami
1. Emanuel King—25, LB, Alabama, from Seattle
2. Carl Zander—43, LB, Tennessee
3. Sean Thomas—70, DB, Texas Christian
4. Anthony Tuggle—97, DB, Nicholls State
5. Tony Degrate—127, DT, Texas
5. Lee Davis—129, DB, Mississipi, from New England
6. Eric Stokes—148, T, Northeastern, from Tampa Bay
6. Keith Lester—154, TE, Murray State
7. Kim Locklin—172, RB, New Mexico State, from Atlanta
7. Joe Walter—181, T, Texas Tech
8. Dave Strobel—211, LB, Iowa
9. Keith Cruise—238, DE, Northwestern
10. Bernard King—265, LB, Syracuse
11. Harold Stanfield—296, TE, Mississippi College
12. Louis Garza—322, T, New Mexico State

CLEVELAND BROWNS

A few years ago, the Cleveland Browns came to be known as the "Kardiac Kids" for their uncanny ability to pull out victories in the final seconds. Unfortunately, what goes around comes around. The 1984 Browns, considered a playoff-caliber team before the season began, could be remembered as the "Kardiac-Arrest Kids."

Cleveland went from being the NFL's only 9-7 team not to make the playoffs in 1983 to 5-11 and almost bottom-rung status in 1984. But in 9 of the 11 defeats, the Browns were in a position to win or tie in the final two minutes. Three times they were beaten by field goals on the last play of the game and a fourth loss came on a field goal with only five seconds left.

Close calls didn't win Sam Rutigliano any sympathy, however. The popular coach was fired after a 1-7 start.

His successor, Marty Schottenheimer, went 4-4, but a black cloud dogged him, too. He was a victim of three of the last-second defeats. And his four victories included two over Houston, plus Buffalo and Atlanta, none of which finished better than 4-12.

Still, Schottenheimer received a contract through 1986 to lift Cleveland from its funk. If his track record as defensive coordinator is an indicator, the Browns' exile from contender status should be short-lived.

The Cleveland defense improved from ninth in the NFL in 1983 in yards-allowed to second behind Chicago in 1984 while giving up the fourth-fewest touchdowns. Subtract blowout losses to Seattle (33-0) and world champion San Francisco (41-7) and the Browns' average yield fell to just 16 points per game. Cleveland was one of only three teams to hold opponents under a

Ozzie Newsome led all AFC receivers with 89 catches.

M. Schottenheimer

300-yard average during the season.

On the down side, the Browns didn't always play as well in the fourth quarter as they did in the first, which led to several of the late defeats.

The offense, in turn, proved inconsistent from start to finish. Paul McDonald became a full-time starter at quarterback for the first time and he went through a difficult period of adjustment. It also didn't help matters that Cleveland's best offensive lineman, Cody Risien, went down with a serious knee injury in the final preseason game and was lost for the year.

That set the tone for the season. Both Rutigliano and owner Art Modell had predicted an AFC Central championship for the Browns before the year began.

Rutigliano's firing didn't temper Schottenheimer's enthusiasm. He is as confident about what he expects of the Browns in the future as Rutigliano was. "We have the intent and the commitment to make this team the best in the league. We have a plan and we have the energy."

OFFENSE

McDonald's first season as full-time successor to departed Brian Sipe (USFL) was a painful one both emotionally and physically. He wound up being sacked a club-record 53 times, 40 coming in the first eight games. His 271 completions for 3,472 yards—fifth-best in club history—and 14 touchdowns were respectable figures, but he also had 23 interceptions. The best thing McDonald did was throw to Ozzie Newsome. The seventh-year Pro Bowl star from Alabama may be a tight end in title, but his job is to catch passes and he is very good at it. He grabbed an AFC-leading 89—matching his 1983 output—for 1,001 yards and 5 touchdowns despite facing double and triple coverages on almost every play. No other Brown had more than 35.

Newsome's 440 career receptions rank third on the NFL's all-time list of tight ends. Over the last six years no other NFL receiver has caught more passes.

It was hoped that Duriel Harris, acquired from Miami, would take some pressure off Newsome, especially as a long-ball threat. But he was a disappointment, with just 32 catches before being waived late in the year. Rookie Brian Brennan helped pick up the slack with 35 receptions, even though he broke a hand.

Ricky Feacher and Willis Adams were next in the pecking order with 22 and 21, respectively, not the kind of contributions expected from wide receivers.

Adding to the problem was converted running back Dwight Walker, a third-year pro who had won a starting wide receiver job with an attention-grabbing preseason, only to wind up on injured reserve after a car wreck the night before the opener. He missed a month and never regained his form, catching just 10.

The running game was even less productive, although Cleveland got the best from what it had. Veteran fullback Mike Pruitt was plagued by a knee problem that required arthroscopic surgery and wound up with his lowest rushing total in seven years, 506 yards. Charles White, who had sat out all of 1983 with a broken ankle, again was injured and contributed even less, carrying just 24 times for 62 yards.

Two low-round draft choices provided what ground attack the Browns had. Boyce Green, picked eleventh in 1983, led the way with 673 yards, while Earnest Byner, chosen tenth in 1984, had 426 and a gaudy 5.9-yard average. He ran for 188 yards—9 per carry—in a flashy finish against Houston.

A Greg Pruitt-type with his ability to slash and weave, Byner will be given the opportunity in 1985 to

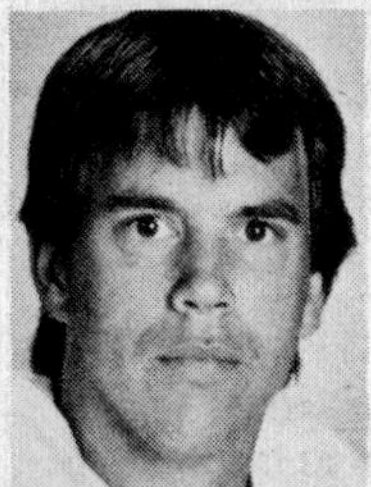

Matt Bahr

Earnest Byner

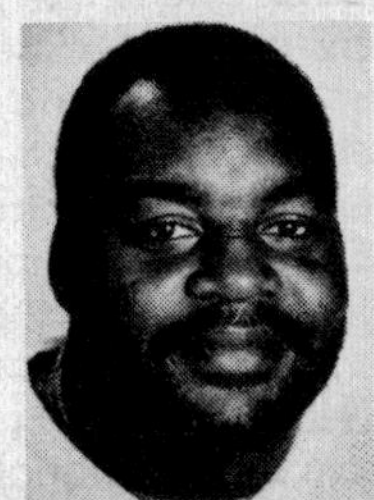

Reggie Camp

prove he's not a fluke. White, in turn, has yet to justify the first-round choice Cleveland used for him in 1980. This season could be the last chance for the former Heisman Trophy winner from USC.

A new face who could make a big splash is Kevin Mack, a USFL refugee.

All of the backs would prosper, as would the passing game in general, if the line can pull itself back together. Risien's return at right tackle, assuming he's back in form, will help considerably. And center Mike Baab, who will be a third-year starter in 1985, is rock solid. Otherwise, it is a question of reversing the aging process.

The retirement of left tackle Doug Dieken, whose consecutive-game streak of 203 was the longest among active NFL players, leaves a gaping hole in an offensive line that has two more veterans, guards Joe DeLamielleure (13 years) and Robert Jackson (11) also well on the downward side of their careers.

When Schottenheimer took over at midseason, he pulled some different strings to shore up the pass protection, but they were temporary fixes. The Browns have to play better up front if they are to improve upon their twenty-fourth-place ranking in 1984.

DEFENSE

The Browns are coming off a season in which they led the AFC in eight defensive categories as diverse as fewest rushing touchdowns allowed and fewest first downs allowed passing. "The Dogs"—the nickname cornerback Hanford Dixon gave them—were anything but, showing a good pass rush, excellent man-to-man coverage in the secondary, and tenacious pursuit on the part of the linebackers.

Opportunistic is another word that fits. Cleveland scored 114 points off the 41 turnovers it forced.

The linebacking was solid all year. Outside backer Clay Matthews made his seventh year his best one, registering 12 sacks, knocking down seven passes, recovering a fumble and forcing three others. He was Pro Bowl-bound until he broke his arm in the final game.

Inside linebacker Eddie Johnson also batted down seven passes and made 100 unassisted tackles. The

Three Years at a Glance

Averages NFL Rank	OFFENSE			DEFENSE		
	1984	1983	1982	1984	1983	1982
Points Rank	**15.6** 25T	**22.3** 13	**15.6** 23	**18.6** 6	**21.4** 14	**20.2** 16
Yards Rank	**301.8** 24	**348.9** 10	**302.2** 17	**290.1** 2	**321.4** 9	**346.0** 23
Rushing Yards Rank	**106.0** 21	**120.1** 19	**97.0** 23	**121.6** 15	**129.1** 14	**143.6** 26
Passing Yards Rank	**195.8** 18	**228.8** 6	**205.0** 12T	**168.5** 3	**192.3** 9	**202.4** 14
Sacks Rank	**3.4** 20T	**2.1** 4T	**2.9** 18	**2.7** 17T	**2.0** 24T	**2.4** 15T
Turnovers Rank	**2.4** 18T	**2.4** 11T	**2.7** 17T	**2.2** 14T	**2.0** 23	**3.1** 2
Punt Returns Rank	**8.1** 17	**7.4** 20	**5.8** 22	**11.4** 26	**10.3** 24	**7.2** 10
Kickoff Returns Rank	**19.0** 20	**20.5** 7	**19.8** 18	**22.3** 28	**18.9** 11	**18.4** 7
Penalty Yards Rank	**58.0** 20	**61.9** 24	**51.2** 15	**47.8** 21	**58.8** 7	**48.4** 16

	W-L Total	Home	Road	Playoffs
1982	4-5	2-2	2-3	0-1, Lost First Round Game
1983	9-7	6-2	3-5	None
1984	5-11	2-6	3-5	None

man beside him, Tom Cousineau, was the overall leader in tackles for the third consecutive year. Matthews, Johnson, Cousineau, and Chip Banks played so well that Dick Ambrose, the veteran of the group, wasn't missed. He spent the entire year on the inactive list after offseason surgery on his ankle failed to heal.

Johnson, a third-year player who stepped in for Ambrose, is a remarkable success story. He is only 6 feet 1-inch, 218 pounds, but Schottenheimer, his biggest fan, says he has "six-inch pop. That is, he takes on a bigger opponent, then gets into him with such quickness and explosion that he controls and neutralizes him."

Where the Browns needed improvement was in the secondary and the line. In both areas, they got it. Second-year defensive end Reggie Camp provided the punch up front, coming into his own as one the AFC's best pass rushers. He had 13 sacks in the last 12 games and his season total of 14, just a half-sack shy of Bill Glass's club record, placed him fourth among defensive linemen in the conference.

Bob Golic was a steady—and steadying—performer at nose tackle, and Keith Baldwin, beginning his fourth season, is a comer at the other end. Veteran Carl Hairston provides experience, and Elvis Franks adds depth in pass-rush situations.

The secondary received the greatest infusion of talent. Frank Minnifield, plucked from the USFL, teamed with Dixon to give Cleveland a pressing pair of cornerbacks cut from the same cloth as the Raiders' Lester Hayes and Mike Haynes. Had Minnifield not been plagued by hamstring problems, he might have gone to the Pro Bowl in his first NFL season.

Dixon, a fourth-year Brown, all but forced opponents to throw Minnifield's way, intercepting five passes and knocking down a team-high 22 others. He also recovered a fumble.

Don Rogers, Cleveland's top draft choice, was another fresh face who made good. He had an awesome first half of the season and, although he tailed off at the finish after suffering a midseason shoulder separation, still won AFC defensive rookie-of-the-year honors.

Strong safety Al Gross, who averaged 20.6 yards on

Hanford Dixon

Clay Matthews

Don Rogers

five interception returns, completes a secondary that should be among the NFL's best for years.

SPECIAL TEAMS

It took Matt Bahr three stops to find himself a niche in the NFL, but he found it with the Browns. After a 101-point year in 1983, he started slowly last season, missing 8 of his first 20 tries. He connected on his last 12 in a row—four shy of Don Cockroft's club record—and his final field goal of the year, number 24, broke Lou Groza's 31-year-old single-season Browns record.

Bahr's career field-goal percentage of .671 ranks him ninth in the NFL standings. He has made 31 straight field goals from inside the 30 and also is working on a streak of 28 points-after in a row. With 97 points, he was Cleveland's leading scorer for the fourth year.

The Browns' kicking game is in good feet all the way around. Steve Cox averaged 43.4 yards per punt, the highest by a Cleveland player since Gary Collins's 46.7 in 1965 and the fourth-best in the AFC. His net of 33.7 was less impressive, but several times he outkicked his coverage.

Cox also gives the Browns a long-range field-goal threat. He was 1-for-3 kicking from beyond the 50, but the one he hit in Cincinnati covered 60 yards, second-longest in NFL history. He owns two of the six longest.

The Browns' return teams were moderately successful—Brennan averaged eight yards per punt return to rank among the conference leaders—but their cover teams were a sore spot with Schottenheimer, who will stress them more than Rutigliano did. Cleveland allowed 22.3 yards per kickoff runback, poorest in the NFL, and 11.4 on punt returns, third from the bottom.

VETERAN ROSTER

No.	Name	Pos.	Ht.	Wt.	NFL Exp.	Birthdate	College	Games in 1984
80	Adams, Willis	TE-WR	6-2	200	6	8/22/56	Houston	16
52	Ambrose, Dick	LB	6-0	228	10	1/17/53	Virginia	0
53	Anderson, Stuart	LB	6-1	225	4	12/25/59	Virginia	6
61	Baab, Mike	C	6-4	270	4	12/6/59	Texas	16
9	Bahr, Matt	K	5-10	175	7	7/6/56	Penn State	16
99	Baldwin, Keith	DE	6-4	270	4	10/13/60	Texas A&M	16
56	Banks, Chip	LB	6-4	233	4	9/18/59	Southern California	16
24	Best, Greg	S	5-10	185	3	1/14/60	Kansas State	5
88	Bolden, Rickey	T-TE	6-6	250	2	9/8/61	Southern Methodist	12
47	Braziel, Larry	CB	6-0	184	7	9/25/54	Southern California	13
86	Brennan, Brian	WR	5-9	178	2	2/15/62	Boston College	15
49	Burrell, Clinton	S	6-1	192	6	9/4/56	Louisiana State	13
44	Byner, Earnest	RB	5-10	215	2	9/15/62	East Carolina	16
96	Camp, Reggie	DE	6-4	270	3	2/28/61	California	16
75	Contz, Bill	T	6-5	260	3	5/12/61	Penn State	15
50	Cousineau, Tom	LB	6-3	225	4	5/6/57	Ohio State	16
15	Cox, Steve	P-K	6-4	195	5	5/11/58	Arkansas	16
	Danielson, Gary	QB	6-2	196	9	9/10/51	Purdue	15
85	Davis, Bruce	WR	5-8	160	2	2/25/63	Baylor	14
38	Davis, Johnny	FB	6-1	235	8	7/17/56	Alabama	16
64	DeLamielleure, Joe	G	6-3	260	13	3/16/51	Michigan State	16
29	Dixon, Hanford	CB	5-11	182	5	12/25/58	Southern Mississippi	16
74	Farren, Paul	T	6-5	260	3	12/24/60	Boston University	15
83	Feacher, Ricky	WR	5-10	180	10	2/11/54	Mississippi Valley State	16
10	Flick, Tom	QB	6-3	190	4	8/30/58	Washington	1
94	Franks, Elvis	DE	6-4	265	6	7/9/57	Morgan State	16
79	Golic, Bob	NT	6-2	260	6	10/26/57	Notre Dame	15
30	Green, Boyce	RB	5-11	215	3	6/24/60	Carson-Newman	16
27	Gross, Al	S	6-3	186	3	1/4/61	Arizona	16
78	Hairston, Carl	DE	6-4	260	10	12/15/52	Maryland (E. Shore)	16
81	Holt, Harry	TE	6-4	230	3	12/29/57	Arizona	12
68	Jackson, Robert	G	6-5	260	11	4/1/53	Duke	16
51	Johnson, Eddie	LB	6-1	215	5	2/3/59	Louisville	16
1	Johnson, Nate	WR-KR	6-0	195	2	5/12/57	Hillsdale	0
90	Jones, Willie	DE	6-4	257	4	11/22/57	Florida State	0
77	Lewis, Darryl	TE	6-6	226	2	4/16/61	Texas-Arlington	2
62	Lilja, George	T	6-4	262	4	3/3/58	Michigan	7
59	Marshall, David	LB	6-3	220	2	1/3/61	Eastern Michigan	16
57	Matthews, Clay	LB	6-2	235	8	3/15/56	Southern California	16
16	McDonald, Paul	QB	6-2	185	6	2/23/58	Southern California	16
31	Minnifield, Frank	CB	5-9	180	2	1/1/60	Louisville	15
82	Newsome, Ozzie	TE	6-2	232	8	3/16/56	Alabama	16
58	Nicolas, Scott	LB	6-3	226	4	8/7/60	Miami	16
7	Nugent, Terry	QB	6-4	218	2	12/5/61	Colorado State	0
43	Pruitt, Mike	FB	6-0	225	10	4/3/54	Purdue	10
72	Puzzuoli, Dave	NT	6-3	260	3	1/12/61	Pittsburgh	16
63	Risien, Cody	T	6-7	280	6	3/22/57	Texas A&M	0
37	Rockins, Chris	S	6-0	195	2	5/18/62	Oklahoma State	16
20	Rogers, Don	S	6-1	206	2	9/17/62	UCLA	15
87	Stracka, Tim	TE	6-3	225	3	9/27/59	Wisconsin	6
12	Taylor, Jim Bob	QB	6-2	200	2	9/9/59	Georgia Tech	0
89	Walker, Dwight	WR	5-10	185	4	1/10/59	Nicholls State	11
55	Weathers, Curtis	LB	6-5	230	7	9/16/56	Mississippi	16
21	Whitwell, Mike	S	6-0	175	3	11/14/58	Texas A&M	0
84	Young, Glen	WR-KR	6-2	205	3	10/11/60	Mississippi State	2

Coaching Staff

Marty Schottenheimer, head coach; **Tom Bettis,** defensive coordinator; **Bill Cowher,** special teams; **Steve Crosby,** assistant to head coach, running backs; **Greg Landry,** quarterbacks; **Richard Mann,** receivers; **Howard Mudd,** offensive line; **Tom Olivadotti,** linebackers; **Joe Pendry,** offensive coordinator; **Tom Pratt,** defensive line; **Dave Redding,** strength and conditioning; **Darvin Wallis,** special assistant, defense.

1985 Schedule

Preseason

Aug. 10	at San Diego	6:00
Aug. 17	PHILADELPHIA	7:30
Aug. 24	at Buffalo	6:00
Aug. 31	LOS ANGELES RAIDERS	7:30

Regular Season

Sept. 8	ST. LOUIS	1:00
Sept. 16	PITTSBURGH (Mon.)	9:00
Sept. 22	at Dallas	12:00
Sept. 29	at San Diego	1:00
Oct. 6	NEW ENGLAND	1:00
Oct. 13	at Houston	12:00
Oct. 20	LOS ANGELES RAIDERS	1:00
Oct. 27	WASHINGTON	1:00
Nov. 3	at Pittsburgh	1:00
Nov. 10	at Cincinnati	1:00
Nov. 17	BUFFALO	1:00
Nov. 24	CINCINNATI	1:00
Dec. 1	at N.Y. Giants	1:00
Dec. 8	at Seattle	1:00
Dec. 15	HOUSTON	1:00
Dec. 22	at N.Y. Jets	1:00

1984 Results

Sept. 3	at Seattle	0-33
Sept. 9	at L.A. Rams	17-20
Sept. 16	DENVER	14-24
Sept. 23	PITTSBURGH	20-10
Sept. 30	at Kansas City	6-10
Oct. 7	NEW ENGLAND	16-17
Oct. 14	N.Y. JETS	20-24
Oct. 21	at Cincinnati	9-12
Oct. 28	NEW ORLEANS	14-16
Nov. 4	at Buffalo	13-10
Nov. 11	SAN FRANCISCO	7-41
Nov. 18	at Atlanta	23-7
Nov. 25	HOUSTON	27-10
Dec. 2	CINCINNATI*	17-20
Dec. 9	at Pittsburgh	20-23
Dec. 16	at Houston	27-20

1985 Draft Choices

1. Choice to Green Bay through Buffalo
2. Greg Allen—35, RB, Florida State
3. Choice To Buffalo
4. Choice to Miami
5. Choice to Dallas through Buffalo
6. Mark Krerowicz—147, G, Ohio State
7. Reginald Langhorne—175, WR, Elizabeth City State
8. Fred Banks—203, WR, Liberty Baptist
9. Choice to Philadelphia
10. Larry Williams—259, G, Notre Dame
11. Travis Tucker—287, TE, Southern Connecticut
12. Shane Swanson—315, WR, Nebraska

HOUSTON OILERS

The good news in Houston is that the Oilers appear to be on the road to recovery. The bad news is that they still have a long and bumpy highway ahead of them.

Since Bum Phillips, coach of three consecutive playoff teams, was fired on New Year's Eve 1980, the Oilers have had three head coaches, four defensive coordinators, three offensive coordinators, and exactly 13 victories—a total of 6 in the last three seasons. From early 1981 through mid-1984, they lost an NFL record 23 road games; over one stretch, they were 2-31.

This will be Hugh Campbell's second season as coach. He made a number of mistakes as an NFL rookie in 1984, but he won five consecutive Canadian Football League championships and still has management's confidence that he can rebuild the Oilers.

It has been a major construction project. Phillips's last Houston team built an 11-5 record, but was long in the tooth. Five years later, only four of Bum's players remained in 1985 training camp. The Oilers' starting offense last season averaged 1.77 years of NFL experience.

That included quarterback Warren Moon, who was part of Campbell's five CFL titles, joining the Oilers as a free agent after back-to-back 5,000-yard-passing seasons with Edmonton. Although not a raw rookie, he had his share of adjusting to do, a contributing factor in Houston's 0-10 start. But a 3-3 finish, which included a satisfying overtime victory against division-champion Pittsburgh, gives reason for optimism in 1985.

The Oilers have gone 1-8, 2-14, and 3-13 in the last three seasons. General manager Ladd Herzeg is expecting more of a quantum leap this season, all the

Quarterback Warren Moon gives Houston a scrambler.

Hugh Campbell

way to 8-8 if his dreams come true. Toward that end, Houston has a new offensive coordinator, Joe Faragalli, and a renewed commitment to playing the take-no-prisoners type of defense that became Houston's trademark in the late seventies, when the Oilers were two-time American Football Conference runners-up.

Faragalli served as Campbell's number-two man in Canada and was Cincinnati's quarterbacks-receivers coach last season.

No one questions that the Oilers have the offensive talent to be an impressive point-scoring machine. Defensively, the personnel is still suspect.

OFFENSE

It was assumed that the addition of Moon, who became the NFL's first $1 million-per-year player in 1984, would immediately pluck the Oilers from their offensive doldrums. No such luck. Instead, their point production fell from a poor 288 in 1983 to a terrible 240 (only Indianapolis, with 239, had fewer), and their offense ranked twenty-third in yards gained.

In many respects, Moon didn't have a bad season individually. He passed for a club-record 3,338 yards and 12 touchdowns—against 14 interceptions—with a completion percentage of 57.6. He endured 47 sacks, but more often than not his quick feet and mind carried him out of trouble. He read defenses deftly and his aptitude for the NFL game seemed to improve weekly.

The Oilers would be better suited for tapping his potential if they had a big-play receiver. Second-year man Eric Mullins, a seventh-round draft choice, looked as though he might fill that role after a brilliant preseason, but he never was given the chance, catching just six passes all year.

Houston's most reliable receiver is Tim Smith. Despite catching 83 passes in 1983, he had to prove himself again to a new coaching staff and, after a so-so preseason, he began the year on the bench. He didn't stay there long, however, and finished the season with

69 receptions for 1,141 yards and four touchdowns. His 16.5-yard average smokescreens his lack of breakaway speed.

Moon also found reliable targets in tight ends Jamie Williams (41 catches) and Chris Dressel (40), while Larry Moriarty and Stan Edwards caught 51 passes between them coming out of the backfield.

Where the Oilers need more productivity is from fifth-year man Mike Holston and fourth-year pro Steve Bryant. Holston, in particular, has been a major disappointment. He caught 26 passes over the last half of his rookie year in 1981 to position himself as Ken Burrough's successor, but he has had just 41 since, scoring only two touchdowns.

The face of the running game changed drastically with the exit of Houston institution Earl Campbell, who was traded to New Orleans six games into the season for the Saints' first-round choice in the 1985 draft. Given his sluggish start—278 yards, 2.9 per carry—after off-season arthroscopic surgery, and the Oilers' lack of success, the move wasn't a gamble.

As further proof, second-year pro Moriarty emerged as a front-line back. Moriarty averaged 102 yards over his last five games and figures to be more effective in the two-back set Houston will use more in 1985. Stan Edwards, another young back once dwarfed by Campbell's presence, figures to be the other starter. He averaged 4.5 yards per carry.

Without a superstar running back, Houston has built a superstar line, instead.

Guards Mike Munchak and Dean Steinkuhler are

Jesse Baker

Larry Moriarty

Mike Munchak

number-one draft choices, as is right tackle Bruce Matthews, while center Jim Romano, acquired from the Raiders, and left tackle Harvey Salem both are second-rounders. Munchak, 25, beginning his fourth season and coming off a Pro Bowl year, is the oldster in the group. Once they really mesh as a unit, they'll move mountains. Each is a potential all-pro.

Steinkuhler, the Oilers' number-one pick a year ago and only the second player selected, missed the last six games after tearing a knee ligament, but that's not a worry. His rehabilitation went smoothly. John Schuhmacher moved over from guard to fill in competently.

DEFENSE

The Oilers ranked twenty-seventh in the NFL in yards allowed and last—for the second season in a row—against the run, surrendering 4.7 yards per carry. It was bad enough that Eric Dickerson ran for 215 against them in the game in which he broke O.J. Simpson's single-season record. It was worse that Cleveland rookie Earnest Byner, a tenth-round draft choice, ran for 188 a week later.

The pass defense placed a more respectable eleventh, but even that figure is deceiving. Teams had such an easy time running against the Oilers they didn't throw more than they had to. But when they did pass, they had a 61 percent success rate.

Giving up yards and completions is one thing. Giving up points is worse. Houston allowed at least 27 in 11 games. In one three-game stretch (against the 49ers, Bengals and Steelers) they surrendered 100 points. Indianapolis, the lowest-scoring team in the league, ran up 35 against them. Atlanta reeled off 42.

The first order of business is rebuilding the line. Jesse Baker had a respectable year at right end, registering 11 sacks, but Mike Stensrud and Brian Sochia were mediocre at nose tackle. And left end was a disaster; five players tried to fill the hole and all failed. Jerome Foster was the best of the lot, but he was hurt early.

The Oilers' rush produced just 32 sacks, third-lowest total in the league. Lack of pressure on the quarterback made a young secondary look worse than it really was. In fact, if the Oilers have a defensive future, it's in the

Three Years at a Glance

Averages NFL Rank	OFFENSE			DEFENSE		
	1984	1983	1982	1984	1983	1982
Points	**15.0**	**18.0**	**15.1**	**27.3**	**28.8**	**27.2**
Rank	27	22	24	26	27	27
Yards	**305.3**	**306.3**	**263.7**	**373.0**	**352.0**	**382.0**
Rank	23	24	28	27	22	28
Rushing Yards	**103.5**	**124.9**	**88.8**	**174.3**	**174.2**	**136.1**
Rank	23	18	26	28	28	23
Passing Yards	**201.8**	**181.4**	**174.9**	**198.7**	**177.8**	**245.9**
Rank	17	23	19	11	4	25
Sacks	**3.1**	**3.1**	**4.3**	**2.0**	**1.9**	**3.4**
Rank	16T	19T	27	25T	26T	6T
Turnovers	**1.9**	**2.9**	**2.9**	**1.5**	**1.8**	**1.9**
Rank	7T	20T	23T	25	27	25
Punt Returns	**5.8**	**8.0**	**5.5**	**10.3**	**7.5**	**8.4**
Rank	28	17	26	23	10	17
Kickoff Returns	**19.6**	**20.2**	**20.1**	**19.3**	**21.0**	**21.7**
Rank	13	12	15	10	23	22
Penalty Yards	**50.8**	**49.0**	**47.1**	**54.8**	**51.6**	**50.4**
Rank	12	9	11	13	13	14

	W-L Total	Home	Road	Playoffs
1982	1-8	1-4	0-4	None
1983	2-14	2-6	0-8	None
1984	3-13	2-6	1-7	None

backfield, where safeties Keith Bostic and Bo Eason and cornerback Steve Brown are potential winners.

Injuries kept Eason—brother of Patriots quarterback Tony—from getting a true test as a rookie, but the coaching staff still is sold on him.

Right corner Willie Tullis is the enigma. When he won a starting job in 1982, a bright future was predicted for him. But, despite his team-leading four interceptions—Houston picked off an AFC low 13 passes—he frequently was caught out of position and beaten deep more often than second-year man Brown.

Linebacker is the most experienced area of the team, with Gregg Bingham, Robert Brazile, and Ted Thompson all holdovers from the glory days. This isn't to say, however, that it's a team strength.

Inside backer Bingham, beginning his thirteenth season, has as sharp a football mind as there is in the game today, but the legs are going and he never had a surplus of speed. He may be best utilized in spot duty, much as the 49ers used Jack Reynolds.

Brazile, a perennial all-pro early in his career, was only a shadow of his former self in 1984, his tenth season. Once a master of the big play, he came up with just two sacks off blitzes in 1984.

Avon Riley and Robert Abraham actually played better among the starters. Abraham, starting his fourth year, had a team-leading 106 unassisted tackles from his inside spot, while Riley picked up 3½ sacks blitzing from the strongside outside position.

Riley, a ninth-round draft choice out of UCLA in 1981, is said to have all-pro physical skills, but he has been hurt as much as anyone by Houston's coaching situation. This will be the first time in five seasons he hasn't had to adjust to a new coordinator and new defensive scheme.

Second-year man John Grimsley, a sixth-round pick last season, may be ready to push Bingham aside if he can build on his promising rookie performance. Seven-year veteran Daryl Hunt will return after missing all last season with a knee injury. Thompson, in his eleventh season, remains the utility man.

Coordinator Jerry Glanville is convinced the Oilers

Avon Riley

Tim Smith

Dean Steinkuhler

can get better. "We have to," he said. "I think everybody knows that."

SPECIAL TEAMS

All eyes are on Florian Kempf and Joe Cooper, the two placekickers who will fight it out to determine who stays and who goes. The job had belonged to Kempf since he unseated Toni Fritsch in 1982, but Kempf suffered a back injury trying to make a tackle on a kickoff return in the ninth game and was left unable to kick.

Enter Cooper, who had spent an unsuccessful summer opposite Rolf Benirschke in San Diego's training camp. When the Oilers called, he was enrolled in law school in Fresno, California. He had given up on playing in the NFL in 1984.

His first official NFL attempt was wide, but he made history the following week in Kansas City. His 44-yard field goal with 90 seconds left provided the winning margin in the Oilers' 17-16 victory, their first of the season and their first on the road after an NFL-record 23 consecutive defeats.

Cooper connected on 10 of his next 11 attempts the rest of the way and all 13 of his PATs.

The punting situation also is unsettled with 14-year veteran John James coming off his poorest season, even if it was a milestone year. James's 88 punts gave him 1,083 for his career, breaking Jerrel Wilson's NFL career record, but he averaged only 39.6 yards and his net of 31.4 tied him for last in the league.

Carl Roaches's 5.8-yard punt-return average, which included a long return of just 18 yards, also ranked dead last. The Oilers' kickoff return and kickoff cover teams also were mediocre.

VETERAN ROSTER

No.	Name	Pos.	Ht.	Wt.	NFL Exp.	Birthdate	College	Games in 1984
56	Abraham, Robert	LB	6-1	230	4	7/13/60	North Carolina State	16
29	Allen, Patrick	CB	5-10	173	2	8/26/61	Utah State	16
75	Baker, Jesse	DE	6-5	271	7	7/10/57	Jacksonville State	16
54	Bingham, Gregg	LB	6-1	232	13	3/13/51	Purdue	16
25	Bostic, Keith	S	6-1	210	3	1/17/61	Michigan	16
52	Brazile, Robert	LB	6-4	253	11	2/7/53	Jackson State	16
24	Brown, Steve	CB	5-11	189	3	5/20/60	Oregon	16
81	Bryant, Steve	WR	6-2	197	4	10/10/59	Purdue	14
8	Cooper, Joe	K	5-10	175	2	10/30/60	California	7
31	Donaldson, Jeff	S	6-0	193	2	4/19/62	Colorado	16
88	Dressel, Chris	TE	6-4	238	3	2/7/61	Stanford	16
21	Eason, Bo	S	6-2	200	2	3/10/61	Cal-Davis	10
32	Edwards, Stan	RB	6-0	210	4	5/20/60	Michigan	14
78	Foster, Jerome	DE	6-2	263	3	7/25/60	Ohio State	9
77	France, Doug	T	6-5	278	10	4/26/53	Ohio State	0
59	Grimsley, John	LB	6-2	232	2	2/25/62	Kentucky	16
90	Hamm, Bob	DE	6-4	263	3	4/24/59	Nevada-Reno	12
36	Hartwig, Carter	S	6-0	203	7	2/2/56	Southern California	14
84	Holston, Mike	WR	6-3	191	5	1/8/58	Morgan State	16
66	Howell, Pat	G	6-6	265	7	3/12/57	Southern California	11
50	Hunt, Daryl	LB	6-3	243	7	11/3/56	Oklahoma	5
97	Johnson, Mike	DE	6-5	253	2	4/24/62	Illinois	16
57	Joiner, Tim	LB	6-4	248	3	1/7/61	Louisiana State	11
38	Joyner, Willie	RB	5-10	200	-2	4/2/62	Maryland	10
4	Kempf, Florian	K	5-9	170	4	5/25/56	Pennsylvania	9
27	Kennedy, Mike	S	6-0	195	3	2/26/59	Toledo	11
10	Luck, Oliver	QB	6-2	196	4	4/5/60	West Virginia	4
28	Lyday, Allen	CB-S	5-10	186	2	9/16/60	Nebraska	4
93	Lyles, Robert	LB	6-1	223	2	3/21/61	Texas Christian	6
74	Matthews, Bruce	T	6-4	280	3	8/8/61	Southern California	16
89	McCloskey, Mike	TE	6-5	246	3	2/2/61	Penn State	15
26	Meadows, Darryl	S	6-1	198	3	2/15/61	Toledo	14
91	Meads, Johnny	LB	6-2	225	2	6/25/61	Nicholls State	16
1	Moon, Warren	QB	6-3	208	2	11/18/56	Washington	16
76	Moran, Eric	T	6-5	282	2	6/10/60	Washington	8
30	Moriarty, Larry	RB	6-1	240	3	4/24/58	Notre Dame	14
80	Mullins, Eric	WR	5-11	181	2	7/30/62	Stanford	13
63	Munchak, Mike	G	6-3	286	4	3/5/60	Penn State	16
12	Ransom, Brian	QB	6-3	202	3	7/9/60	Tennessee State	0
53	Riley, Avon	LB	6-3	236	5	2/10/58	UCLA	16
85	Roaches, Carl	KR-WR	5-8	170	6	10/2/53	Texas A&M	16
55	Romano, Jim	C	6-3	255	4	9/7/59	Penn State	8
73	Salem, Harvey	T	6-6	285	3	1/15/61	California	16
62	Schuhmacher, John	G	6-3	277	6	9/23/55	Southern California	16
83	Smith, Tim	WR	6-2	206	6	3/20/57	Nebraska	16
72	Sochia, Brian	NT	6-3	254	3	7/21/61	Northwest Oklahoma St.	16
70	Steinkuhler, Dean	T	6-3	273	2	1/27/61	Nebraska	10
67	Stensrud, Mike	NT	6-5	280	7	2/19/56	Iowa State	16
98	Studaway, Mark	DE	6-3	269	2	9/20/60	Tennessee	6
51	Thompson, Ted	LB	6-1	218	11	1/17/53	Southern Methodist	16
20	Tullis, Willie	CB	6-0	195	5	4/5/58	Troy State	16
82	Walls, Herkie	WR	5-8	160	3	7/18/61	Texas	14
87	Williams, Jamie	TE	6-4	232	3	2/25/60	Nebraska	16
33	Woolfolk, Butch	RB	6-1	207	4	3/1/60	Michigan	15

Coaching Staff

Hugh Campbell, head coach; **John Devlin,** linebackers; **Joe Faragalli,** offensive coordinator; **Gene Gaines,** special teams; **Jerry Glanville,** defensive coordinator; **Kenny Houston,** defensive backfield; **Bruce Lemmerman,** receivers; **Bob Padilla,** defensive line; **Al Roberts,** running backs; **Bill Walsh,** offensive line.

1985 Schedule

Preseason

Aug. 3	N.Y. Giants at Canton	2:30
Aug. 10	at Los Angeles Rams	7:00
Aug 17	at New Orleans	7:00
Aug. 24	KANSAS CITY	8:00
Aug. 31	at Dallas	8:00

Regular Season

Sept. 8	MIAMI	12:00
Sept. 15	at Washington	1:00
Sept. 22	at Pittsburgh	1:00
Sept. 29	DALLAS	12:00
Oct. 6	at Denver	2:00
Oct. 13	CLEVELAND	12:00
Oct. 20	CINCINNATI	12:00
Oct. 27	at St. Louis	12:00
Nov. 3	KANSAS CITY	12:00
Nov. 10	at Buffalo	1:00
Nov. 17	PITTSBURGH	12:00
Nov. 24	SAN DIEGO	12:00
Dec. 1	at Cincinnati	1:00
Dec. 8	N.Y. GIANTS	3:00
Dec. 15	at Cleveland	1:00
Dec. 22	at Indianapolis	4:00

1984 Results

Sept. 2	L.A. RAIDERS	14-24
Sept. 9	INDIANAPOLIS	21-35
Sept. 16	at San Diego	14-31
Sept. 23	at Atlanta	10-42
Sept. 30	NEW ORLEANS	10-27
Oct. 7	at Cincinnati	3-13
Oct. 14	at Miami	10-28
Oct. 21	SAN FRANCISCO	21-34
Oct. 28	CINCINNATI	13-31
Nov. 4	at Pittsburgh	7-35
Nov. 11	at Kansas City	17-16
Nov. 18	N.Y. JETS	31-20
Nov. 25	at Cleveland	10-27
Dec. 2	PITTSBURGH*	23-20
Dec. 9	at L.A. Rams	16-27
Dec. 16	CLEVELAND	20-27

1985 Draft Choices

1. Choice to Atlanta through Minnesota
1. Ray Childress—3, DE, Texas A&M, from Minnesota
1. Richard Johnson—11, DB, Wisconsin, from New Orleans
2. Choice to Denver
2. Richard Byrd—36, DE, So. Mississippi, from Tampa Bay through Denver
3. Choice to New York Giants
3. Mike Kelley—82, C, Notre Dame, from Denver
4. Tom Briehl—87, LB, Stanford
5. Choice to Dallas

5. Frank Bush—133, LB, North Carolina State, from L.A. Rams through Kansas City
5. Lee Johnson—138, K, Brigham Young, from Denver
6. Choice to L.A. Raiders
6. Joe Krakoski—153, LB, Washington, from Kansas City
7. Mike Akiu—170, WR, Hawaii
8. Chuck Thomas—199, C, Oklahoma
9. Steve Tasker—226, KR, Northwestern
10. Mike Golic—255, DE, Notre Dame
11. Willie Drewrey—281, KR, West Virginia
12. Mark Vonder Haar—311, DT, Minnesota

PITTSBURGH STEELERS

No NFL team has won more division championships since the 1970 merger with the American Football League than the Pittsburgh Steelers. Nevertheless, the script for Pittsburgh's ninth AFC Central title in 1984 hardly was predictable.

The Steelers rode a crazy roller-coaster from start to finish, ruining Cincinnati's victory party at the last possible moment with an upset of the defending Super Bowl champion Raiders in Los Angeles on the final afternoon of the regular season. Yet, two weeks earlier, they had been upset themselves, by 3-13 Houston.

The Steelers followed their title-clinching win in Los Angeles with an even more unanticipated 24-17 playoff victory over Denver (13-3) to charge into the AFC Championship Game against the Dolphins. Pittsburgh fell in Miami, but the season had to be judged a success.

"We had our ups and downs," veteran wide receiver John Stallworth admitted. "But we'd like to believe the team you saw beat Denver was the team we really were, not the team that lost to Houston."

Who knows? The Steelers also were a team that gave Super Bowl XIX champion San Francisco its lone defeat one weekend and lost to the Indianapolis Colts the next.

It was that kind of year in Steeltown, where the faces and the story line have changed, if the tradition hasn't.

Chuck Noll has had 13 consecutive non-losing seasons and has made the playoffs 11 of those years. But many think the man who was the architect of the Steelers' four world championships in the 1970s did his finest coaching job in 1984, Pittsburgh's 9-7 record notwithstanding.

Mark Malone takes over as quarterback for the Steelers.

Chuck Noll

Four of Pittsburgh's five road losses were by a total of nine points. Plus, the Steelers were one of the NFL's five youngest teams, playing without veterans Terry Bradshaw, Franco Harris, and Mel Blount, as well as Jack Lambert for the first time. Bradshaw and Blount retired, Harris got himself waived after a training-camp contract holdout, and Lambert sat out all but a few quarters of the season with a broken toe.

By year's end, only three participants in the Steelers' four Super Bowls—Stallworth, center Mike Webster, and safety Donnie Shell—still were on the roster. Four rookies started on offense in the playoffs.

After claiming the job at midseason from David Woodley (who had been obtained from Miami), quarterback Mark Malone wound up playing in more games than he had in his four previous seasons combined. He typified the new wave of Steelers stars. "This is a young football team with potential," Noll said before the season began. "Our whole problem is reaching that potential. We have some young players who want to play very badly. Now we're going to play the season to see if they can."

They could, although it took Noll most of the year to find out. But now the young players have experience and, in the AFC Central, 1985 would seem to be their year once again.

As usual.

OFFENSE

If Malone can build from the foundation he laid in 1984, Pittsburgh's immediate quarterback future is secure. Bradshaw's former back-up lacks his predecessor's strength, but he has the requisite sharp mind and leadership qualities to be a consistent winner. He went 6-3 as a starter in the regular season, completing 54 percent of his passes for 2,137 yards and 16 touchdowns as the Steelers' passing game rose from twenty-seventh in the NFL in 1983 to fifteenth.

Malone goes to training camp as the number-one

man, although Noll hasn't yet written off Woodley, who was assumed to be the heir-apparent to Bradshaw after the Steelers took the trouble to trade for him. Woodley fumbled two center snaps in a season-opening loss to Kansas City, but then directed consecutive victories over the Jets and the Rams. He suffered a concussion, which allowed Malone to move in.

Once Malone took over, he got considerable help from one oldtimer and one newcomer. Stallworth, a non-factor a year earlier because of injuries, saved his best season for his eleventh, breaking Steelers records for catches (80) and yards gained (1,395). His seven 100-yard games led all NFL receivers, and he scored 11 touchdowns, one-fifth of his career total.

Stallworth prospered in part because defenses suddenly had another Lynn Swann-type to worry about opposite him. Louis Lipps, Pittsburgh's top draft choice, rewarded the club's faith in him with a rookie-of-the-year season that included 45 receptions for 860 yards. His nine touchdowns included one rushing and one on a punt return, making him the NFL's only triple-threat scorer.

The resurgence of the passing game overshadowed a productive rushing attack that carried on competently without Harris, tying the Bengals for sixth-best in the NFL. Frank Pollard, a former eleventh-round draft choice with a journeyman's reputation, stepped in as a starter and ran for with 851 yards and a 4.0 average. He added 99 more on 16 carries in the Denver playoff victory, scoring two touchdowns.

Running mate Walter Abercrombie, a 1982 first-

Robin Cole

Tunch Ilkin

Louis Lipps

round pick with an injury-prone reputation, also came into his own over the final five weeks and finished with 610 yards, giving Pittsburgh the league's only all-Baylor University starting backfield. Second-year man Rich Erenberg, a surprise in training camp last summer, provides solid relief at either position.

The Steelers averaged 136.2 rushing yards per game behind an offensive line that lost both starting tackles and a starting guard during the course of the season. At one point, only two Steelers linemen were completely free of injury. Pittsburgh got a big boost from rookie Terry Long, who wound up as the starting right guard.

Playing beside veteran center Webster didn't hurt his development. Webster, in his twelfth season in 1985, remains one of the NFL's most reliable, consistent centers. Right tackle Tunch Ilkin also had a Pro Bowl-type season, even if he didn't get the recognition.

Ilkin and left guard Craig Wolfley are next behind Webster in experience with five years apiece. It's a nice mix of youthful exuberance and veteran sophistication.

DEFENSE

If someone had told Noll before the 1984 season began that he wouldn't have Lambert's services, he might have predicted disaster. As it turned out, the Steelers played as well defensively as any of their teams since the Steel Curtain days. They finished fourth overall in the NFL in fewest yards allowed and were first in the AFC against the run, giving up just one 100-yard game.

The defense thought—and played—offensively, scoring six touchdowns.

Lambert, a nine-time all-pro, broke a big toe in the season opener and spent most of the year on injured reserve. However, four-year veteran David Little proved to be more than a stop-gap replacement and earned the right to inherit the left inside linebacker position for good when Lambert retires.

Little was aided by playing between fleet outside backer Mike Merriweather and Robin Cole, an eight-year veteran. Merriweather, in only his fourth year, went to the Pro Bowl on the strength of 15 quarterback sacks, 98 tackles, and 2 interceptions and was the dom-

Three Years at a Glance

Averages NFL Rank	OFFENSE			DEFENSE		
	1984	1983	1982	1984	1983	1982
Points	**24.2**	**22.2**	**22.7**	**19.4**	**18.9**	**16.2**
Rank	8	14	8	11T	7	4
Yards	**338.8**	**313.4**	**330.0**	**307.3**	**295.8**	**319.3**
Rank	8	22	8	5	3	17
Rushing Yards	**136.2**	**163.1**	**131.9**	**101.1**	**114.6**	**84.7**
Rank	6T	4	8	4	7	1
Passing Yards	**202.6**	**150.3**	**198.1**	**206.2**	**181.2**	**234.7**
Rank	15	27	17	15	5	23
Sacks	**2.2**	**3.3**	**2.1**	**2.9**	**3.1**	**3.8**
Rank	5T	22	8	14	8	2
Turnovers	**2.5**	**2.7**	**2.8**	**2.6**	**2.8**	**2.8**
Rank	22	19	22	5T	8	7T
Punt Returns	**11.4**	**8.3**	**8.8**	**9.5**	**9.5**	**6.5**
Rank	4	14	9	18	18	9
Kickoff Returns	**19.0**	**18.1**	**20.3**	**21.9**	**23.2**	**22.8**
Rank	19	25	13	26	28	26
Penalty Yards	**59.3**	**52.3**	**51.0**	**59.1**	**48.9**	**39.4**
Rank	22	15	14	8	20	24

	W-L Total	**Home**	**Road**	**Playoffs**
1982	6-3	4-0	2-3	0-1, Lost First Round Game
1983	10-6	4-4	6-2	0-1, Lost First Round Game
1984	9-7	6-2	3-5	1-1, Lost AFC Championship Game

inant defensive player in the AFC Central.

Cole, moved inside for the first time in his career, responded with a Pro Bowl season of his own. He is a fearsome hitter, in the best Lambert tradition.

The Steelers didn't get a lot of quarterback pressure from their front three, but ends John Goodman and Edmund Nelson and nose tackle Gary Dunn are workhorse types who hold their ground. Dunn was an anchor up front. Keith Gary added bulk in passing situations and is just now beginning to come into his own.

When 1984 began, the biggest defensive hole to fill was at Blount's right cornerback spot. Future Hall of Famers aren't easily replaced, especially when the leading candidate is a 5-foot 8-inch former free agent from Mississippi Valley State University. But Sam Washington proved he belonged—and then some—by intercepting six passes over the first half of the season. Defenses tested him early in order not to have to throw to Dwayne Woodruff's side. Woodruff, a seventh-year pro, has become one of the NFL's top cover men.

Strong safety Shell, beginning his twelfth year, hasn't showed any major signs of deterioration, intercepting seven passes—he is the NFL career leader among active players with 43—and still hitting with the tenacity of a decade ago.

Free safety Eric Williams will be battling fourth-year pro Rick Woods to keep his spot.

The Steelers' secondary intercepted 25 of the team's 31 passes—second in the NFL—and played with a controlled recklessness encouraged by 29-year-old defensive coordinator Tony Dungy.

"We try to stay basic and we don't gamble much," Dungy said. "But because we're always hustling around the ball we make some big plays."

Dungy fits in perfectly with Pittsburgh's new youthful image. He has been a protege of Noll since he was 24, and he's a likely candidate to become the NFL's first modern-day black head coach.

SPECIAL TEAMS

Pittsburgh's special teams were very special indeed, particularly with Lipps getting loose and sinking opponents. The NFL's top rookie missed two games with an

Frank Pollard   *Donnie Shell*   *John Stallworth*

ankle injury but still fell just 12 yards short of Greg Pruitt's league punt-return yardage record—and he had runs of 73 and 61 called back.

However proficient and valuable Lipps might be at receiver, the Steelers will be hard-pressed to take him out of their return game. His 12.4-yard average, best in the league among players with more than 30 attempts, was the highest by a rookie since Neil Colzie's 13.6 for the Raiders in 1975.

Rookies Todd Spencer and Erenberg were far less spectacular returning kickoffs, but their 20.7- and 20.5-yard averages were adequate.

Pittsburgh was less successul defending against kickoff and punt returns. They tied for next-to-last in the former category with a 21.9-yard yield and ranked in the bottom half of the latter with a 9.5.

If not for Lipps, placekicker Gary Anderson would have stood out as the Steelers' special teams star. The third-year pro led the AFC in scoring for the second consecutive season with 117 points, hitting all 45 of his points-after touchdowns and 24 of 32 field goals, including 2 of 3 from beyond 50 yards.

Anderson's field goal, with 1:42 left in Candlestick Park, felled the champion 49ers 20-17, San Francisco's lone loss in 19 games. He was 16 for 21 on the road, and 5 of 6 on grass, a bane of most kickers.

Punter Craig Colquitt, starting his seventh season, might not have quite as much job security. His 41.2-yard average placed him only eleventh among AFC punters, although his net of 34.7 rated a couple notches higher. Also on the plus side, 21 of his punts died inside the 20-yard line.

VETERAN ROSTER

No.	Name	Pos.	Ht.	Wt.	NFL Exp.	Birthdate	College	Games in 1984
34	Abercrombie, Walter	RB	6-0	210	4	9/26/59	Baylor	14
1	Anderson, Gary	K	5-11	170	4	7/16/59	Syracuse	16
77	August, Steve	T	6-5	258	9	9/4/54	Tulsa	11
54	Bingham, Craig	LB	6-2	220	4	9/29/59	Syracuse	11
71	Boures, Emil	G-T	6-1	261	4	1/29/60	Pittsburgh	8
23	Brown, Chris	CB-S	6-0	195	2	4/11/62	Notre Dame	16
79	Brown, Larry	T	6-4	270	15	6/16/49	Kansas	7
10	Campbell, Scott	QB	6-0	201	2	4/15/62	Purdue	5
80	Capers, Wayne	WR	6-2	193	3	5/17/61	Kansas	16
78	Catano, Mark	DE	6-3	265	2	1/26/62	Valdosta State	16
33	Clayton, Harvey	CB	5-9	180	3	4/4/61	Florida State	14
56	Cole, Robin	LB	6-2	225	9	9/11/55	New Mexico	16
5	Colquitt, Craig	P	6-1	182	7	6/9/54	Tennessee	16
40	Corley, Anthony	RB	6-0	210	2	8/10/60	Nevada-Reno	14
89	Cunningham, Bennie	TE	6-5	255	10	12/23/54	Clemson	7
67	Dunn, Gary	NT	6-3	265	9	8/24/53	Miami	16
	Echols, Terry	LB	6-0	220	2	1/10/62	Marshall	4
24	Erenberg, Rich	RB-KR	5-10	200	2	4/17/62	Colgate	16
92	Gary, Keith	DE	6-3	260	3	9/14/59	Oklahoma	16
26	Gillespie, Scoop	RB	5-10	185	2	2/26/62	William Jewell	14
95	Goodman, John	DE	6-6	255	5	11/12/58	Oklahoma	14
53	Hinkle, Bryan	LB	6-2	220	4	6/4/59	Oregon	15
62	Ilkin, Tunch	T	6-3	255	6	9/23/57	Indiana State	16
29	Johnson, Ron	S	5-11	195	8	6/8/56	Eastern Michigan	15
90	Kohrs, Bob	LB	6-3	235	5	11/8/58	Arizona State	10
84	Kolodziejski, Chris	TE	6-3	231	2	1/5/61	Wyoming	7
58	Lambert, Jack	LB	6-4	220	12	7/8/52	Kent State	8
83	Lipps, Louis	WR-KR	5-10	190	2	8/9/62	Southern Mississippi	14
50	Little, David	LB	6-1	230	5	1/3/59	Florida	16
74	Long, Terry	G	5-11	272	2	7/21/59	East Carolina	12
16	Malone, Mark	QB	6-4	218	6	11/22/58	Arizona State	13
57	Merriweather, Mike	LB	6-2	215	4	11/26/60	Pacific	16
81	Nelson, Darrell	TE	6-2	235	2	10/27/61	Memphis State	11
64	Nelson, Edmund	NT-DE	6-3	270	4	4/3/60	Auburn	16
30	Pollard, Frank	RB	5-10	218	6	6/15/57	Baylor	15
60	Rasmussen, Randy	C-G	6-1	253	2	9/27/60	Minnesota	16
88	Rodgers, John	TE	6-2	238	4	2/7/60	Louisiana Tech	6
63	Rostosky, Pete	T	6-4	255	2	7/29/61	Connecticut	8
59	Seabaugh, Todd	LB	6-4	225	2	3/16/61	San Diego State	16
31	Shell, Donnie	S	5-11	190	12	8/26/51	South Carolina State	16
72	Snell, Ray	T	6-4	265	6	2/24/58	Wisconsin	13
36	Spencer, Todd	RB	6-0	200	2	7/26/62	Southern California	7
82	Stallworth, John	WR	6-2	191	12	7/15/52	Alabama A&M	16
85	Sweeney, Calvin	WR	6-2	190	6	1/12/55	Southern California	9
87	Thompson, Weegie	WR	6-6	210	2	3/21/61	Florida State	16
38	Veals, Elton	RB	5-11	230	2	3/26/61	Tulane	15
41	Washington, Sam	CB	5-8	180	4	3/7/60	Miss.Valley State	14
52	Webster, Mike	C	6-1	250	12	3/18/52	Wisconsin	16
21	Williams, Eric	S	6-1	183	3	2/21/60	North Carolina State	16
28	Williams, Robert	S	5-11	202	2	9/26/62	Eastern Illinois	2
93	Willis, Keith	DE	6-1	260	4	7/29/59	Northeastern	12
61	Wingle, Blake	G	6-2	267	3	4/17/60	UCLA	15
73	Wolfley, Craig	G	6-1	255	6	5/19/58	Syracuse	9
19	Woodley, David	QB	6-2	204	6	10/25/58	Louisiana State	7
49	Woodruff, Dwayne	CB	6-0	198	7	2/18/57	Louisville	16
22	Woods, Rick	S	6-0	191	4	11/16/59	Boise State	15

Coaching Staff

Chuck Noll, head coach; **Ron Blackledge,** offensive line, tackles; **Tony Dungy,** defensive coordinator; **Walt Evans,** assistant conditioning coach; **Dennis Fitzgerald,** inside linebackers; **Dick Hoak,** offensive backfield; **Jed Hughes,** outside linebackers; **Hal Hunter,** offensive line; **John Kolb,** defensive line, conditioning; **Tom Moore,** offensive coordinator.

1985 Schedule

Preseason

Aug. 10	at Tampa Bay	8:00
Aug. 17	at Minnesota	7:00
Aug. 23	at St. Louis.	7:30
Aug. 30	N.Y. GIANTS	7:30

Regular Season

Sept. 8	INDIANAPOLIS	1:00
Sept. 16	at Cleveland (Mon.)	1:00
Sept. 22	HOUSTON	1:00
Sept. 30	CINCINNATI	9:00
Oct. 6	at Miami	1:00
Oct. 13	at Dallas.	12:00
Oct. 20	ST. LOUIS	1:00
Oct. 27	at Cincinnati.	4:00
Nov. 3	CLEVELAND.	1:00
Nov. 10	at Kansas City.	12:00
Nov. 17	at Houston	12:00
Nov. 24	WASHINGTON	1:00
Dec. 1	DENVER	1:00
Dec. 8	at San Diego.	6:00
Dec. 15	BUFFALO.	1:00
Dec. 21	at N.Y. Giants (Sat.)	12:30

1984 Results

Sept. 2	KANSAS CITY	27-37
Sept. 6	at N.Y. Jets (Thurs.)	23-17
Sept. 16	L.A. RAMS.	24-14
Sept. 23	at Cleveland	10-20
Oct. 1	CINCINNATI (Mon.)	38-17
Oct. 7	MIAMI.	7-31
Oct. 14	at San Francisco	20-17
Oct. 21	at Indianapolis	16-17
Oct. 28	ATLANTA.	35-10
Nov. 4	HOUSTON	35-7
Nov. 11	at Cincinnati.	20-22
Nov. 18	at New Orleans (Mon.).	24-27
Nov. 25	SAN DIEGO	52-24
Dec. 2	at Houston*	20-23
Dec. 9	CLEVELAND (Sat.)	23-20
Dec. 16	at L.A. Raiders	13-7
Dec. 30	Denver.	24-17
Jan. 6	Miami	28-45

1985 Draft Choices

1. Darryl Sims—20, DE, Wisconsin
2. Mark Behning—47, T, Nebraska
3. Liffort Hobley—74, DB, Louisiana State
4. Dan Turk—101, C, Wisconsin
5. Choice to Seattle
5. Cam Jacobs—136, LB, Kentucky, from Washington
6. Gregg Carr—160, LB, Auburn
7. Alan Andrews—187, TE, Rutgers
8. Harry Newsome—214, P, Wake Forest
9. Fred Small—241, LB, Washington
9. Andre Harris—242, DB, Minnesota, from New England
10. Oliver White—268, TE, Kentucky
11. Terry Matichak—300, DB, Missouri
12. Jeff Sanchez—327, DB, Georgia

DENVER BRONCOS

The Denver Broncos present an interesting paradox.

They were not the best offensive team in the National Football League last season. Not by a long shot. They ranked twenty-second in the league in total offense. Denver wasn't the best defensive team, either. Only three teams allowed more yards than the Broncos did in 1984.

But Denver was, in fact, the *best* team in its own division and the second-best team in the conference. The Broncos won a club-record 13 games to overhaul the defending Super Bowl champion Los Angeles Raiders for the AFC West title and finish with the second-best record in the conference behind Miami's 14-2 mark.

The success of the Broncos can be traced to mistakes: Their defense caused them and their offense stopped making them. The result—the bottom line—surprised even coach Dan Reeves.

"There was no way I felt we'd win our division," Reeves said. "I felt we'd be competitive and we'd fight for a playoff berth. But we played better than I thought we would. We had a lot of young people who came around, who played quicker than we thought they would.

"Our offensive line had an excellent year and we were able to run the ball. We didn't play well defensively yardage-wise, but we were tough in terms of not giving up points. We caused more errors than we made. And we played well within our division. We wound up beating the Raiders and San Diego twice and splitting with both Kansas City and Seattle. If you want to win this division, you'd better be successful in it or you'll get eaten up."

Sammy Winder finished third among AFC rushers with 1,153.

Dan Reeves

Reeves doesn't think his Broncos should be favored to repeat in the AFC West in 1985. "I don't know if you ever can pick a favorite in this division," he said. And if he's looking for reasons why, there are plenty of them in 1985.

Seattle finished one game out of first place a year ago without 1983 AFC rushing leader Curt Warner. Now he's back. Kansas City figures to have quarterback Bill Kenney for more than half the season, as was the case in 1984. A third-place finish won't sit well with the Raiders, and the Chargers can't possibly have as many injuries as in 1984.

The Broncos no longer are an unknown commodity. Their success came so quietly last season that in the Pro Bowl balloting by the AFC players last December, only one Denver player was named to participate in the postseason all-star game—running back Sammy Winder. And he was selected as a reserve.

"If you continue to have success, the recognition will come," Reeves said. "Our players learned last year they can compete with anyone. They don't have to back up to anybody. If we have the same sort of year [in 1985], we'll get recognition.

"I don't think anybody took us seriously last year. We snuck up on a lot of people. The true test of how good a team we are will be this season. We won our division and people will be shooting for us. We'll be a better football team this year but we're going to have to be."

OFFENSE

When quarterback John Elway reaches his potential—and that could be soon—the Broncos will not need to rely on their defense as much.

The former Stanford All-America made great strides between his first and second seasons, moving from the seventeenth-rated passer to eighth, increasing his yardage from 1,663 to 2,598, and his touchdowns from 7 to 18. He also threw only one more interception (15) than he did in 1983, though he threw 121 more passes.

"Experience will make John Elway better," Reeves

said, "and he'll continue to improve as we surround him with better people. If you compare Elway to [Miami quarterback Dan] Marino, we don't have the same type of people around him. We don't have the speed and the big-play capability Miami has in [Mark] Duper and [Mark] Clayton. We have to work a little harder.

"But John has done an excellent job. He makes the people around him better. We know that he's still got a long way to go to get to where he wants to be. But he'll get there; there's no question in my mind he'll get there. If we can come up with a speed receiver and a back to catch the ball out of the backfield, we can help him get there a little quicker."

Wide receiver Steve Watson has helped Elway come a long way already. Watson is one of the best-kept secrets in the league. He has topped 1,000 yards in receiving three of the last four seasons, with only the strike year preventing him from making it four in a row. Yet Watson has gone to only one Pro Bowl; he was bypassed in 1984, despite 69 receptions for 1,170 yards.

But Reeves hit Watson's relative obscurity on the head when he said the Broncos need a speed guy on the flank. Watson is not the burner, the home-run threat whose name leaps out at his peers when they vote the Pro Bowl teams each December.

"Somebody who is a technician like myself can be just as effective as someone with speed," Watson said. "I hope so, because I'm not fast. I don't know whether it's by instinct or not."

The Broncos acquired wide receiver Butch Johnson from the Houston Oilers late in the preseason last year

John Elway   *Steve Foley*   *Tom Jackson*

when Dave Logan didn't pan out, and Johnson gave Reeves a 42-catch, six-touchdown season. He'll hold down the other flank until Denver can find a sprinter. The Broncos also rotate three tight ends in two positions because of their one-back offense. Clarence Kay, Jim Wright, and John Sawyer are better blockers than receivers.

Winder has withstood a three-year challenge from 1982 first-round draft pick Gerald Willhite to emerge as one of the AFC's premier runners. He finished third in the conference last season with 1,153 yards rushing and also caught 44 passes in a safety-valve capacity to earn his first trip to the Pro Bowl.

On the offensive line, center Billy Bryan and tackle Dave Studdard have emerged as star-quality. After getting beaten up the previous two seasons as apprentice starters, tackles Keith Bishop and Ken Lanier began to hand out some punishment of their own in 1984. Paul Howard gives the Broncos 11 years of experience at right guard. As a group, those linemen do an effective job. Elway was sacked only 24 times in 1984.

DEFENSE

The key statistic for the Denver defense was not the 5,687 yards it allowed in 1984. It was the 241 points the Broncos yielded—the fewest points allowed in the AFC and the second-fewest in the NFL behind the 227 of the Super Bowl champion San Francisco 49ers.

A defense can allow yards with regularity when it can force turnovers with the regularity that Denver's revived Orange Crush did. The Broncos finished second in the NFL to the Seahawks a year ago in both turnovers (55) and turnover ratio (a plus-21). Denver intercepted 31 passes, and set club records with 24 fumble recoveries and 57 sacks. In addition, eight turnovers were converted into defensive touchdowns. "We teach a scrambling, swarming defense," said veteran linebacker Tom Jackson. "We figure the more hands and helmets you have on the ball, the better the chances of getting a turnover. I don't care what people say, either the ball is bouncing your way or it isn't. But the more it bounces your way, the more you look for it."

Denver's defensive opportunism was evident in a

Three Years at a Glance

Averages NFL Rank	OFFENSE			DEFENSE		
	1984	1983	1982	1984	1983	1982
Points Rank	**22.1** 11	**18.9** 21	**16.4** 20	**15.1** 2	**20.4** 9	**25.1** 25
Yards Rank	**308.4** 22	**300.7** 26	**315.2** 15	**355.4** 25	**350.6** 21	**352.1** 24
Rushing Yards Rank	**129.8** 10	**111.5** 23	**113.1** 17	**104.0** 5	**121.1** 10	**103.9** 7
Passing Yards Rank	**178.7** 23	**189.2** 20	**202.1** 15	**251.4** 27	**229.4** 23	**248.2** 26
Sacks Rank	**2.2** 5T	**3.4** 24T	**2.7** 15	**3.6** 5T	**2.4** 20	**1.8** 24
Turnovers Rank	**2.1** 10T	**2.6** 18	**4.0** 28	**3.4** 2	**2.9** 7	**2.1** 22
Punt Returns Rank	**7.8** 18	**11.1** 3T	**14.5** 1	**7.6** 8	**9.5** 19	**9.1** 20
Kickoff Returns Rank	**19.9** 10	**19.2** 17	**20.5** 12	**21.5** 23	**17.9** 5	**20.8** 17
Penalty Yards Rank	**39.8** 3	**50.3** 11	**57.3** 19	**55.7** 11	**68.6** 2	**63.4** 5

	W-L Total	**Home**	**Road**	**Playoffs**
1982	2-7	1-4	1-3	None
1983	9-7	6-2	3-5	0-1, Lost First Round Game
1984	13-3	7-1	6-2	0-1, Lost Divisional Playoff Game

Monday night game against the Green Bay Packers during a freak mid-October blizzard. The Broncos returned fumbles for touchdowns on Green Bay's first two plays of the game to take a 14-0 lead after 37 seconds on a field that quickly made offense virtually impossible. Safety Steve Foley ran 22 yards with the first fumble, and cornerback Louis Wright 27 yards with the second. The Broncos went on to win 17-14.

Foley and cornerback Mike Harden each intercepted six passes, and Nickel back Steve Wilson had four for the Broncos last season. Still, the best of the deep defenders may be safety Dennis Smith, who will be starting his fifth season. Nose tackle Rubin Carter fell on three fumbles, with Foley, Wright, Harden, and end Rulon Jones recovering two apiece. Jones had 11 sacks among his 105 tackles.

One problem Denver faces on defense is age. In 1985, Jackson and end Barney Chavous are entering their thirteenth seasons, Wright and Carter their eleventh, and Foley his tenth. But Reeves already has begun the rebuilding process.

The Broncos replaced perennial Pro Bowl middle linebacker Randy Gradishar last fall with fourth-year man Steve Busick, and Busick responded with a team-leading 195 tackles. Reeves also has begun to phase in linemen Walt Boyers, Scott Garnett, and Andre Townsend, linebackers Karl Mecklenburg and Ricky Hunley and defensive backs Randy Robbins and Tony Lilly. All have been added to the roster since 1983.

The Broncos categorize Hunley, as a steal. He was a first-round draft choice by Cincinnati in 1984, but he couldn't come to contract terms with the Bengals. So, last October, Denver traded a third-round pick in 1985 and a first-round pick in 1986 for the 6-2, 238-pound former Arizona All-America.

Hunley was activated in the ninth game of the season and played almost exclusively on the special teams while he learned the intricate system of defensive coordinator Joe Collier. But he should be a factor in 1985.

"I like this defense," Hunley said. "I'd be crazy not to. It's built on speed. The players are all fast and they run to the football. They preach aggression and there's no

Rulon Jones   *Dennis Smith*   *Steve Watson*

hesitancy about making mistakes. When the ball is loose, you're always going to see Broncos around it."

Linebackers always have been the cornerstone of the Orange Crush defense, and Hunley, Busick, Rick Dennison, and Mecklenburg have the potential to play at the same level as the 1977 foursome of Gradishar, Jackson, Bob Swenson, and Joe Rizzo. That group helped take the Broncos to Super Bowl XII.

SPECIAL TEAMS

The Broncos might have had a 15-victory season if placekicker Rich Karlis hadn't been star-crossed in two games down the stretch. He hit the upright with a 25-yard field-goal attempt in the closing minutes of a 27-24 loss to the Seahawks, then hit another upright the following week with a 42-yard field-goal try in the final minute of a 16-13 loss to the Chiefs.

That didn't shake Denver's faith in Karlis. He came back the next week to kick three field goals, including one of 50 yards in a 16-13 victory over the Chargers, and wound up with the first 100-point season of his career. Despite the misses against Seattle and Kansas City, Karlis is as reliable as he is productive; he has converted 80 percent of his career field-goal tries (53 of 66).

Punter Chris Norman had a nondescript rookie season, averaging only 40.1 yards per kick. But he managed a respectable 35.4 net average while punting 96 times, the third-highest figure in the conference.

Willhite gives the Broncos explosiveness on kick returns that the club figured to miss when a neck injury forced Rick Upchurch to retire in 1984. Willhite averaged 10 yards for 20 punt returns with a long run of 35. He averaged 27.3 on four kickoff returns.

VETERAN ROSTER

No.	Name	Pos.	Ht.	Wt.	NFL Exp.	Birthdate	College	Games in 1984
80	Alexander, Ray	WR	6-3	180	2	1/8/62	Florida A&M	8
54	Bishop, Keith	G-C	6-3	265	5	3/10/57	Baylor	16
65	Bowyer, Walt	DE	6-4	252	3	9/8/60	Arizona State	16
26	Brewer, Chris	RB	6-1	193	2	1/23/62	Arizona	13
64	Bryan, Billy	C	6-2	255	8	9/21/55	Duke	16
58	Busick, Steve	LB	6-4	227	5	12/10/58	Southern California	16
68	Carter, Rubin	NT	6-0	256	11	12/12/52	Miami	15
79	Chavous, Barney	DE	6-3	258	13	3/22/51	South Carolina State	15
59	Comeaux, Darren	LB	6-1	227	4	4/15/60	Arizona State	16
63	Cooper, Mark	G	6-5	267	3	2/14/60	Miami	15
55	Dennison, Rick	LB	6-3	220	4	6/22/58	Colorado State	16
7	Elway, John	QB	6-3	202	3	6/28/60	Stanford	15
43	Foley, Steve	S	6-2	190	9	11/11/53	Tulane	16
62	Freeman, Mike	G	6-3	256	2	10/13/61	Arizona	9
66	Garnett, Scott	NT	6-2	271	2	12/3/62	Washington	16
72	Graves, Marsharne	T	6-3	272	2	7/8/62	Arizona	1
31	Harden, Mike	CB	6-1	192	6	2/16/58	Michigan	16
74	Hood, Winford	G	6-3	262	2	3/29/62	Georgia	16
60	Howard, Paul	G	6-3	260	12	9/12/50	Brigham Young	16
98	Hunley, Ricky	LB	6-2	238	2	11/11/61	Arizona	8
66	Hyde, Glenn	G-C	6-3	255	9	3/14/51	Pittsburgh	0
28	Jackson, Roger	S	6-0	186	4	2/28/59	Bethune-Cookman	16
57	Jackson, Tom	LB	5-11	220	13	4/4/51	Louisville	16
86	Johnson, Butch	WR	6-1	187	10	5/28/54	Cal-Riverside	16
75	Jones, Rulon	DE	6-6	260	6	3/25/58	Utah State	16
3	Karlis, Rich	K	6-0	180	4	5/23/59	Cincinnati	16
88	Kay, Clarence	TE	6-2	237	2	7/30/61	Georgia	16
8	Kubiak, Gary	QB	6-0	192	3	8/15/61	Texas A&M	7
33	Lang, Gene	RB	5-10	196	2	3/15/62	Louisiana State	16
76	Lanier, Ken	T	6-3	269	5	7/8/59	Florida State	16
22	Lilly, Tony	S	6-0	199	2	2/16/62	Florida	13
	Manning, Wade	CB	5-11	190	4	7/25/55	Ohio State	0
69	Manor, Brison	DE	6-4	248	9	8/10/52	Arkansas	10
77	Mecklenburg, Karl	DE-LB	6-3	250	3	9/1/60	Minnesota	16
29	Myers, Wilbur	S	5-11	195	2	8/17/61	Delta State	0
39	Myles, Jesse	RB	5-10	210	3	9/28/60	Louisiana State	7
1	Norman, Chris	P	6-2	198	2	5/25/62	South Carolina	16
24	Parros, Rick	RB	5-11	200	5	6/14/58	Utah State	15
48	Robbins, Randy	CB	6-2	189	2	9/14/62	Arizona	16
50	Ryan, Jim	LB	6-1	215	7	5/18/57	William & Mary	16
84	Sampson, Clint	WR	5-11	183	3	1/4/61	San Diego State	12
83	Sawyer, John	TE	6-2	230	10	7/26/53	Southern Mississippi	10
	Shaffer, Craig	LB	6-1	227	4	3/31/59	Indiana State	4
56	Smith, Aaron	LB	6-2	225	2	8/10/62	Utah State	10
49	Smith, Dennis	S	6-3	200	5	2/3/59	Southern California	15
70	Studdard, Dave	T	6-4	260	7	11/22/55	Texas	16
85	Summers, Don	TE	6-4	226	2	2/2/61	Boise State	16
51	Swenson, Bob	LB	6-3	225	9	7/1/53	California	0
61	Townsend, Andre	DE-NT	6-3	265	2	10/8/62	Mississippi	16
81	Watson, Steve	WR	6-4	195	7	5/28/57	Temple	16
47	Willhite, Gerald	RB	5-10	200	4	5/30/59	San Jose State	16
45	Wilson, Steve	CB	5-10	195	7	8/25/57	Howard	15
23	Winder, Sammy	RB	5-11	203	4	7/15/59	Southern Mississippi	16
52	Woodard, Ken	LB	6-1	218	4	1/22/60	Tuskegee Institute	16
87	Wright, Jim	TE	6-3	240	6	9/1/56	Texas Christian	16
20	Wright, Louis	CB	6-2	200	11	1/31/53	San Jose State	16

Coaching Staff

Dan Reeves, head coach; **Marvin Bass,** special assistant; **Joe Collier,** assistant head coach, defense; **Chan Gailey,** special teams, defensive assistant; **Alex Gibbs,** offensive line; **Stan Jones,** defensive line; **Al Miller,** strength and conditioning; **Myrel Moore,** linebackers; **Nick Nicolau,** running backs; **Mike Shannon,** wide receivers; **Doc Urich,** tight ends, assistant offensive line; **Charlie West,** defensive backs.

1985 Schedule

Preseason

Aug. 10	N.Y. GIANTS	7:00
Aug. 19	at San Francisco	6:00
Aug. 24	INDIANAPOLIS	7:00
Aug. 30	MINNESOTA	7:00

Regular Season

Sept. 8	at L.A. Rams	1:00
Sept. 15	NEW ORLEANS	2:00
Sept. 22	at Atlanta	1:00
Sept. 29	MIAMI	2:00
Oct. 6	HOUSTON	2:00
Oct. 13	at Indianapolis	12:00
Oct. 20	SEATTLE	2:00
Oct. 27	at Kansas City	12:00
Nov. 3	at San Diego	1:00
Nov. 11	SAN FRANCISCO (Mon.)	7:00
Nov. 17	SAN DIEGO	2:00
Nov. 24	at L.A. Raiders	1:00
Dec. 1	at Pittsburgh	1:00
Dec. 8	L.A. RAIDERS	2:00
Dec. 14	KANSAS CITY (Sat.)	2:00
Dec. 22	at Seattle (Fri.)	5:00

1984 Results

Sept. 2	CINCINNATI	20-17
Sept. 9	at Chicago	0-27
Sept. 16	at Cleveland	24-14
Sept. 23	KANSAS CITY	21-0
Sept. 30	L.A. RAIDERS	16-13
Oct. 7	at Detroit	28-7
Oct. 15	GREEN BAY (Mon.)	17-14
Oct. 21	at Buffalo	37-7
Oct. 28	at L.A. Raiders*	22-19
Nov. 4	NEW ENGLAND	26-19
Nov. 11	at San Diego	16-13
Nov. 18	MINNESOTA	42-21
Nov. 25	SEATTLE	24-27
Dec. 2	at Kansas City	13-16
Dec. 9	SAN DIEGO	16-13
Dec. 15	at Seattle (Sat.)	31-14
Dec. 30	PITTSBURGH	17-24

1985 Draft Choices

1. Steve Sewell—26, RB, Oklahoma
2. Vance Johnson—31, WR, Arizona, from Houston
2. Simon Fletcher—54, DE, Houston
3. Choice to Houston
4. Keli McGregor—110, TE, Colorado State
5. Choice to Houston
5. Billy Hinson—139, G, Florida, from Miami
6. Choice to N.Y. Jets
7. Dallas Cameron—194, NT, Miami
8. Eric Riley—222, DB, Florida State
9. Daryl Smith—249, DB, North Alabama
10. Buddy Funck—269, QB, New Mexico, from New England
10. Ron Anderson—278, LB, Southern Methodist
11. Gary Rolle—306, WR, Florida
12. Dan Lynch—334, G, Washington State

KANSAS CITY CHIEFS

The Kansas City Chiefs have not gone to the playoffs since 1971. That 13-year drought is the longest in the AFC and the second-longest in the NFL behind the New Orleans Saints, who never have played a post-season game in their 18-year history.

Only six teams have failed to win a divisional title during the last 13 years—the New York Jets, Houston Oilers, Seattle Seahawks, New York Giants, the Saints, and the Chiefs—yet the Jets, Oilers, Seahawks, and Giants all have managed to gain wild-card trips to the playoffs in a normal season (not including the strike year, 1982). The Seahawks, who didn't even come along until five years after Kansas City's last postseason appearance, made their playoff debut in 1983.

The Chiefs have had only three winning seasons in the last 13 years and only one since 1973. They have finished in last place in the AFC West four times and have not been as high as second place since 1972. They also are playing under their third head coach since Hank Stram last took them to the playoffs.

The Chiefs continued their unfulfilling course in 1984 with an 8-8 record and a fourth-place finish. There wouldn't appear to be much reason for optimism in 1985: The three teams that finished above Kansas City in the AFC West all won 11 or more games and all went to the playoffs.

But there *is* optimism. Kansas City managed a .500 record despite playing without quarterback and offensive catalyst Bill Kenney for seven games because of injuries.

The Chiefs managed that .500 finish by scoring three consecutive victories in December—their first three-

Carlos Carson came up with another 1,000-yard year.

John Mackovic

game winning streak since 1981 and the first such streak to end a season since 1972.

It wasn't just a three-game winning streak. It was a three-game winning streak against AFC West rivals, including victories over the eventual division champion Denver Broncos and the eventual runner-up Seahawks. And in the cases of Seattle, and San Diego in the season finale, they weren't just victories, they were blowouts. Kenney simply tore them apart offensively and the defense played as if Bobby Bell, Willie Lanier, and Buck Buchanan were back from the Chiefs teams of the sixties.

The Chiefs upset Denver 16-13 on the fourteenth weekend, then blasted the Seahawks 34-7, both victories coming at home, and defeated the Chargers 42-21 to avoid another last-place finish. The road victory at San Diego forced the Chargers to settle for fifth place with a 7-9 record. Kansas City was the only team in the AFC West to win its final three games.

"I really feel those last three games stood for our season—where we are and where we hope to go," Kansas City coach John Mackovic said. "I'm proud of our players. I believe in them a great deal and they believe in themselves even more than before. I think they've developed a true confidence and a true feeling of building a great team."

But the Chiefs got an unusual reward for finishing fourth—road games in 1985 against Super Bowl finalists San Francisco and Miami. The Chiefs will play host to AFC Central champion Pittsburgh, plus an NFC wild-card qualifier, the Los Angeles Rams. Then, of course, don't forget two games each in the AFC West against Denver (13-3), Seattle (12-4), and Los Angeles (11-5).

OFFENSE

There is hope in 1985 because there is Kenney. In 1983, when he played his first complete 16-game schedule as the number-one quarterback, Kenney passed for a club-record 4,348 yards and 24 touchdowns to earn a trip to the AFC-NFC Pro Bowl.

But Kenney broke the thumb on his passing hand in the final preseason game of 1984 and did not return until the seventh weekend of the season. He relieved Todd Blackledge in the second half of that game and passed for 238 yards and two touchdowns in roughly 25 minutes, helping Kansas City post a 31-13 triumph over San Diego.

Kenney took a physical beating in a November game against the Seahawks, suffering knee and shoulder injuries while being sacked three times and flattened on countless other plays in a 45-0 setback. He did not play the following week against the Houston Oilers, who wound up beating the Chiefs 17-16 for their first victory of 1984.

But Kenney returned to start the last five games, and he was spectacular in the final four. He passed for 286 yards in a 28-27 loss to the New York Giants, then threw for 281 yards against Denver, 312 against Seattle, and 245 against San Diego before leaving the game early in the third quarter with a 42-0 lead. He threw nine touchdown passes and only two interceptions in those final four weeks.

The receiving corps has blossomed along with Kenney. Carlos Carson has caught 137 passes over the last two years and has had back-to-back 1,000-yard seasons. He is Kansas City's game-breaker. Henry Marshall has played for the Chiefs for nine seasons but he never reached his potential until Mackovic took over in 1983.

Marshall has set personal bests the last two seasons with 50 catches in 1983 and 62 in 1984. He was the team

Brad Budde

Deron Cherry

Bill Kenney

leader in receptions a year ago and also posted a career-high 912 yards. The 6-2, 220-pound Marshall is the most versatile of Kansas City's wide receivers.

Marshall had two 100-yard games a year ago and they were big ones—166 yards against Seattle and 148 against Denver; Carson had four 100-yard days. Anthony Hancock also had a 109-yard day against Cincinnati in the second game of the season but he sprained an ankle the following week and never returned to form. Stephone Paige, who plays almost exclusively on third downs, has contributed 60 catches and 10 touchdowns during the Mackovic era.

Kenney likes to throw downfield and he's going to have to look in that direction even more in 1985 because of the absence of fullback Theotis Brown, the club's efficient safety-valve receiver. Brown, who had 85 receptions over the last two seasons, suffered a heart attack last winter and may be forced to give up professional football at age 27. That will shift the burden in the backfield to diminutive halfback Herman Heard, who led the team with 684 rushing yards as a rookie last season. But at 184 pounds, he's going to need some help.

Tight end Willie Scott is a much better blocker than receiver and provides a fine complement to an offensive line that has developed into a solid unit after years of instability. Center Bob Rush, guard Tom Condon, and tackle Matt Herkenhoff give the Chiefs a combined 27 years of experience, with 1980 number-one draft pick Brad Budde at guard and 1983 number-two pick David Lutz at tackle ensuring a quality future.

DEFENSE

The pieces are in place for a defense that could rival those of the Broncos, Seahawks, and Raiders. Kansas City has three former first-round draft choices on its defensive line—ends Art Still (1978) and Mike Bell (1979), and nose tackle Bill Maas (1984)—plus one of the most talented, young secondaries in the league in cornerbacks Albert Lewis and Kevin Ross, and safeties Deron Cherry and Lloyd Burruss. And all 11 starters are hitters.

Mackovic is particularly pleased with what he has

Three Years at a Glance

Averages NFL Rank	OFFENSE			DEFENSE		
	1984	1983	1982	1984	1983	1982
Points Rank	**19.6** 17	**24.1** 8	**19.6** 16	**20.3** 15	**22.9** 21	**20.4** 17
Yards Rank	**318.4** 17	**349.7** 9	**277.6** 25	**351.6** 24	**336.6** 14	**303.6** 10
Rushing Yards Rank	**95.4** 27	**78.4** 28	**104.8** 21	**123.8** 16	**142.2** 20	**118.3** 19
Passing Yards Rank	**223.0** 7	**271.3** 3	**172.8** 21	**227.8** 23	**194.4** 10	**185.2** 10
Sacks Rank	**2.1** 4	**2.9** 16	**4.4** 28	**3.1** 12	**2.2** 22	**1.7** 25T
Turnovers Rank	**2.3** 15T	**2.4** 11T	**1.3** 1	**2.6** 7	**3.2** 3	**2.4** 14T
Punt Returns Rank	**8.2** 15	**7.3** 21	**8.6** 11	**7.7** 9	**10.4** 25	**15.4** 28
Kickoff Returns Rank	**18.9** 21	**17.2** 26	**21.3** 5	**21.2** 20	**20.4** 21	**18.9** 8
Penalty Yards Rank	**50.1** 11	**56.9** 20	**41.3** 7	**59.4** 7	**52.3** 11T	**54.0** 10

	W-L Total	Home	Road	Playoffs
1982	3-6	2-2	1-4	None
1983	6-10	5-3	1-7	None
1984	8-8	5-3	3-5	None

up front. Still returned to his Pro Bowl form in 1984 when he led the team in both sacks with 14½ and in tackles with 131. He capped his season by returning a fumble 83 yards late in the fourth quarter for the winning AFC touchdown in the Pro Bowl.

If Bell had not been hampered by a knee injury throughout the second half of the season, he also might have been selected to play in the AFC-NFC Pro Bowl. He managed to make 13½ sacks but only three came after October 28. But he still was voted as a second alternate to the Pro Bowl.

Maas provided the missing link. His presence forced offensive lines to stop double-teaming Still and Bell. Maas added five sacks, even though he missed three complete games and was severely limited in several others because of a fractured fibula suffered in an early-season game. That trio helped the Chiefs set a club record with 50 sacks in 1984.

"In Art Still, Bill Maas, and Mike Bell," Mackovic said, "we have three players on our front line who are among the very best in the NFL and play that way on a regular basis when they're healthy. That's a great starting point for any defense. Just as your offense starts with your quarterback, defense starts with your line."

The secondary isn't far behind talent-wise. Cherry was selected to his second consecutive Pro Bowl, and Mackovic feels Burruss and Lewis play at that level as well. Ross started every game last season and wound up with a team runner-up six interceptions in earning a spot on the NFL all-rookie team. Cherry chipped in seven interceptions and Lewis four.

Gary Spani has been solid at inside linebacker in Kansas City's 3-4 scheme, and second-year man Scott Radecic, a product of the Penn State linebacking factory, has a bright future. Outside linebackers Calvin Daniels and Ken McAlister both are capable of spectacular play, but they have to show it more consistently.

The Chiefs allowed only 29 touchdowns running and passing, an average of fewer than two per game, in 1984 and forced 41 turnovers to pave a turnover ratio of a plus-4. Mackovic is looking for continued improvement in that area.

Nick Lowery

Bill Maas

Art Still

SPECIAL TEAMS

Kansas City's special teams were among the league's best during the Marv Levy coaching era from 1978 through 1982. That was to be expected—Levy was one of the original special teams coaches in the early 1970s with the Washington Redskins, who uplifted the standards for special teams play in that era.

Mackovic's strength as a coach is his offensive mind. He doesn't put nearly the emphasis on special teams that Levy did. But after a 6-10 finish in 1983 and after a review of his team's failings, Mackovic decided to make special teams a more important portion of Kansas City's football package.

The Chiefs tried to make punter Jim Arnold a directional kicker as a rookie in 1983, but the project was a bust; he averaged 39.9 yards per kick and had the worst net in the conference at 32.6. So Mackovic let the former Vanderbilt All-America kick away in 1984, concentrating on hang time rather than location, and Arnold wound up leading the AFC with an average of 44.9 yards per kick. He also increased his net by almost five yards to 37.5.

Placekicker Nick Lowery had his third 100-point season in the last four years, kicking 23 field goals en route to a team-leading 104 points. J.T. Smith gives Kansas City sure hands on returns but he no longer is the breakaway threat he once was. He averaged 20.6 yards per kickoff return, but his 8.5-yard average on punt returns was two yards fewer than his career average. A healthy Hancock, with his soft, receiver's hands and 4.4 speed, could be Kansas City's answer to a solid return game.

VETERAN ROSTER

No.	Name	Pos.	Ht.	Wt.	NFL Exp.	Birthdate	College	Games in 1984
76	Alt, John	T	6-7	278	2	5/30/62	Iowa	15
6	Arnold, Jim	P	6-2	212	3	1/31/61	Vanderbilt	16
87	Arnold, Walt	TE	6-3	234	6	8/31/58	New Mexico	10
68	Auer, Scott	G-T	6-4	255	2	10/4/61	Michigan State	16
77	Baldinger, Rich	T-G	6-4	285	4	12/31/59	Wake Forest	14
99	Bell, Mike	DE	6-4	250	6	8/30/57	Colorado State	15
14	Blackledge, Todd	QB	6-3	225	3	2/25/61	Penn State	11
57	Blanton, Jerry	LB	6-1	236	7	12/10/56	Kentucky	10
27	Brown, Theotis	RB	6-2	225	7	4/20/57	UCLA	14
66	Budde, Brad	G	6-4	260	6	5/9/58	Southern California	16
34	Burruss, Lloyd	S	6-0	202	5	10/31/57	Maryland	16
88	Carson, Carlos	WR	5-11	180	6	12/28/58	Louisiana State	16
20	Cherry, Deron	S	5-11	190	5	9/12/59	Rutgers	16
65	Condon, Tom	G	6-3	275	12	12/26/52	Boston College	16
50	Daniels, Calvin	LB	6-3	236	4	12/26/58	North Carolina	16
73	Dawson, Mike	NT	6-3	245	10	10/16/53	Arizona	9
38	Gunter, Michael	RB	5-11	205	2	1/18/61	Tulsa	4
82	Hancock, Anthony	WR-KR	6-0	200	4	6/10/60	Tennessee	14
44	Heard, Herman	RB	5-10	184	2	11/24/61	Southern Colorado	16
60	Herkenhoff, Matt	T	6-4	275	10	4/2/51	Minnesota	15
23	Hill, Greg	CB	6-1	189	3	2/12/61	Oklahoma State	15
93	Holle, Eric	DE-NT	6-4	250	2	9/5/60	Texas	16
43	Jackson, Billy	RB	5-10	215	5	9/13/59	Alabama	16
52	Jolly, Ken	LB	6-2	220	2	2/28/62	Mid-America Nazarene	16
9	Kenney, Bill	QB	6-4	211	7	1/20/55	Northern Colorado	9
91	Kremer, Ken	NT	6-4	260	7	7/16/57	Ball State	16
40	Lacy, Ken	RB	6-0	222	2	11/1/60	Tulsa	15
26	Lane, Skip	CB-S	6-1	208	2	1/30/60	Mississippi	4
29	Lewis, Albert	CB	6-2	190	3	10/6/60	Grambling	15
71	Lindstrom, Dave	DE	6-6	255	8	11/16/54	Boston University	16
62	Lingner, Adam	C-G	6-4	250	3	11/2/60	Illinois	16
84	Little, Dave	TE	6-2	239	2	4/18/61	Middle Tennessee State	10
8	Lowery, Nick	K	6-4	189	6	5/27/56	Dartmouth	16
72	Lutz, David	T	6-5	285	3	12/30/59	Georgia Tech	7
63	Maas, Bill	NT	6-4	265	2	3/2/62	Pittsburgh	14
94	McAlister, Ken	LB	6-5	220	4	4/15/60	San Francisco	15
89	Marshall, Henry	WR	6-2	220	10	8/9/54	Missouri	16
11	Osiecki, Sandy	QB	6-5	202	2	5/18/60	Arizona State	4
83	Paige, Stephone	WR	6-1	180	3	10/15/61	Fresno State	16
95	Paine, Jeff	LB	6-2	224	2	8/19/61	Texas A&M	14
21	Parker, Kerry	CB	6-1	200	2	10/3/55	Grambling	15
97	Radecic, Scott	LB	6-3	240	2	6/14/62	Penn State	16
30	Robinson, Mark	S	5-10	206	2	9/13/62	Penn State	16
31	Ross, Kevin	CB	5-9	180	2	1/16/62	Temple	16
70	Rourke, Jim	T-G	6-5	263	6	2/10/57	Boston College	13
53	Rush, Bob	C	6-5	264	8	2/27/55	Memphis State	16
81	Scott, Willie	TE	6-4	245	5	2/13/59	South Carolina	15
86	Smith, J. T.	WR-KR	6-2	185	8	10/29/55	North Texas State	15
59	Spani, Gary	LB	6-2	228	8	1/9/56	Kansas State	14
67	Still, Art	DE	6-7	257	8	12/5/55	Kentucky	16
35	Thomas, Ken	RB	5-9	211	2	2/11/60	San Jose State	0
56	Zamberlin, John	LB	6-2	226	7	2/13/56	Pacific Lutheran	8

Coaching Staff

John Mackovic, head coach; **David Brazil,** defensive assistant; **Walt Corey,** defensive line; **Dan Daniel,** inside linebackers; **Marty Galbraith,** offensive line; **Doug Graber,** defensive backs, defensive quality control; **J.D. Helm,** offensive assistant; **C.T. Hewgley,** offensive and defensive lines coordinator; **Pete McCulley,** quarterbacks; **Willie Peete,** offensive backs; **Jim Vechiarella,** outside linebackers, special teams; **Richard Williamson,** receivers.

1985 Schedule

Preseason

Aug. 10	at Cincinnati	7:00
Aug. 17	NEW ENGLAND	7:30
Aug. 24	at Houston	8:00
Aug. 31	ST. LOUIS	7:30

Regular Season

Sept. 8	at New Orleans	12:00
Sept. 12	L.A. RAIDERS (Thurs.)	7:00
Sept. 22	at Miami	4:00
Sept. 29	SEATTLE	12:00
Oct. 6	at L.A. Raiders	1:00
Oct. 13	at San Diego	1:00
Oct. 20	L.A. RAMS	12:00
Oct. 27	DENVER	12:00
Nov. 3	at Houston	12:00
Nov. 10	PITTSBURGH	12:00
Nov. 17	at San Francisco	1:00
Nov. 24	INDIANAPOLIS	3:00
Dec. 1	at Seattle	1:00
Dec. 8	ATLANTA	12:00
Dec. 14	at Denver (Sat.)	2:00
Dec. 22	SAN DIEGO	12:00

1984 Results

Sept. 2	at Pittsburgh	37-27
Sept. 9	at Cincinnati	27-22
Sept. 16	L.A. RAIDERS	20-22
Sept. 23	at Denver	0-21
Sept. 30	CLEVELAND	10-6
Oct. 7	N.Y. JETS	16-17
Oct. 14	SAN DIEGO	31-13
Oct. 21	at N.Y. Jets	7-28
Oct. 28	TAMPA BAY	24-20
Nov. 4	at Seattle	0-45
Nov. 11	HOUSTON	16-17
Nov. 18	at L.A. Raiders	7-17
Nov. 25	at N.Y. Giants	27-28
Dec. 2	DENVER	16-13
Dec. 9	SEATTLE	34-7
Dec. 16	at San Diego	42-21

1985 Draft Choices

1. Ethan Horton—15. RB. North Carolina
2. Jonathan Hayes—41. TE. Iowa
3. Choice to San Diego
4. Bob Olderman—99. G. Virginia
5. Bruce King—126. RB. Purdue
6. Jonathan Bostic—149. DB. Bethune-Cookman. from Philadelphia
6. Choice to Houston
7. Vince Thomson—180. DE. Missouri Western. from San Diego
7. Dave Heffernan—183. G. Miami
8. Ira Hillary—210. WR. South Carolina
9. Mike Armentrout—237. DB. S.W. Missouri
10. Jeff Smith—267. RB. Nebraska
11. Chris Jackson—293. C. Southern Methodist
12. Le Bel. Harper—321. C. Colorado State

LOS ANGELES RAIDERS

The AFC West respects running back Marcus Allen, who annually gains more yards and scores more points than anyone else in the AFC. The division respects the Pro Bowl cornerback tandem of Lester Hayes and Mike Haynes for their attack style of defense. It also respects the pass rush of defensive end Howie Long, the maneuverability of tight end Todd Christensen, and the leadership of quarterback Jim Plunkett.

There are plenty more players on the Los Angeles Raiders who command the *respect* of the AFC West. But the one person in the organization whom the division *fears* does not even suit up on Sundays. That person is the pulse of the Raiders, managing general partner Al Davis.

And 1985 is the type of year when Davis is to be most feared. That's because the Raiders weren't good enough last season. The Raiders won the Super Bowl in 1983 but they didn't in 1984. They won 11 games but managed only a third-place finish in the AFC West behind Denver and Seattle. The Raiders went to the playoffs but they were eliminated in their first game by the Seahawks.

If Davis needs to tinker with the engine, he will. If he needs parts, he'll get them. Some how, some way, he'll make it right again—and often in a subtle way. The AFC West knows Davis will be busy rebuilding the Raiders this season, even though an 11-victory season does not normally call for an overhaul.

"I don't think I've ever heard of the Raiders organization having a youth movement, a rebuilding period," Haynes said. "You never see twenty-five rookies around here. There's always a good mix of young guys

Running back Marcus Allen scored 18 touchdowns for Raiders.

Tom Flores

and old guys. That's a tribute to Al Davis. He does a good job of filling in the blanks. If they need a quarterback or a linebacker or a cornerback, he's not afraid to go get the best guy available. And he's not afraid to pay the price.

"You hear a lot of teams say, 'We're going to build through the draft.' That's a mistake. If you're one or two guys away, you can't sit and wait for them [in the draft] because they might never come along. When I was at New England they drafted the best player available regardless of his position. You can get stacked up that way. At one time we had five number-ones [draft picks] in the secondary. You don't use your number-one on a guy who's going to sit.

"If the Raiders need an outside linebacker, they draft one. He might not be the best athlete available but if he's got talent and he can fill the need, they'll take him. The Raiders do what they feel they have to do."

OFFENSE

The most pressing need is for a sure-handed receiver with speed. The Raiders always have had a big-play offense, and Cliff Branch was the guy who gave it to them. He came out of the University of Colorado as a world-class sprinter in 1972 with a 9.1 clocking in the 100-yard dash.

Branch had his first 1,000-yard season in 1974, then averaged a devastating 24.2 yards on 46 catches in 1976. Even at 35 years of age in 1983, Branch averaged 17.8 yards for his 39 receptions and recorded the longest touchdown catch of his career, 99 yards.

But at 36 years of age, Branch slowed in 1984. He caught fewer passes (27) than any season since 1973 and averaged only 14.9 yards per reception. He also failed to score a touchdown for the first time since his rookie season. His lack of effectiveness on the flank allowed defenses to gang up inside on possession receiver Christensen.

Christensen, former Brigham Young fullback, still managed 80 catches for 1,007 yards to earn his second

AFC Pro Bowl invitation. But he had to work a lot harder than he did in 1983 when he had 92 catches for 1,247 yards and 12 touchdowns.

"Defenses have been designed to stop me," Christensen said. "I can't recall the last time I saw single coverage."

Malcolm Barnwell is a threat on the other flank—but not the threat of a younger Branch. Although he averaged 18.9 yards on his 45 catches in 1984, Barnwell got into the end zone only twice. Dokie Williams averaged 23.1 yards per catch, but only had 22 receptions.

The trump card the Raiders have used lately to cure all of their offensive ailments has been Allen, arguably the most versatile running back in the game today. The former USC Heisman Trophy winner can beat you with his hands, legs, or arm.

Allen caught more passes (64) for more yards (758) than any running back in the AFC last season. He also shared the league-lead in non-kick scoring with 18 touchdowns and 108 points, and he missed out on the conference rushing crown by 12 yards to San Diego's Earnest Jackson. Nonetheless, his 1,168 rushing yards were a career high. And although he didn't throw an option pass for a touchdown last year, he has four in his three-year career.

Allen had three 100-yard rushing days last season, including a 155-yard effort against the Miami Dolphins, and one 100-yard receiving day, a 173-yard explosion against the Seahawks. But it is not possible to break down Allen's contribution into segments; the complete package tells a better story.

Todd Christensen   *Dave Dalby*   *Mike Haynes*

Allen had 11 games in which his total yardage exceeded 100 yards last season; he was over 90 on four other occasions. That consistency was the reason he led the AFC in total offense a year ago with 1,926 yards. And he was just as tough in close—9 of his 13 rushing touchdowns were power plunges of two yards—as he was from afar—he caught touchdown passes of 73, 58, and 36 yards in 1984.

"Marcus has great feel and vision for what's going on," Kansas City coach John Mackovic said. "He's a great competitor. He does not like to be denied yardage. If it's third-and-three and they give him the ball, he's going to get the three. If it's first-and-ten he wants ten not three or four [yards]. When they're on the goal line, he walks on people's backs to get into the end zone. He wants whatever there is to get."

The Raiders still have to resolve a quarterback controversy. The 37-year-old Plunkett and 28-year-old Marc Wilson both have long-term contracts. Wilson would seem to be the future, but Los Angeles continues to cling to Plunkett. And for good reason: The former Stanford Heisman Trophy winner has a 42-14 record in career starts with the Raiders and has delivered two Super Bowl championships in five years.

Neither quarterback performed particularly well in 1984. Wilson threw 15 touchdown passes but offset that with 17 interceptions. Plunkett passed for only 6 touchdowns in 198 passes and was intercepted 10 times. The lack of mobility by both also resulted in 49 sacks.

Raiders linemen generally are huge and experienced and the team certainly can win with their current collection. Not only that, the Raiders have a stockpile of them, which allows Los Angeles to withstand injuries up front better than any team in the NFL.

Eleven-year veteran tackle Henry Lawrence weighs 275 pounds and he toted that bulk to Hawaii for the 1985 Pro Bowl. Center Dave Dalby has 13 years of experience and 255 pounds, tackle Bruce Davis six years and 280 pounds. Guard Mickey Marvin has eight years and 260 pounds, guard Curt Marsh three years and 270 pounds. Tackle Don Mosebar is going into his third season; he weighs 260 pounds. Charley Hannah provides

Three Years at a Glance

Averages NFL Rank	OFFENSE			DEFENSE		
	1984	1983	1982	1984	1983	1982
Points Rank	**23.0** 9	**27.6** 3	**28.9** 2	**17.4** 4	**21.1** 13	**22.2** 21
Yards Rank	**327.8** 15	**355.4** 7	**328.3** 10	**290.3** 3	**296.8** 4	**340.7** 22
Rushing Yards Rank	**117.9** 17	**140.0** 10	**120.0** 13	**118.3** 13	**99.1** 4	**86.4** 2
Passing Yards Rank	**209.9** 12	**215.4** 9	**208.3** 10	**172.0** 4	**197.6** 13	**254.2** 27
Sacks Rank	**3.4** 19	**3.4** 24T	**2.6** 12T	**4.0** 3	**3.6** 2T	**4.2** 1
Turnovers Rank	**3.0** 3T	**3.1** 25	**2.7** 17T	**2.1** 16T	**2.3** 17T	**3.2** 1
Punt Returns Rank	**10.0** 6	**11.5** 1	**7.7** 17	**10.1** 22	**9.5** 20	**4.2** 5
Kickoff Returns Rank	**21.7** 3	**19.3** 16	**20.9** 8	**17.4** 4	**18.0** 6	**19.8** 14
Penalty Yards Rank	**75.6** 28	**62.0** 25	**93.3** 28	**66.3** 3	**59.2** 6	**65.3** 4

	W-L Total	**Home**	**Road**	**Playoffs**
1982	8-1	4-0	4-1	1-1, Lost Second Round Game
1983	12-4	6-2	6-2	3-0, Won Super Bowl XVIII
1984	11-5	6-2	5-3	0-1, Lost First Round Game

depth at guard with his eight years and 260 pounds. Shelby Jordan is a 6-7, 285-pound reserve tackle.

DEFENSE

The Raiders aren't hurting on defense—not with five of their starters earning Pro Bowl berths last season. Los Angeles allowed only 278 points in 1984, the second-lowest total in the AFC, and held 10 of its regular-season opponents to 17 points or less. Ironically, the Raiders lost four of those games and also suffered elimination from the playoffs despite holding Seattle to 13 points in the Kingdome.

Teams don't want to find themselves in a position where they have to pass against the Raiders. In addition to Hayes and Haynes, free safety Vann McElroy went to the Pro Bowl and Mike Davis is a rugged counterpart. Only two NFL defenses allowed a lower completion percentage than the 50 percent by the Raiders.

Quarterbacks have to be concerned with more than Hayes and Haynes on passing downs. Beware the blindside hit: The Raiders led the AFC in sacks last season with 64. Long and outside linebacker Rod Martin, a pair of two-time Pro Bowl picks, had 12 and 11, respectively. Bill Pickel led the team with 12½.

Los Angeles coach Tom Flores relies heavily on situation substitution up front with Reggie Kinlaw and Pickel interchangeable at nose tackle. Lyle Alzado, Sean Jones, and Greg Townsend rotate at the end opposite Long and also step inside when the line changes from a three- to a four-man front. Despite his 36 years, Alzado continues to wreak havoc on passing downs and wound up with eight sacks a year ago.

Matt Millen and Martin rank among the best at their respective linebacking positions in the NFL, and when Brad Van Pelt, who was acquired to replace Ted Hendricks last year, adapts to the system, he'll give the Raiders a solid two-down linebacker against the run. Jeff Barnes comes in for Van Pelt in passing situations. Their experience has allowed three-year veteran Jack Squirek, a Super Bowl XVIII hero, to develop at his own pace as an inside linebacker.

The Raiders also like size on defense. Van Pelt is large as linebackers go at 6-5, 235. Millen was once a de-

Henry Lawrence

Howie Long

Vann McElroy

fensive tackle at Penn State. But the key size is on the corners, where neither Hayes nor Haynes fit the NFL stereotype: Neither is 5-10, 185 pounds. Hayes is 6-0, 200 pounds and Haynes 6-2, 190, and they use their size to punish receivers, both at the line and after the catch. That's why the Raiders still are able to use man-to-man coverage as their basic defense while almost everyone else is shifting to zone.

SPECIAL TEAMS

The Raiders always have prided themselves on their kicking game and it was superb again in 1984.

Chris Bahr scored 100 points for the second consecutive season, kicking 20 of 27 field goals along the way, and, although he is no longer a Pro Bowl automatic, punter Ray Guy contributes quality. His 41.9-yard average may have been below his career standards but he had a net of 35.4, and 25 of his 91 punts were downed inside the 20. He still is the master of field position.

Williams and Cle Montgomery combined to return 50 kickoffs for an average of 23.5 yards a year ago, and the Raiders were considerably stingier on their own kickoffs. Opponents had a tough time even getting back to the 20 when Bahr kicked off, averaging only 17.4 yards on 61 returns.

But Los Angeles was sub-par in its punt returns as Greg Pruitt started showing his age (32). He averaged only 8.9 yards per return and was not nearly as sure-handed as he was in 1983, when he averaged 11.5 yards to earn a trip to the Pro Bowl.

The Raiders began working Montgomery in as the deep back on punts late in the season and he responded with a 13.9-yard average on 14 runbacks.

VETERAN ROSTER

No.	Name	Pos.	Ht.	Wt.	NFL Exp.	Birthdate	College	Games in 1984
97	Ackerman, Rick	NT	6-4	250	4	6/16/59	Memphis State	15*
59	Adams, Stanley	LB	6-2	215	2	5/22/60	Memphis State	4
32	Allen, Marcus	RB	6-2	205	4	3/22/60	Southern California	16
77	Alzado, Lyle	DE	6-3	260	14	4/3/49	Yankton	16
10	Bahr, Chris	K	5-10	170	10	2/3/53	Penn State	16
56	Barnes, Jeff	LB	6-2	230	9	3/1/55	California	16
80	Barnwell, Malcolm	WR	5-11	185	5	6/28/58	Virginia Union	16
86	Belk, Rocky	WR	6-0	185	2	6/20/60	Miami	0*
21	Branch, Cliff	WR	5-11	170	14	8/1/48	Colorado	14*
66	Bryant, Warren	T	6-7	285	9	11/11/55	Kentucky	9
54	Byrd, Darryl	LB	6-1	220	3	9/3/60	Illinois	16
57	Caldwell, Tony	LB	6-1	225	3	4/1/61	Washington	16
19	Campbell, Rich	QB	6-4	219	5	12/21/58	California	3
87	Casper, Dave	TE	6-4	240	12	2/2/52	Notre Dame	7
46	Christensen, Todd	TE	6-3	230	7	8/3/56	Brigham Young	16
50	Dalby, Dave	C	6-3	255	14	8/19/50	UCLA	16
79	Davis, Bruce	T	6-6	280	7	6/21/56	UCLA	16
45	Davis, James	CB	6-0	190	4	6/12/57	Southern	15
36	Davis, Mike	S	6-3	205	8	4/15/56	Colorado	16
8	Guy, Ray	P	6-3	195	13	12/22/49	Southern Mississippi	16
73	Hannah, Charley	G	6-5	260	9	7/26/55	Alabama	15
27	Hawkins, Frank	RB	5-9	210	5	7/3/59	Nevada-Reno	16
37	Hayes, Lester	CB	6-0	200	9	1/22/55	Texas A&M	16
22	Haynes, Mike	CB	6-2	190	10	7/1/53	Arizona State	16
11	Humm, David	QB	6-2	190	11	4/2/52	Nebraska	3
31	Jensen, Derrick	TE-RB	6-1	215	7	4/27/56	Texas-Arlington	16
99	Jones, Sean	DE	6-7	265	2	12/19/62	Northeastern	16
74	Jordan, Shelby	T	6-7	280	10	1/23/52	Washington, Mo.	11
52	Junkin, Trey	LB	6-2	220	3	1/23/61	Louisiana Tech	14*
33	King, Kenny	RB	5-11	205	7	3/7/57	Oklahoma	16
62	Kinlaw, Reggie	NT	6-2	245	6	1/9/57	Oklahoma	13
	Krimm, John	S	6-1	190	2	5/30/60	Notre Dame	0*
70	Lawrence, Henry	T	6-4	270	12	9/26/51	Florida A&M	16
75	Long, Howie	DE	6-5	270	5	1/6/60	Villanova	16
60	Marsh, Curt	G	6-5	270	4	8/25/59	Washington	16
53	Martin, Rod	LB	6-2	225	9	4/7/54	Southern California	16
65	Marvin, Mickey	G	6-4	265	9	10/5/55	Tennessee	9
43	McCall, Joe	RB	6-0	195	2	2/17/62	Pittsburgh	3
26	McElroy, Vann	S	6-2	190	4	1/13/60	Baylor	16
23	McKinney, Odis	S	6-2	190	8	5/19/57	Colorado	16
55	Millen, Matt	LB	6-2	250	6	3/12/58	Penn State	16
28	Montgomery, Cle	WR	5-8	180	5	7/1/56	Abilene Christian	16
72	Mosebar, Don	G	6-6	260	3	9/11/61	Southern California	10
51	Nelson, Bob	LB	6-4	235	9	6/30/53	Nebraska	12
81	Parker, Andy	TE	6-5	240	2	9/8/61	Utah	9
71	Pickel, Bill	NT	6-5	260	3	11/5/59	Rutgers	16
16	Plunkett, Jim	QB	6-2	220	15	12/5/47	Stanford	8
34	Pruitt, Greg	RB	5-10	190	13	8/18/51	Oklahoma	15
88	Seale, Sam	WR	5-9	175	2	10/6/62	Western State, Colo.	12
58	Squirek, Jack	LB	6-4	230	4	2/16/59	Illinois	12
30	Toran, Stacey	S	6-2	200	2	11/10/61	Notre Dame	16
93	Townsend, Greg	DE	6-3	240	3	11/3/61	Texas Christian	16
91	Van Pelt, Brad	LB	6-5	235	13	4/5/51	Michigan State	9
20	Watts, Ted	CB	6-0	190	5	5/29/59	Texas Tech	16
67	Wheeler, Dwight	C-T	6-3	275	7	1/3/55	Tennessee State	4
85	Williams, Dokie	WR	5-11	180	3	8/25/60	UCLA	16
38	Willis, Chester	RB	5-11	200	5	5/2/58	Auburn	16
6	Wilson, Marc	QB	6-6	205	6	2/15/57	Brigham Young	16

Coaching Staff

Tom Flores, head coach; **Sam Boghosian,** offensive line; **Willie Brown,** defensive backfield; **Chet Franklin,** defensive backfield; **Larry Kennan,** quarterbacks; **Earl Leggett,** defensive line; **Bob Mischak,** tight ends, strength and conditioning; **Steve Ortmayer,** football operations and special teams; **Art Shell,** offensive line; **Tom Walsh,** receivers; **Ray Willsey,** offensive backfield; **Bob Zeman,** linebackers.

1985 Schedule

Preseason

Aug. 10	SAN FRANCISCO	6:00
Aug. 18	WASHINGTON	1:00
Aug. 24	MIAMI	6:00
Aug. 30	at Cleveland	7:30

Regular Season

Sept. 8	N.Y. JETS	1:00
Sept. 12	at Kansas City (Thurs.)	7:00
Sept. 22	SAN FRANCISCO	1:00
Sept. 29	at New England	1:00
Oct. 6	KANSAS CITY	1:00
Oct. 13	NEW ORLEANS	1:00
Oct. 20	at Cleveland	1:00
Oct. 28	SAN DIEGO (Mon.)	6:00
Nov. 3	at Seattle	1:00
Nov. 10	at San Diego	1:00
Nov. 17	CINCINNATI	1:00
Nov. 24	DENVER	1:00
Dec. 1	at Atlanta	4:00
Dec. 8	at Denver	2:00
Dec. 15	SEATTLE	1:00
Dec. 23	at L.A. Rams (Mon.)	6:00

1984 Results

Sept. 2	at Houston	24-14
Sept. 6	GREEN BAY	28-7
Sept. 16	at Kansas City	22-20
Sept. 24	SAN DIEGO (Mon.)	33-30
Sept. 30	at Denver	13-16
Oct. 7	SEATTLE	28-14
Oct. 14	MINNESOTA	23-20
Oct. 21	at San Diego	44-37
Oct. 28	DENVER*	19-22
Nov. 4	at Chicago	6-17
Nov. 12	at Seattle (Mon.)	14-17
Nov. 18	KANSAS CITY	17-7
Nov. 25	INDIANAPOLIS	21-7
Dec. 2	at Miami	45-34
Dec. 10	at Detroit (Mon.)	24-3
Dec. 16	PITTSBURGH	7-13
Dec. 22	Seattle	7-13

1985 Draft Choices

1. Jessie Hester—23, WR, Florida State
2. Choice to New England
3. Tim Moffett—79, WR, Mississippi
3. Stefon Adams—80, DB, East Carolina, from Washington through Houston
4. Jamie Kimmel—107, LB, Syracuse, from Washington
4. Choice to New England
5. Dan Reeder—135, RB, Delaware
6. Rusty Hilger—143, QB, Oklahoma State, from Houston
6. Choice to Minnesota
7. Kevin Belcher—186, T, Wisconsin, from N.Y. Giants
7. Mark Pattison—188, WR, Washington, from New England
7. Bret Clark—191, DB, Nebraska
7. Nick Haden—192, C, Penn State, from Washington through New England
8. Leonard Wingate—220, DT, South Carolina State
9. Chris Sydnor—246, DB, Penn State
10. Reggie McKenzie—275, LB, Tennessee, from Washington
10. Albert Myres—276, DB, Tulsa
11. Steve Strachan—303, RB, Boston College
12. Raymond Polk—332, DB, Oklahoma State

SAN DIEGO CHARGERS

The San Diego Chargers had more—far more—than their share of injuries in 1984. Coach Don Coryell had a potential playoff contender until it was dismantled by injuries—and the quality of players those injuries struck hurt as much as the quantity.

First, the quantity. The Chargers had to make 47 player moves after finalizing their 49-man roster in late August. Only eight players from the opening-day depth chart started all 16 games. San Diego suited up 66 different players during the season, and 19 of them wound up on the injured-reserve list.

Now, the quality. Dan Fouts, a five-time Pro Bowl quarterback and the NFL's most prolific passer over the past five years, finished the season on injured reserve. So did Kellen Winslow, a four-time AFC Pro Bowl tight end who was on a pace to break the NFL single-season receiving record. And so did starting cornerbacks Gill Byrd and Danny Walters and linebacker Ray Preston.

Second-round draft pick Mike Guendling, a linebacker from Northwestern, didn't play a down after suffering a knee injury in the opening week of training camp—even before the veterans showed up.

"I've never been through a season with so many injuries in key positions," said Coryell, who was forced to endure a 7-9 record and a last-place finish in the rugged AFC West.

If there is one player the Chargers cannot afford to be without, it's Fouts. San Diego rode his passing arm to four consecutive postseason appearances from 1979 through 1982. But a series of injuries knocked him out of the lineup for six games during the 1983 season and San Diego wound up losing five of them to finish 6-10.

Charlie Joiner moved into top spot in NFL in career receiving.

Don Coryell

Fouts then sat out the final 3½ games of the 1984 season after suffering shoulder, knee, and groin injuries on the same second-quarter play against the Pittsburgh Steelers in week 13 when he was sacked by linebacker Mike Merriweather.

Winslow was on his way to his best year ever with an NFL-leading 55 catches when he suffered torn knee ligaments on the eighth weekend of the 1984 season against the Los Angeles Raiders. He was so far ahead on the league receiving list that no one was able to overtake him until the tenth week of the season.

Starting cornerbacks Walters (knee) and Byrd (hamstring) also missed eight and three games, respectively...and when a team is vulnerable at cornerback, everyone in the stadium knows it quickly.

In the season finale against Kansas City, when San Diego was forced to start late-season, free-agent signees Bill Kay and Lucious Smith at cornerback, the Chiefs' Bill Kenney passed for 245 yards and three touchdowns in just 33 minutes. The Chiefs scored the first 42 points of the game, then coasted to a 42-21 victory.

San Diego may have been a last-place team a year ago but it certainly didn't have last-place talent. At least not on paper. A return to good health—and the ability to stay in good health—would give Coryell and the Chargers the chance to prove they still belong among the league's elite. After all, they *were* 7-1 in games outside the AFC West last season.

So this season bring on the Miami Dolphins—the Chargers handed the AFC champions one of only two losses they suffered in 1984. Bring on the Chicago Bears—the Chargers delivered the NFC Central champions a 20-7 setback. And bring on the Denver Broncos—the Chargers dropped two 16-13 games to the AFC West champions. Just don't bring on injuries—or at least not as many of them—in 1985.

OFFENSE

Even with only partial seasons from Fouts and Winslow, the Chargers still finished with the fourth-best offense in the NFL. San Diego set a league record with 401 pass completions, and running back Earnest Jackson led the AFC with 1,179 yards—the first time a Charger has finished on top in rushing since Dickie Post in 1969.

Despite missing all of December, Fouts still finished with more completions (317) for more yards (3,740) than any quarterback in the AFC except Dan Marino of the Dolphins. He also threw 19 touchdown passes and finished third in the conference in passing.

Fouts ranks fourth on the all-time passing list with 33,854 yards and fifth with 2,585 completions. The prospect of a 16-game season out of Fouts alarms the entire AFC West.

"There are a few players in our league who could help any team be a winner," Kansas City coach John Mackovic said. "Dan Fouts is one. He could turn a nonwinner into a winner or help a good team become a great team. You can't say that about every quarterback in this league. He has remarkable talent."

Fouts's long-time back-up, Ed Luther, jumped to the USFL during the offseason. To replace him, the Chargers obtained Mark Herrmann from Indianapolis in an offseason trade. Herrmann started two games for the Colts in 1984 and completed 51 percent of his passes last season (29 of 56) for 352 yards. Bruce Mathison also is available, but he has thrown only 38 "live" passes in the last six seasons; he threw only 33 as a career-long back-up at the University of Nebraska and has thrown just five passes in his two years as San Diego's number-three quarterback.

Rolf Benirschke

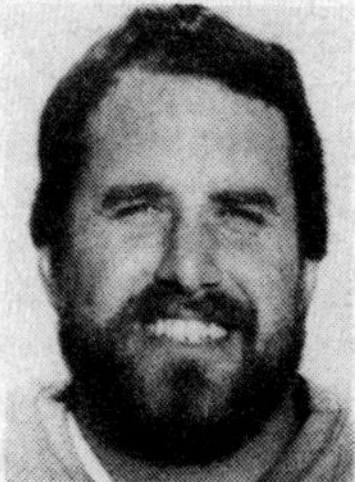

Dan Fouts

Mike Green

The Chargers will continue to throw the football in 1985, whether it's Fouts, Herrmann, or Mathison, taking the snaps from center.

"The name of the game on offense is scoring—moving the ball down the field and into the end zone," Fouts said. "Whether you do it by running or throwing really doesn't matter...just as long as you do it. We average seven yards per attempt—that's *attempt*, not completion. Our completion average is around ten [yards]. Seven yards a pass—that's greater than you ever can do running the ball."

Charlie Joiner became the all-time leading receiver in league history last season when he bumped his career total to 657 catches. He's had four career 1,000-yard seasons, and Wes Chandler has two. They become even more effective when Winslow is roaming the underbelly of zone defenses.

Although he is expected to return this season, team doctors do not expect Winslow to be ready for the 1985 opener. Back-up tight ends Pete Holohan and Eric Sievers caught 56 and 41 passes, respectively, in 1984, but Winslow's absence leaves an empty trapeze in San Diego's aerial circus.

"He's a momentum-maker," Fouts said. "He can go on a roll and destroy a football team. He allows the quarterback to throw the ball to him even when he's covered because of his great athletic talent and size. It's like throwing a ball in to a post man [center] in basketball. You can give him a high lob in traffic and he can snatch it with one hand. It's too bad we can't throw bounce passes [in the NFL] or we'd use those, too."

Jackson only can get better—last season was his first as a starting running back and only his second as a professional. The Chargers also are looking for increased productivity from speedy wide receiver Bobby Duckworth, who scored four touchdowns and averaged a stunning 28.6 yards on his 25 catches a year ago. He's being groomed to replace Joiner, who enters his seventeenth season this fall.

The line that protects Fouts so well and opens the holes for Jackson returns intact and as big as ever. Center Don Macek goes 260 pounds, guards Doug Wilker-

Three Years at a Glance

Averages NFL Rank	OFFENSE			DEFENSE		
	1984	1983	1982	1984	1983	1982
Points Rank	**24.6** 6	**22.4** 12	**32.0** 1	**25.8** 24	**28.9** 28	**24.6** 24
Yards Rank	**393.6** 4	**387.3** 1	**449.8** 1	**371.0** 26	**372.2** 26	**361.4** 25
Rushing Yards Rank	**103.4** 24	**96.0** 25	**124.6** 11	**115.7** 10	**135.8** 18	**106.8** 9
Passing Yards Rank	**290.2** 2	**291.3** 1	**325.2** 1	**255.3** 28	**236.4** 25	**254.7** 28
Sacks Rank	**2.3** 7T	**1.8** 3	**1.3** 3T	**2.1** 24	**1.9** 26T	**2.1** 20
Turnovers Rank	**2.4** 17	**3.4** 27	**2.2** 10	**2.3** 12T	**2.1** 22	**2.8** 7T
Punt Returns Rank	**6.4** 25	**6.5** 26	**11.5** 2	**9.3** 17	**8.5** 15	**12.3** 26
Kickoff Returns Rank	**20.9** 6	**18.6** 22	**19.8** 19	**20.0** 13	**20.4** 20	**19.4** 12
Penalty Yards Rank	**63.9** 25	**60.1** 21	**58.9** 22	**56.6** 9	**59.6** 5	**68.0** 2

	W-L Total	Home	Road	Playoffs
1982	6-3	3-1	3-2	1-1, Lost Second Round Game
1983	6-10	4-4	2-6	None
1984	7-9	4-4	3-5	None

son and Dennis McKnight 253 and 263, respectively, and tackles Ed White and Sam Claphan 284 and 282.

DEFENSE

Defense, as always, is where San Diego needs to make the most improvement. The Chargers allowed 413 points last season, including a club-record 52 against Pittsburgh. Opponents ran up 30 or more points six times against San Diego.

Linebacking is the strength of the San Diego defense, with a dependable veteran tandem of Linden King and Woodrow Lowe manning the outside and a youthful and at-times spectacular twosome of Mike Green and Billy Ray Smith on the inside. Green and Smith combined for 260 tackles, four fumble recoveries, three sacks, and three interceptions a year ago.

Both Smith and Green were selected by San Diego in the 1983 draft, with Smith coming in the first round and Green in the ninth round. Green is only 6 feet, but he has proved a steal for the Chargers. He has led the team in tackles each of his first two seasons and was voted the club's defensive MVP in 1984. When you can't play big, play emotional.

San Diego should get immediate help from 6-foot 3-inch, 241-pound Mike Guendling, who can play either inside or outside, and also from nose tackle Dewey Forte, whom the Chargers signed from Los Angeles of the USFL. He brings 285 pounds to the middle of the defensive line.

Forte figures to make San Diego stronger against the run, but what the Chargers need is a more consistent pass rush up front. The defensive line recorded only 20 sacks last season, which was two fewer than Mark Gastineau's individual league-leading total for the New York Jets.

The absence of a strong pass rush had a direct effect on the secondary as the Chargers wound up twenty-eighth (last) in the NFL against the pass with an average yield of 255.3 yards per game. San Diego defensive backs intercepted only 11 passes in 1984, with Byrd the team leader with a modest 4.

"We have to improve our pass rush and coverage," Coryell said. "If you only have one, you're in trouble."

Earnest Jackson   *Linden King*   *Ed White*

Safeties Tim Fox and Ken Greene have a combined 16 years of experience in NFL secondaries and still have the savvy to get the job done. But with the lack of a pass rush (team-leader Keith Ferguson, a defensive end, had only eight sacks) and the instability on the corners a year ago, they were like two buckets of water in a forest fire.

SPECIAL TEAMS

If Fouts can manuever San Diego into scoring range, the Chargers know that with Rolf Benirschke around they'll probably come away with something. He has converted 73 percent of the 183 field-goal tries in his eight-year career, including 17 of 26 in 1984. Benirschke finished with 92 points and undoubtedly would have topped 100 for the third time in his career had he not missed two games at midyear because of an operation to remove kidney stones. Benny Ricardo provided 13 kicking points in his absence.

The Chargers also can win with Maury Buford as their punter. He averaged 42 yards on 66 kicks last season, but, more important, only three of his punts went for touchbacks and he wound up with a net average of 35 yards. No punter in the league had fewer touchbacks than Buford in 1984.

Lionel James did a commendable job returning kickoffs for the Chargers, averaging 22.3 yards per runback, and he also carried a punt back 58 yards for a touchdown against the Steelers. James averaged only 5.2 yards on his remaining 29 punt returns, however.

But with an offense as explosive as Air Coryell, field position isn't as mandatory for the Chargers as it would be for a more conservative attack.

AFC WEST

VETERAN ROSTER

No.	Name	Pos.	Ht.	Wt.	NFL Exp.	Birthdate	College	Games in 1984
86	Bendross, Jesse	WR	6-0	197	2	5/19/61	Alabama	16
6	Benirschke, Rolf	K	6-1	184	9	2/7/55	Cal-Davis	14
50	Bradley, Carlos	LB	6-0	226	5	4/27/60	Wake Forest	8
7	Buford, Maury	P	6-1	191	4	2/18/60	Texas Tech	16
22	Byrd, Gill	CB	5-10	201	3	2/20/61	San Jose State	13
89	Chandler, Wes	WR	6-0	182	8	8/22/56	Florida	15
91	Chickillo, Tony	NT	6-3	259	2	7/8/60	Miami	1
77	Claphan, Sam	T	6-6	282	5	10/10/56	Oklahoma	16
82	Duckworth, Bobby	WR	6-3	196	4	11/27/58	Arkansas	16
84	Egloff, Ron	TE	6-5	227	9	10/2/55	Wisconsin	12
78	Ehin, Chuck	DE	6-4	260	3	7/1/61	Brigham Young	16
68	Elko, Bill	NT	6-5	280	3	12/28/59	Louisiana State	15
76	Ferguson, Keith	DE	6-5	255	5	4/3/59	Ohio State	16
14	Fouts, Dan	QB	6-3	203	13	6/10/51	Oregon	13
48	Fox, Tim	S	5-11	186	10	11/1/53	Ohio State	11
75	Gissinger, Andrew	C-T	6-5	282	4	7/4/59	Syracuse	16
69	Gofourth, Derrel	G-C	6-3	250	9	3/20/55	Oklahoma State	16
58	Green, Mike	LB	6-0	239	3	6/29/61	Oklahoma State	16
28	Greene, Ken	S	6-2	196	8	5/8/56	Washington State	15
43	Gregor, Bob	S	6-2	191	5	2/10/57	Washington State	7
73	Guthrie, Keith	NT	6-3	267	2	8/17/62	Texas A&M	11
20	Henderson, Reuben	CB	6-0	196	5	10/3/58	San Diego State	12
9	Herrmann, Mark	QB	6-5	199	5	1/8/59	Purdue	3
88	Holohan, Pete	TE	6-4	249	5	7/25/59	Notre Dame	15
41	Jackson, Earnest	RB	5-10	206	3	12/18/59	Texas A&M	16
26	James, Lionel	KR-RB	5-6	172	2	5/25/62	Auburn	16
18	Joiner, Charlie	WR	5-11	180	17	10/14/47	Grambling	16
31	Kay, Bill	CB	6-1	190	5	1/10/60	Purdue	15
57	King, Linden	LB	6-4	250	8	6/28/55	Colorado State	16
64	Loewen, Chuck	G-T	6-4	268	5	1/23/57	South Dakota State	13
51	Lowe, Woodrow	LB	6-0	219	10	6/9/54	Alabama	15
62	Macek, Don	C	6-2	260	10	7/2/54	Boston College	13
12	Mathison, Bruce	QB	6-3	203	3	4/25/59	Nebraska	2
21	McGee, Buford	RB	6-0	206	2	8/16/60	Mississippi	16
60	McKnight, Dennis	C-G	6-3	272	4	9/12/59	Drake	16
24	McPherson, Miles	CB-S	5-11	191	4	3/30/60	New Haven University	9
83	Micho, Bob	TE	6-3	227	2	3/7/62	Texas	6
25	Morris, Wayne	RB	6-0	208	10	5/3/54	Southern Methodist	10
46	Muncie, Chuck	RB	6-8	230	9	3/17/53	California	1
55	Nelson, Derrie	LB	6-1	238	3	2/8/58	Nebraska	6
93	Nelson, Shane	LB	6-1	232	8	5/25/55	Baylor	0
56	Osby, Vince	LB	6-0	222	2	7/8/61	Illinois	16
52	Preston, Ray	LB	6-0	221	10	1/25/54	Syracuse	10
90	Robinson, Fred	DE	6-4	240	2	10/22/61	Miami	16
85	Sievers, Eric	TE	6-3	236	5	11/9/58	Maryland	14
54	Smith, Billy Ray	LB	6-3	231	3	8/10/61	Arkansas	16
45	Smith, Johnny Ray	CB	5-9	190	4	9/7/57	Lamar	1
33	Smith, Lucious	CB	5-10	190	6	1/17/57	Cal State-Fullerton	13
32	Thomas, Jewerl	RB	5-10	230	6	9/10/57	San Jose State	7
59	Thrift, Cliff	LB	6-1	237	7	5/3/56	East Central Oklahoma	16
27	Turner, John	CB-S	6-0	193	8	2/22/56	Miami	15
23	Walters, Danny	CB	6-1	180	3	11/4/60	Arkansas	8
67	White, Ed	T	6-2	284	17	4/4/47	California	15
63	Wilkerson, Doug	G	6-3	253	16	3/27/47	North Carolina Central	16
92	Williams, Eric	LB	6-2	235	9	6/17/55	Southern California	13
99	Williams, Lee	DE	6-6	270	2	10/15/62	Bethune-Cookman	8
80	Winslow, Kellen	TE	6-5	242	7	11/5/57	Missouri	7
49	Young, Andre	S	6-0	190	4	11/22/60	Louisiana Tech	13

Coaching Staff

Don Coryell, head coach; **Dave Adolph,** assistant coach; **Tom Bass,** defensive coordinator; **Hank Bauer,** special offensive assistant; **Marv Braden,** special offensive assistant; **Gunther Cunningham,** defensive line; **Earnel Durden,** offensive backs; **Dave Levy,** offensive coordinator; **Al Saunders,** receivers; **Jim Wagstaff,** defensive backfield; **Chuck Weber,** linebackers; **Ernie Zampese,** quarterbacks, passing game.

1985 Schedule

Preseason

Aug. 10	CLEVELAND	6:00
Aug. 17	DALLAS	6:00
Aug. 24	at San Francisco	Noon
Aug. 30	NEW ORLEANS	7:00

Regular Season

Sept. 8	at Buffalo	4:00
Sept. 15	SEATTLE	1:00
Sept. 22	at Cincinnati	1:00
Sept. 29	CLEVELAND	1:00
Oct. 6	at Seattle	1:00
Oct. 13	KANSAS CITY	1:00
Oct. 20	at Minnesota	12:00
Oct. 28	at L.A. Raiders (Mon.)	6:00
Nov. 3	DENVER	1:00
Nov. 10	L.A. RAIDERS	1:00
Nov. 17	at Denver	2:00
Nov. 24	at Houston	12:00
Dec. 1	BUFFALO	1:00
Dec. 8	PITTSBURGH	6:00
Dec. 15	PHILADELPHIA	1:00
Dec. 22	at Kansas City	12:00

1984 Results

Sept. 2	at Minnesota	42-13
Sept. 9	at Seattle	17-31
Sept. 16	HOUSTON	31-14
Sept. 24	at L.A. Raiders (Mon.)	30-33
Sept. 30	DETROIT	27-24
Oct. 7	at Green Bay	34-28
Oct. 14	at Kansas City	13-31
Oct. 21	L.A. RAIDERS	37-44
Oct. 29	SEATTLE (Mon.)	0-24
Nov. 4	at Indianapolis	38-10
Nov. 11	DENVER	13-16
Nov. 18	MIAMI*	34-28
Nov. 25	at Pittsburgh	24-52
Dec. 3	CHICAGO (Mon.)	20-7
Dec. 9	at Denver	13-16
Dec. 16	KANSAS CITY	21-42

1985 Draft Choices

1. Jim Lachey—12, G, Ohio State
2. Wayne Davis—39, DB, Indiana State
2. Jeffery Dale—55, DB, Louisiana State, from Miami
3. Choice to Minnesota
3. John Hendy—69, DB, Cal State-Long Beach, from Kansas City
4. Ralf Mojsiejenko—96, K, Michigan State
5. Choice to Seattle
6. Terry Lewis—150, DB, Michigan State
7. Choice to Kansas City
7. Mark Fellows—196, LB, Montana State, from San Francisco
8. Curtis Adams—207, RB, Central Michigan
9. Paul Berner—234, QB, Pacific
9. Dan Remsberg—252, T, Abilene Christian, from San Francisco
10. David King—264, DB, Auburn 11. Jeff Smith—291, NT, Kentucky
12. Tony Simmons—318, DE, Tennessee
12. Bret Pearson—329, TE, Wisconsin, from Chicago

SEATTLE SEAHAWKS

It was like making an omelet without all the ingredients. But head coach Chuck Knox still had the Seattle Seahawks cookin' in 1984.

Knox had guided the Seahawks to a 9-7 record and the first playoff berth in franchise history in his first season in the Pacific Northwest in 1983. Seattle figured to be in postseason contention again in 1984 and possibly reach double figures in victories for the first time in club history.

But that was before running back Curt Warner, the 1983 AFC rookie of the year who had produced 35 percent of Seattle's offense that season with his club-record 1,449 rushing yards and 325 receiving yards, suffered a knee injury in the second quarter of the 1984 season opener against the Cleveland Browns.

When Warner went out for the year, Seattle's playoff hopes figured to depart with him. The Seahawks never did establish a running game in 1984, but 15 weeks after Warner was helped off the field, Seattle was on its way to the playoffs, riding a club-record 12 victories.

"A lot of people were surprised by how we finished," Seattle quarterback Dave Krieg said, "but that's a tribute to our coaching staff. They found ways for us to win. When Curt went down, Chuck said, 'Hey, listen: Curt is an excellent runner and pass receiver...but he doesn't cover [kicks] on special teams. He doesn't make any tackles on defense. One man does not make a team.'

"The team is the most important thing. No one individual is more important than the team. That's Chuck's motto. That's the team's motto. Obviously we've got some very talented players like Kenny Easley, Steve Largent, and Curt Warner. But they know they only

Steve Largent has caught passes in 107 consecutive games.

Chuck Knox

can be as good as the guys around them. We are a team in every sense."

Knox has parlayed his we're-all-in-this-together philosophy into a career of coaching quick fixes. He took over the Los Angeles Rams following a 6-7-1 season and guided them to a 12-2 record and an NFC West championship in his first season in 1973. He took over at Buffalo in 1978 and, in his third season, directed the Bills to an 11-5 mark and an AFC East title. Seattle had gone seven years without qualifying for the playoffs before Knox showed up.

"There's no one in Seattle who doesn't put the team first," Pro Bowl safety Easley said. "Chuck Knox preaches team, team, team, team, team....It's funny, but it wasn't until about a week after the whole season was over that I realized we weren't in the Super Bowl. That's how positive and optimistic and team-oriented Chuck Knox is. The team's the thing.

"Individual success is not very important to me. I don't think it's very important to any of us. The important thing is that the team does well. Last season it was very rewarding for our team to have seven guys on the Pro Bowl team. That was a tremendous honor. But individual success is predicated on team success. If we are all playing well to make the team successful, that's when you get individual accolades."

Krieg, wide receiver Largent, nose tackle Joe Nash, cornerback Dave Brown, placekicker Norm Johnson, and special teams standout Fredd Young all were on the AFC Pro Bowl squad along with Easley. Except for Easley, Largent, and possibly Johnson, Seattle's Pro Bowl contingent was a cast of overachievers. In fact, the Seahawks have an entire roster of players who seem to achieve beyond their ability.

OFFENSE

Seattle scored only 10 touchdowns on the ground last season and its leading rusher, Hughes, gained only 327 yards. That's what made Krieg's performance even more incredible.

In his first full season as a starting NFL quarterback, with defenses both expecting and waiting for him to pass, Krieg threw for a club-record 3,671 yards and 32 touchdowns. Only Dan Marino of the Miami Dolphins threw more touchdown passes in 1984.

The experience of having read secondaries for a season figures to make Krieg that much better in 1985. So does the return to the backfield of Warner, which will force linebackers to focus on the run.

"Curt gives us a breakaway threat," Krieg said. "If there's a small hole, some runners might get four or five yards, but Curt can turn it into fourteen or sixteen yards. He'll take the pressure off our passing game. The defense won't be able to dictate when we pass now. With Curt, we won't have as many second-and-seven and third-and-eight situations."

Warner became the first Seattle running back ever to gain 1,000 yards in a season in 1983 and he did it with such style that he led the AFC in rushing. He scored 13 touchdowns on the ground and had six 100-yard days—just three fewer than all Seattle running backs had amassed in the club's first seven years of existence. He is a franchise back.

"Warner is the closest I've seen to O.J.," said Seattle guard Reggie McKenzie, who has blocked for both Warner and O.J. Simpson. "He has that wiggle, wobble. O.J. used to call it his shimmy.

"When the hole is not where it's supposed to be, the great running backs have the ability to find it. The great ones have the quick feet that enable them to find the daylight. O.J. and Curt both could jump in and then

Dave Brown

Kenny Easley

Norm Johnson

jump back out of a hole. That's the shimmy and Curt has a whole lot of shimmy."

Although Knox historically has been a ball-control coach and in Warner has an ideal ball-control running back, the Seahawks will continue to throw because they have the best 1-2 receiving punch in their history with wide receivers Largent and Daryl Turner.

Largent went to his fourth Pro Bowl following a 1,164-yard, 12-touchdown season. He has caught passes in 107 consecutive games, the third-longest streak in NFL history. If he catches passes in all 16 games this fall, he will overtake Mel Gray in the number-two spot and would be in a position to break Harold Carmichael's record of 127 in the fifth game of the 1986 season.

"We're only interested in individual records if they can help us win," Knox said. "That comes first. We would like all of our players to maintain and perpetuate an individual record but winning is the bottom line. Nothing should interfere with winning."

But that isn't the only record Largent is pursuing as he enters his tenth season. He ranks ninth all-time in both catches (545) and yards (8,722), and tenth in touchdowns (72). His seven 50-catch seasons give him a share of an NFL record and his six 1,000-yard seasons are one short of another mark held by Lance Alworth. He's third in career 100-yard games with 32 and would need nine such days in 1985 to tie Alworth for second.

Largent will be even more effective now that the Seahawks finally have found a standout receiver to operate on the other flank. Turner, a second-round draft pick out of Michigan State a year ago, stepped in when Paul Johns suffered a season-ending neck injury and caught 35 passes for 715 yards in 10 starts. Ten of his receptions went for touchdowns and he averaged 20.4 yards per catch. He also could turn in a 1,000-yard season in 1985.

A major problem still is the lack of a good tight end.

The offensive line is mostly made of veterans. Guard Edwin Bailey is the youngster in his fifth year, and guard Robert Pratt the oldster in his twelfth. Center Blair Bush and tackle Bob Cryder both are entering

Three Years at a Glance

Averages NFL Rank	OFFENSE			DEFENSE		
	1984	1983	1982	1984	1983	1982
Points Rank	**26.1** 5	**25.2** 6	**14.1** 27	**17.6** 5	**24.8** 24	**16.3** 5
Yards Rank	**316.8** 18	**318.3** 19	**288.2** 22	**310.2** 6	**376.8** 27	**310.4** 12
Rushing Yards Rank	**102.8** 25	**132.4** 14	**88.3** 27	**111.8** 6	**137.4** 19	**162.3** 27
Passing Yards Rank	**213.9** 10	**185.8** 21	**199.9** 16	**198.4** 10	**239.4** 26	**148.1** 3
Sacks Rank	**2.6** 9T	**2.9** 17T	**4.0** 26	**3.4** 7T	**2.7** 13T	**1.9** 23
Turnovers Rank	**2.4** 18T	**2.4** 11T	**2.7** 17T	**3.9** 1	**3.4** 2	**2.4** 14T
Punt Returns Rank	**11.0** 5	**10.8** 5	**10.9** 6	**6.4** 6	**5.1** 1	**3.6** 3
Kickoff Returns Rank	**18.6** 24	**22.2** 2	**18.8** 24	**16.7** 2	**16.1** 1	**15.0** 1
Penalty Yards Rank	**73.7** 27	**55.6** 19	**58.1** 20	**55.1** 12	**45.3** 23	**45.1** 21

	W-L Total	Home	Road	Playoffs
1982	4-5	3-2	1-3	None
1983	9-7	5-3	4-4	2-1, Lost AFC Championship Game
1984	12-4	7-1	5-3	1-1, Lost Divisional Playoff Game

their eighth seasons, tackle Ron Essink his sixth, and McKenzie comes off the bench with 13 years of experience.

DEFENSE

The Seattle defense also stepped forward to address Warner's injury a year ago. Without a ball-control running back on their side, those defenders knew they would have to spend more time on the field in 1984. They worked up a reasonable compromise—turnovers.

The Seahawks forced 63 turnovers last season. Only two teams in NFL history ever forced more, the 1961 Denver Broncos with 68, and the 1961 San Diego Chargers with 66. The Seattle defense returned eight of those turnovers for touchdowns, including an NFL-record four interceptions for touchdowns against the Kansas City Chiefs in a November game.

The Seahawks allowed the fewest points in franchise history (282) and also set a club record with 55 sacks. They posted back-to-back shutouts of San Diego and Kansas City in November to fuel an eight-game, mid-season winning streak.

The Seahawks led the NFL in interceptions with 38, and Easley was tops individually with 10. Dave Brown chipped in a career-high eight interceptions to earn the first Pro Bowl bid of his 10-year career, safety John Harris had six interceptions, and cornerback Keith Simpson four.

Ends Jeff Bryant and Jacob Green had 14½ and 13 sacks, respectively, and linebacker Shelton Robinson had a team-leading 93 tackles. Green and Robinson each contributed four of Seattle's league-leading 25 fumble recoveries. Nash made 82 tackles from his nose position. He recorded seven sacks, recovered three fumbles, and blocked two field goals en route to a starter's spot in the Pro Bowl. Keith Butler is the other inside linebacker, with Bruce Scholtz and Greg Gaines on the outside. Michael Jackson adds depth to the position.

The statistics might not be as glossy for the Seattle defense in 1985, but, with Warner back, they might not need to be. About the only thing that is predictable is that Easley, the heart and soul of the Seahawks' de-

Dave Krieg

Joe Nash

Fredd Young

fense, will be a better player in 1985 than he was a year ago. Just as he was a better player in 1984 than he was in 1983 and a better player in 1983 than he was in 1982. And he went to the Pro Bowl all three of those seasons.

SPECIAL TEAMS

Special teams are special in Seattle. They also are good. Young's tackles were so spectacular on kick coverages that he was selected to the Pro Bowl in his rookie season as the AFC's special teams player. In his NFL debut against Cleveland, he blocked a punt and made four tackles inside the 20-yard line on kickoffs, forcing one fumble. Young wound up with two blocked punts and 20 tackles in 1984.

Johnson handled the AFC Pro Bowl squad's kicking chores following his 110-point season. He also emerged as the most accurate field-goal kicker in the conference by converting 20 of his 24 opportunities, with two of his misses coming from beyond 50 yards. At 25, his best seasons should still be ahead of him.

Johns had a career average of 11.3 yards per punt return prior to suffering his neck injury in the fourth game of the 1984 season. That's the ninth-best return average in NFL history and you don't replace that type of productivity with just anyone. So the Seahawks summoned the versatile Easley, who averaged 12.1 yards on his 16 returns. Hughes also gave Seattle a solid 20.5-yard return average on kickoffs.

The only gray area for Seattle is at punter, where Jeff West averaged just 37.5 yards per kick in 1984. The Seahawks have signed former Pro Bowl punter Luke Prestridge (Denver, 1983) to compete with him in training camp.

VETERAN ROSTER

No.	Name	Pos.	Ht.	Wt.	NFL Exp.	Birthdate	College	Games in 1984
69	Abramowitz, Sid	T	6-6	280	3	5/21/60	Tulsa	4
65	Bailey, Edwin	G	6-4	265	5	5/15/59	South Carolina State	12
22	Brown, Dave	CB	6-2	190	11	1/16/53	Michigan	16
77	Bryant, Jeff	DE	6-5	270	4	5/22/60	Clemson	16
59	Bush, Blair	C	6-3	252	8	11/25/56	Washington	16
96	Butler, Chuck	LB	6-0	220	2	12/18/61	Boise State	8
53	Butler, Keith	LB	6-4	238	8	5/16/56	Memphis State	16
83	Castor, Chris	WR	6-0	170	3	8/13/60	Duke	15
78	Cryder, Bob	T	6-4	282	8	9/7/56	Alabama	16
31	Dixon, Zachary	RB	6-1	204	7	3/5/57	Temple	13
33	Doornink, Dan	FB	6-3	210	8	2/1/56	Washington State	16
35	Dufek, Don	S	6-0	195	9	4/28/54	Michigan	9
45	Easley, Kenny	S	6-3	206	5	1/15/59	UCLA	16
68	Edwards, Randy	DE	6-4	255	2	3/9/61	Alabama	13
64	Essink, Ron	T	6-6	275	6	7/30/58	Grand Valley State	16
74	Fanning, Mike	DE	6-6	255	11	2/2/53	Notre Dame	16
56	Gaines, Greg	LB	6-3	220	4	10/16/58	Tennessee	16
79	Green, Jacob	DE	6-3	255	6	1/21/57	Texas A&M	16
44	Harris, John	S	6-2	200	8	6/13/56	Arizona State	16
63	Hicks, Mark	LB	6-2	225	2	11/7/60	Arizona State	0
46	Hughes, David	FB	6-0	220	5	6/1/59	Boise State	16
55	Jackson, Michael	LB	6-1	220	7	7/15/57	Washington	8
24	Jackson, Terry	CB	5-11	197	8	12/9/55	San Diego State	16
85	Johns, Paul	WR	5-11	170	5	11/14/58	Tulsa	4
9	Johnson, Norm	K	6-2	193	4	5/31/60	UCLA	16
60	Kaiser, John	LB	6-3	221	2	6/6/62	Arizona	16
62	Kauahi, Kani	C	6-2	260	4	9/6/59	Hawaii	16
17	Krieg, Dave	QB	6-1	185	6	10/20/58	Milton	16
37	Lane, Eric	RB	6-0	195	5	1/6/59	Brigham Young	15
80	Largent, Steve	WR	5-11	184	10	9/28/54	Tulsa	16
73	Mangiero, Dino	NT	6-2	270	6	12/19/58	Rutgers	15
67	McKenzie, Reggie	G	6-5	255	14	7/27/50	Michigan	10
51	Merriman, Sam	LB	6-3	225	3	5/5/61	Idaho	16
88	Metzelaars, Pete	TE	6-7	240	4	5/24/60	Wabash	9
71	Millard, Bryan	T	6-5	284	2	12/2/60	Texas	14
43	Morris, Randall	RB	6-0	190	2	4/22/61	Tennessee	10
21	Moyer, Paul	S	6-1	201	3	7/26/61	Arizona State	16
72	Nash, Joe	NT	6-2	250	4	10/11/60	Boston College	16
61	Pratt, Robert	G	6-4	250	12	5/25/51	North Carolina	16
57	Robinson, Shelton	LB	6-2	233	4	9/14/60	North Carolina	16
84	Scales, Dwight	WR	6-2	182	9	5/30/53	Grambling	4
58	Scholtz, Bruce	LB	6-6	240	4	9/26/58	Texas	16
75	Schreiber, Adam	G	6-4	284	2	2/20/62	Texas	6
42	Simpson, Keith	CB	6-1	195	8	3/9/56	Memphis State	15
82	Skansi, Paul	WR	5-11	190	3	1/11/61	Washington	7
20	Taylor, Terry	CB	5-10	175	2	7/18/61	Southern Illinois	16
86	Tice, Mike	TE	6-7	250	5	2/2/59	Maryland	16
81	Turner, Daryl	WR	6-3	198	2	12/15/61	Michigan State	16
89	Walker, Byron	WR	6-4	190	4	7/28/60	Citadel	16
28	Warner, Curt	RB	5-11	205	2	3/18/61	Penn State	1
8	West, Jeff	P	6-2	205	10	4/6/53	Cincinnati	16
54	Williams, Eugene	LB	6-1	220	3	6/15/60	Tulsa	0
87	Young, Charle	TE	6-4	234	13	2/5/51	Southern California	15
50	Young, Fredd	LB	6-1	225	2	11/14/61	New Mexico State	16
10	Zorn, Jim	QB	6-2	200	10	5/10/53	Cal Poly-Pomona	16

Coaching Staff

Chuck Knox, head coach; **Tom Catlin,** assistant head coach, defensive coordinator, linebackers; **George Dyer,** defensive line; **Chick Harris,** offensive backfield; **Ralph Hawkins,** defensive backfield; **Ken Meyer,** quarterbacks; **Steve Moore,** receivers; **Ray Prochaska,** offensive coordinator; **Kent Stephenson,** offensive line; **Rusty Tillman,** tight ends, special teams; **Joe Vitt,** special assignments.

1985 Schedule

Preseason

Aug. 10	at Indianapolis	7:30
Aug. 16	DETROIT	7:30
Aug. 24	at Minnesota	7:00
Aug. 30	SAN FRANCISCO	6:00

Regular Season

Sept. 8	at Cincinnati	1:00
Sept. 15	at San Diego	1:00
Sept. 23	L.A. RAMS (Mon.)	6:00
Sept. 29	at Kansas City	12:00
Oct. 6	SAN DIEGO	1:00
Oct. 13	ATLANTA	1:00
Oct. 20	at Denver	2:00
Oct. 27	at N.Y. Jets	1:00
Nov. 3	L.A. RAIDERS	1:00
Nov. 10	at New Orleans	12:00
Nov. 17	NEW ENGLAND	1:00
Nov. 25	at San Francisco (Mon.)	6:00
Dec. 1	KANSAS CITY	1:00
Dec. 8	CLEVELAND	1:00
Dec. 15	at L.A. Raiders	1:00
Dec. 22	DENVER (Fri.)	5:00

1984 Results

Sept. 3	CLEVELAND	33-0
Sept. 9	SAN DIEGO	31-17
Sept. 16	at New England	23-38
Sept. 23	CHICAGO	38-9
Sept. 30	at Minnesota	20-12
Oct. 7	at L.A. Raiders	14-28
Oct. 14	BUFFALO	31-28
Oct. 21	vs. Green Bay at Milw	30-24
Oct. 29	at San Diego (Mon.)	24-0
Nov. 4	KANSAS CITY	45-0
Nov. 12	L.A. RAIDERS (Mon.)	17-14
Nov. 18	at Cincinnati	26-6
Nov. 25	at Denver	27-24
Dec. 2	DETROIT	38-17
Dec. 9	at Kansas City	7-34
Dec. 15	DENVER (Sat.)	14-31
Dec. 22	L.A. RAIDERS	13-7
Dec. 29	Miami	10-31

1985 Draft Choices

1. Choice to Cincinnati
2. Owen Gill—53, RB, Iowa
3. Danny Greene—81, WR, Washington
4. Tony Davis—109, TE, Missouri
5. Mark Napolitan—123, C, Michigan State, from San Diego
5. Arnold Brown—128, DB, N. Carolina Central, from Pittsburgh
5. Johnnie Jones—137, RB, Tennessee
6. Choice to N.Y. Giants
7. Ron Mattes—193, T, Virginia
8. Judious Lewis—221, WR, Arkansas State
9. Bob Otto—248, DE, Idaho State
10. John Conner—277, QB, Arizona
10. James Bowers—280, DB, Memphis State, from San Francisco
11. Louis Cooper—305, LB, Western Carolina
12. Choice to Buffalo

NATIONAL FOOTBALL CONFERENCE

EAST: Jim Dent
CENTRAL: Kevin Lamb
WEST: Bud Shaw

DALLAS COWBOYS

What went wrong with the Dallas Cowboys in 1984?

Was it the Quarterback Controversy, or, more specifically, the Great Quarterback Shuffle between Danny White and Gary Hogeboom? Was it Tony Dorsett, who had only two 100-yard games? Was it the offensive line, which lost three starters to injuries? Or should Tom Landry have blamed the battered and bruised wide receivers who performed far below Cowboys standards?

It was all these problems and more. The Cowboys simply lacked the talented players who were around for five Super Bowls in the 1970s. Only three players—Doug Cosbie, Randy White, and Bill Bates—were selected to the NFC Pro Bowl team in 1984.

The Cowboys will miss middle linebacker Bob Breunig, who retired at the end of the season, and 10-year veteran guard Herb Scott, who announced his retirement in March. Each played in three Pro Bowls.

Landry, who agreed to a three-year contract after the 1984 season, prays that he never again will experience so many changes as in 1984. Dallas lost 10 players to retirement, injuries, and defections to the USFL. Among them were Pro Bowl players including Drew Pearson,

Michael Downs has established himself at safety for Dallas.

Tom Landry

Harvey Martin, Billy Joe DuPree, and Pat Donovan.

Many folks in Dallas blame the quarterback controversy for the Cowboys' 9-7 season, the first non-playoff year since 1974. Landry was constantly second-guessed over a decision to bench White, the number-two passer of all time (84.5 rating) after the 1983 season. With White as the starting quarterback, Dallas had compiled a 45-18 record.

White relieved Hogeboom halfway through the season and started six games, including the final four. Now, Landry must make another crucial decision about the quarterback situation. The coach has said he will commit himself to one starting quarterback in 1985.

Along with filling holes in his roster, Landry must mend the psyche of the team. The low point of 1984 was a 14-3 loss to winless Buffalo (0-11). After losing to the Bills, team president Tex Schramm said the Cowboys should trade "finger-pointers," those players who publicly blamed their teammates for losses.

Landry now believes that the Cowboys are on the mend. The evidence could be found in Dallas's offseason conditioning program, which drew a record attendance.

"Our players came out of the 1983 season with a pretty bad overall attitude," Landry said. "But I can see the changes now. I think they now are willing to work, willing to take a lot more responsibility for winning and losing on themselves. We need a healthy attitude if we're going to get back into the hunt for the division championship." (Dallas has not won a division title since 1981).

OFFENSE

Hogeboom has perhaps the strongest arm in the NFL since Terry Bradshaw. What Hogeboom lacked in 1984, though, was the proper passing touch.

With Dallas and Washington tied 7-7 during a game at RFK Stadium, Hogeboom had fullback Timmy Newsome open 30 yards downfield. It would have been a

certain touchdown because linebacker Monte Coleman had followed the wrong receiver. But Hogeboom
overthrew Newsome by more than 10 feet.

No doubt, Hogeboom has the physical talents to become an outstanding NFL quarterback and, perhaps,
to lead Dallas to a Super Bowl. The question is whether
Landry and staff can convince Hogeboom to throw the
ball with more finesse.

"Gary had his first test and he performed pretty well,
but he still has to learn quite a bit about what he can do
in the passing game," Landry said. "He did not pro-
duce the touchdowns and big plays we need at that position, although I think he will in time. His number-one
objective is to score, to take his team into the end zone
when he gets inside the twenty-yard line."

Hogeboom finished the season as the NFC's thir-
teenth-ranked passer with a rating of 63.7. He had only
seven touchdown passes in 10 starts. Still, the Cowboys
did not hesitate to offer Hogeboom a new contract that
will pay him close to $550,000, the salary currently
earned by White.

It is Landry's long-standing policy that the quarterback who finishes the season as the starter begins training camp number-one on the depth chart. White, who
started the last four games, will enter training camp
ahead of Hogeboom.

"Danny had a very difficult year last year," Landry
said. "He was our number-one man for four years and
it's pretty tough on a guy when someone else takes his
place. He had a tough mental situation to overcome
and I think he peformed well. He came back strong in

Bill Bates

Doug Cosbie

Tony Dorsett

the end. He still was not where he wanted to be. But at least he regained the confidence of the team and everyone felt he could win for them."

In 1984, Dallas averaged only 19.3 points per game, its lowest figure in 20 years. The division champion Redskins averaged a touchdown more per game.

Of the 28 NFL teams, Dallas ranked twentieth in rushing and twenty-fourth in passing.

The two wide receivers Landry had counted on—Doug Donley and Tony Hill—spent parts of the season sidelined with injuries. Landry said he admired Donley for trying to play hurt, but admitted the Cowboys need to obtain another wide receiver.

Hill finished the season with 58 receptions, his third-most productive season. If Landry can find another Drew Pearson-type receiver to complement Hill, the receiver situation would brighten.

There is hope for Duriel Harris, who was claimed late in the season from Cleveland. Harris has developed a reputation for dropping passes, but coaches were impressed with the way he ran pass patterns in practice. Mike Renfro (35 for 583 yards) started several games, but is considered a role player.

Defenses learned quickly to double-cover tight end Cosbie, who still finished with a club tight end record of 60 catches for 789 yards. Cosbie is capable of catching 80 or 90 passes a season if Landry decides to center the passing game on one receiver.

Tony Dorsett had his least-productive rushing season since 1979 (1,189 yards), although Landry doled out more praise for Dorsett than ever before in his career.

"Tony actually ran the ball better than any time I can remember since he's been here," Landry said. "We just didn't have any consistency in the running game and we had 'way too many injuries in the offensive line."

Landry named Dorsett one of the team captains and called him "one of the best leaders we've had in a long time."

The career of running back Ron Springs had a snag in 1984. One year after catching a club record 73 passes, Springs had 46 receptions and finished the year on the bench.

Three Years at a Glance

Averages NFL Rank	OFFENSE			DEFENSE		
	1984	1983	1982	1984	1983	1982
Points	**19.3**	**29.9**	**25.1**	**19.3**	**22.5**	**16.1**
Rank	18	2	5T	9	20	3
Yards	**332.5**	**372.4**	**355.4**	**314.8**	**339.2**	**305.9**
Rank	11	5	5	7	17	11
Rushing Yards	**107.1**	**132.3**	**145.9**	**139.1**	**93.7**	**112.3**
Rank	20	15	5	24	2T	13
Passing Yards	**225.4**	**240.1**	**209.6**	**175.6**	**245.5**	**193.6**
Rank	6	4	9	5	27	11
Sacks	**3.0**	**2.3**	**2.8**	**3.6**	**3.6**	**3.6**
Rank	14T	8T	16T	5T	2T	3T
Turnovers	**2.7**	**2.4**	**2.9**	**2.8**	**3.0**	**2.8**
Rank	26T	15T	23T	3	4T	7T
Punt Returns	**8.3**	**9.0**	**8.1**	**4.2**	**11.1**	**5.6**
Rank	14	11	14	1	26	7
Kickoff Returns	**19.0**	**19.0**	**19.7**	**20.2**	**23.2**	**22.8**
Rank	18	18	20	14	27	27
Penalty Yards	**59.2**	**52.9**	**33.8**	**54.3**	**54.6**	**47.9**
Rank	21	17	4	15	9	17

	W-L Total	**Home**	**Road**	**Playoffs**
1982	6-3	3-2	3-1	2-1, Lost NFC Championship Game
1983	12-4	6-2	6-2	0-1, Lost First Round Game
1984	9-7	5-3	4-4	None

Timmy Newsome is the "fullback" of the Cowboys' future. Once considered too tentative as a runner, Newsome took charge of the position when Springs landed in Landry's doghouse. Landry now believes in using bigger fullback-type runners. Newsome stands 6 feet 3 inches, weighs 240 pounds, and has breakaway speed. Landry should have known the offensive line was destined for a bad year when right tackle Jim Cooper broke his leg while walking across a dance floor at a Dallas disco. Howard Richards's knee required surgery midway through the season, and starting left offensive tackle Phil Pozderac also missed some games with an injured knee.

DEFENSE

While the offense was costing Dallas a shot at the playoffs, the defense was having its best season since 1978, the Cowboys' last Super Bowl year.

Although Landry still is stubbornly loyal to the Flex defense, he did adjust the parameters and allowed his players to be more aggressive. Like most NFL teams, Dallas played an "attack" defense in 1984. Free safety Michael Downs became a terror on the safety blitz. He also led the team with seven interceptions.

Dallas finished the season with 28 interceptions and 15 fumble recoveries.

After missing training camp, defensive tackle Randy White struggled early in the season, but finished with 12½ sacks. He was almost unstoppable in the second half of the schedule. After making the Pro Bowl for three consecutive years, defensive end Ed (Too Tall) Jones had a subpar year and missed a trip to Hawaii. He did, however, bat away 16 passes at the line of scrimmage.

Right defensive end Jim Jeffcoat (11½ sacks) was the most improved player in the defensive unit. He was more than an adequate replacement for the retired Harvey Martin.

The biggest surprise, however, was rookie middle linebacker Eugene Lockhart, a sixth-round draft choice who proved it doesn't take a veteran to play middle linebacker in the Flex.

His nickname is "Mean Gene the Hittin' Machine."

Mike Hegman   *Rafael Septien*   *Randy White*

Mike Hegman had his best season at strongside line-backer, but there is some question about the starter at weakside linebacker. Last year's starter, Anthony Dickerson, played out his option, and the 1984 number-one draft choice, Billy Cannon, has been ruled out of further participation in the game because of a spinal injury.

Cornerback Everson Walls, who led the league in interceptions in 1981 and 1982, finished with just three. Teams learned how to take advantage of his relative lack of speed. The Cowboys found a strong safety in 1984 when Dextor Clinkscale, who had been prone to injury, did not miss a game.

SPECIAL TEAMS

"We've got to find a punter," Landry said. "It's hard to believe that we still haven't found one consistent enough to replace Danny White."

Even if White remains the number-one quarterback, Landry wants a new punter in 1985. He believes that a starting quarterback shouldn't have to worry about punting.

There will be no need to replace Rafael Septien, who made 23 of 29 field goals and is the fourth-most accurate kicker in NFL history. Septien scored 102 points and kicked the winning 41-yard field goal in overtime to beat the New Orleans Saints.

As for a non-kicking special teams player, Dallas probably has the best in the league. Bill Bates was a member of seven of the eight special teams units, made almost 80 percent of the tackles, and went to the Pro Bowl as the NFC's special teamer. Bates also will challenge for the starting job at strong safety.

VETERAN ROSTER

No.	Name	Pos.	Ht.	Wt.	NFL Exp.	Birthdate	College	Games in 1984
36	Albritton, Vince	S	6-2	209	2	7/23/62	Washington	16
31	Allen, Gary	RB	5-10	179	4	4/23/60	Hawaii	16
76	Aughtman, Dowe	G	6-3	258	2	1/28/61	Auburn	7
62	Baldinger, Brian	G-T	6-4	258	4	1/7/59	Duke	16
40	Bates, Bill	S	6-1	201	3	6/6/61	Tennessee	12
47	Clinkscale, Dextor	S	5-11	189	5	4/13/58	South Carolina State	15
61	Cooper, Jim	T	6-5	267	9	9/28/55	Temple	7
85	Cornwell, Fred	TE	6-6	237	2	8/7/61	Southern California	14
84	Cosbie, Doug	TE	6-6	235	7	2/27/56	Santa Clara	16
55	DeOssie, Steve	LB	6-2	248	2	11/22/62	Boston College	16
51	Dickerson, Anthony	LB	6-2	222	6	6/9/57	Southern Methodist	16
33	Dorsett, Tony	RB	5-11	185	9	4/7/54	Pittsburgh	16
26	Downs, Michael	S	6-3	195	5	6/9/59	Rice	16
78	Dutton, John	DT	6-7	267	12	2/6/51	Nebraska	16
27	Fellows, Ron	CB	6-0	174	5	11/7/58	Missouri	16
28	Granger, Norm	RB	5-9	220	2	9/14/61	Iowa	15
86	Harris, Duriel	WR	5-11	176	10	11/27/54	New Mexico State	16
58	Hegman, Mike	LB	6-1	231	10	1/17/53	Tennessee State	16
15	Hewko, Bob	QB	6-3	195	2	6/8/60	Florida	0
80	Hill, Tony	WR	6-2	198	9	6/23/56	Stanford	11
14	Hogeboom, Gary	QB	6-4	200	6	8/21/58	Central Michigan	16
97	Hopkins, Thomas	T	6-6	260	2	1/13/60	Alabama A&M	0
21	Howard, Carl	CB	6-2	188	2	9/20/61	Rutgers	10
79	Hunt, John	G	6-4	253	2	11/6/62	Florida	2
77	Jeffcoat, Jim	DE	6-5	257	3	4/1/61	Arizona State	16
72	Jones, Ed	DE	6-9	287	11	2/23/51	Tennessee State	16
23	Jones, James	RB	5-10	189	5	12/6/58	Mississippi State	9
73	Kitson, Syd	G	6-4	262	5	9/27/58	Wake Forest	9
56	Lockhart, Eugene	LB	6-2	233	2	3/8/61	Houston	15
35	McSwain, Chuck	RB	6-0	190	3	2/21/61	Clemson	15
30	Newsome, Timmy	RB	6-1	232	6	5/17/58	Winston-Salem State	15
16	Pelluer, Steve	QB	6-4	210	2	7/29/62	Washington	1
65	Petersen, Kurt	G	6-4	267	6	6/17/57	Missouri	13
81	Phillips, Kirk	WR	6-1	202	2	7/31/60	Tulsa	8
75	Pozderac, Phil	T	6-9	276	4	12/19/59	Notre Dame	15
64	Rafferty, Tom	C	6-3	254	10	8/2/54	Penn State	16
82	Renfro, Mike	WR	6-0	188	8	6/19/55	Texas Christian	16
70	Richards, Howard	T	6-6	260	5	8/7/59	Missouri	11
50	Rohrer, Jeff	LB	6-3	225	4	12/25/58	Yale	16
89	Salonen, Brian	TE	6-2	227	2	7/29/61	Montana	16
66	Schultz, Chris	T	6-8	265	2	2/16/60	Arizona	0
22	Scott, Victor	CB-S	5-11	196	2	6/1/62	Colorado	16
1	Septien, Rafael	K	5-10	180	9	12/12/53	Southwest Louisiana	16
60	Smerek, Don	DT	6-7	255	4	12/20/57	Nevada-Reno	16
20	Springs, Ron	RB	6-1	224	7	11/1/56	Ohio State	16
32	Thurman, Dennis	CB	5-11	175	8	4/13/56	Southern California	16
63	Titensor, Glen	G	6-4	264	5	2/21/58	Brigham Young	15
71	Tuinei, Mark	DT	6-5	274	3	3/31/60	Hawaii	16
57	Turner, Jimmie	LB	6-2	220	2	2/16/62	Presbyterian	5
24	Walls, Everson	CB	6-1	190	5	12/28/59	Grambling	16
5	Warren, John	P	6-0	207	3	11/8/60	Tennessee	3
11	White, Danny	QB-P	6-2	197	10	2/9/52	Arizona State	14
54	White, Randy	DT	6-4	260	11	1/15/53	Maryland	16

Coaching Staff

Tom Landry, head coach; **Neill Armstrong,** research and development; **Al Lavan,** running backs; **Alan Lowry,** special teams; **Jim Myers,** assistant head coach, offensive line; **Dick Nolan,** receivers; **Jim Shofner,** quarterbacks; **Gene Stallings,** defensive backs; **Ernie Stautner,** defensive coordinator, defensive line; **Jerry Tubbs,** linebackers; **Bob Ward,** conditioning.

1985 Schedule

Preseason

Aug. 10	GREEN BAY	8:00
Aug. 17	at San Diego	6:00
Aug. 26	CHICAGO	7:00
Aug. 31	HOUSTON	8:00

Regular Season

Sept. 9	WASHINGTON (Mon.)	8:00
Sept. 15	at Detroit	1:00
Sept. 22	CLEVELAND	12:00
Sept. 29	at Houston	12:00
Oct. 6	at N.Y. Giants	9:00
Oct. 13	PITTSBURGH	12:00
Oct. 20	at Philadelphia	1:00
Oct. 27	ATLANTA	12:00
Nov. 4	at St. Louis (Mon.)	8:00
Nov. 10	at Washington	4:00
Nov. 17	CHICAGO	12:00
Nov. 28	PHILADELPHIA	3:00
Dec. 1	ST. LOUIS (Thanks.)	3:00
Dec. 8	at Cincinnati	1:00
Dec. 15	N.Y. GIANTS	12:00
Dec. 22	at San Francisco	1:00

1984 Results

Sept. 3	at L.A. Rams (Mon.)	20-13
Sept. 9	at N.Y. Giants	7-28
Sept. 16	PHILADELPHIA	23-17
Sept. 23	GREEN BAY	20-6
Sept. 30	at Chicago	23-14
Oct. 7	ST. LOUIS	20-31
Oct. 14	at Washington	14-34
Oct. 21	NEW ORLEANS*	30-27
Oct. 28	INDIANAPOLIS	22-3
Nov. 4	N.Y. GIANTS	7-19
Nov. 11	at St. Louis	24-17
Nov. 18	at Buffalo	3-14
Nov. 22	NEW ENGLAND (Th.)	20-17
Dec. 2	at Philadelphia	26-10
Dec. 9	WASHINGTON	28-30
Dec. 17	at Miami (Mon.)	21-28

1985 Draft Choices

1. Kevin Brooks—17, DE, Michigan
2. Jesse Penn—44, LB, Virginia Tech
3. Crawford Kerr—76, G, Florida
4. Robert Lavette—103, RB, Georgia Tech
5. Herschel Walker—114, RB, Georgia, from Houston
5. Matt Darwin—119, C, Texas A&M, from Cleveland through Buffalo
5. Choice to Buffalo
6. Kurt Ploeger—144, DE, Gustavus Adolphus, from Indianapolis
6. Matt Moran—157, G, Stanford
7. Karl Powe—178, WR, Alabama State, from N.Y. Jets through Kansas City
7. Jim Herrmann—184, DE, Brigham Young
8. Leon Gonzales—216, WR, Bethune-Cookman
9. Scott Strasburger—243, LB, Nebraska
10. Joe Jones—270, TE, Virginia Tech
11. Neal Dellocono—297, LB, UCLA
12. Karl Jordan—324, LB, Vanderbilt

NEW YORK GIANTS

After losing to New Orleans on Saturday of the final weekend of the 1984 season, New York needed victories by Washington over St. Louis and Miami over Dallas to make the playoffs as a wild-card team.

Washington's Mark Moseley delivered one victory with a 37-yard field goal to beat the Cardinals. On Monday night, a 61-yard pass from Miami's Dan Marino to Mark Clayton in the final minute knocked Dallas out of the playoffs.

When it was over, Giants players were standing in front of a giant TV screen, waving their arms. And they weren't complaining about the NFL tie-breaker rules (Dallas, New York, and St. Louis finished the regular season with 9-7 records).

"Rooting against Dallas was easy," said defensive end Casey Merrill. "It's a lot easier than pulling for Washington."

"I don't think we backed into the playoffs," nose tackle Jim Burt said. "Maybe the people who said we backed in are the same ones who said we wouldn't win five games all season."

New York proved it deserved playoff status by defeating the Rams 16-13 in Anaheim the following weekend. It was especially significant in light of the Rams' 33-12 victory over New York in Anaheim during the regular season.

The Giants' defense performed well the following Sunday, holding the multi-faceted San Francisco offense to zero points in the second half after allowing 21 in the first quarter. But the New York offense, which scored only one touchdown in the playoffs, let the defense down.

Phil Simms was injury-free and passed for 4,044 yards.

Bill Parcells

After a 21-10 loss to the 49ers, coach Bill Parcells was asked if he had been satisfied with the Giants' trip through the playoffs. It was the wrong question.

"It was *not* a great season," Parcells snapped. "Any of you people who think that are full of bull."

Safety Bill Currier had the same message.

"We should be mad enough about this to get us fired up," he said. "There's just no excuse for the way we handled the playoffs."

The biggest story of the Giants' year was that quarterback Phil Simms finished the season without a debilitating injury. Simms learned to scramble and to throw on the run. He also received more protection from his offensive line.

"Every time I got hurt in previous years, I was always standing back in the pocket," Simms says. "I learned that moving around doesn't hurt you."

Simms broke Y.A. Tittle's club record for a season with 4,044 yards. He had 22 touchdown passes and finished with a rating of 78.1, ninth in the National Football Conference.

It also was a good year for the Giants' Lionel Manuel, Bobby Johnson, Andy Headen, Zeke Mowatt, and Burt—"no-name" players—who became heroes in a 9-7 season, which was a dramatic improvement over the 3-12-1 of 1983.

Manuel, a rookie, caught 33 passes and was a major reason the Giants defeated Dallas twice in the same season for the first time since 1963. Manuel was called the "best young receiving prospect in the league" by Dallas cornerback Everson Walls.

By NFL standards, Burt is too short for a nose tackle at 6 feet 1. But the Giants were eleventh in the NFL in total yardage allowed and held the Rams' Eric Dickerson to 107 yards in the playoff game.

Even with all-pro cornerback Mark Haynes on injured reserve at the end of the season, the defense still was the heart of the team. Rookie linebacker Gary Reasons intercepted two passes by Montana in the playoff game.

"You don't have to be a genius on this team to realize that we've got youth and we've something to build on," said Pro Bowl linebacker Harry Carson, who didn't have a bad season himself. "Don't count the Giants out in the future."

Carson, who angered Parcells by walking out of training camp, became a leader in the latter part of the season. Giants players won't forget his pregame speech before the playoff game against the Rams in Anaheim.

OFFENSE

Other than turnovers, the Giants showed almost no statistical improvement from the 3-12-1 season. They finished thirteenth in total offense and twenty-second in rushing offense.

Still, they had enough confidence in their running backs to trade former number-one draft choice Butch Woolfolk to the Houston Oilers during the offseason.

If the Giants ever establish a running game, Simms's talents really may begin to shine. The club's leading rusher was Rob Carpenter, who had 795 yards, followed by Joe Morris with 510.

Believe it or not, Simms was the number-three rusher with 162 yards.

Two rookies—tackles William Roberts and Karl Nelson—were starters in the offensive line. As Roberts and Nelson develop, the Giants' running game should continue to improve. There is hope for the 5-foot 7-inch Morris, but the Giants need a durable runner with speed. Morris is quick, but he lacks the breakaway

Harry Carson

Mark Haynes

Bobby Johnson

speed to deliver the big strike. The Giants' longest run of the season (by Morris) was only 28 yards.

Bobby Johnson, a free-agent rookie wide receiver in 1984, led the club with 48 receptions and provided speed that the Giants desperately need. Johnson was a steal. Most clubs thought he was under contract to the Philadelphia Stars, but he had been released by the USFL club.

When teams ignored the Giants' tight ends, Simms went to Mowatt, who finished with 48 receptions for 698 yards.

"The passing game will work when you can keep your quarterback healthy," Parcells said. "We knew everything was eventually going to work out for Phil. Nobody around here had given up on him."

Simms had missed parts of three seasons with a surgically repaired knee, separated shoulder, and broken thumb. Passing for more than 4,000 yards was like running in a marathon for the first time and finishing in the top 10.

One of the more interesting signees by the Giants was wide receiver-kick returner Phil McConkey, a 27-year-old rookie who had not played football since the 1978 season with the Naval Academy. He had been a Naval helicopter pilot the previous five years.

"He levitates, or whatever those helicopter guys do," Giants public relations director Ed Croke said.

Trying to draw a comparison to flying helicopters and playing football, McConkey said, "Football can't ever be as dangerous as trying to land a chopper on a carrier in the Mediterranean during a storm."

Another free-agent receiver who made his mark was Byron Williams, who had been released by the Green Bay Packers. During the second week of the season, he scored a dashing, swerving 62-yard touchdown against the Dallas Cowboys. Williams finished with 24 receptions for 471 yards.

DEFENSE

Is there any question now that the Giants have the best linebackers in the NFL?

Adding to the misery of opposing running backs were rookies Carl Banks (first round) and Reasons

Three Years at a Glance

Averages NFL Rank	OFFENSE			DEFENSE		
	1984	1983	1982	1984	1983	1982
Points	**18.7**	**16.7**	**18.2**	**18.8**	**21.7**	**22.9**
Rank	19	25	17	8	16	22T
Yards	**330.8**	**330.3**	**303.2**	**324.6**	**312.1**	**298.2**
Rank	13	15	16	11	5	7
Rushing Yards	**103.8**	**112.1**	**93.6**	**113.6**	**108.3**	**124.2**
Rank	22	22	24	9	5	20
Passing Yards	**227.0**	**218.2**	**209.7**	**210.9**	**203.8**	**174.0**
Rank	5	8	8	16	16	6
Sacks	**3.4**	**3.1**	**1.9**	**3.0**	**2.8**	**3.4**
Rank	20T	19T	7	13	12	6T
Turnovers	**1.7**	**3.6**	**2.1**	**2.2**	**2.3**	**2.0**
Rank	2	28	8T	14T	17T	23T
Punt Returns	**6.7**	**6.9**	**8.5**	**9.6**	**6.0**	**8.3**
Rank	23	24	12	19	3	15
Kickoff Returns	**18.3**	**18.8**	**20.1**	**19.8**	**19.3**	**18.1**
Rank	25	21	16	11	14	6
Penalty Yards	**43.9**	**63.8**	**41.0**	**43.7**	**57.9**	**46.3**
Rank	6	26	6	26	8	20

	W-L Total	Home	Road	Playoffs
1982	4-5	2-3	2-2	None
1983	3-12-1	1-7	2-5-1	None
1984	9-7	6-2	3-5	1-1, Lost Divisional Playoff Game

(fourth round). Reasons and Banks joined a group that includes superstars Lawrence Taylor and Carson. This is not to ignore Andy Headen or Byron Hunt, who could start for several other NFL teams.

A roving linebacker on passing downs, Taylor finished the season with 11½ sacks, and was followed by defensive ends Casey Merrill with 9 and Leonard Marshall with 7½.

Taylor again led the team in tackles with 114 and his mere presence forces quarterbacks to continually look for him before they take the snap.

"I believe that Lawrence Taylor is the most intimidating player in the NFL," says St. Louis quarterback Neil Lomax. "I don't know of any other player who can stop you in so many ways. He is across the line of scrimmage faster than any player I've ever seen."

Even the absence of cornerback Mark Haynes late in the season did not deter the Giants. Haynes led the club in interceptions with seven, followed by Perry Williams with three and Terry Kinard with two.

Kinard has become one of the NFC's best safeties. He was third on the club's tackle charts with 86. Strong safety Bill Currier, despite his lack of size, is a good tackler, but he can be beaten by a swift tight end.

What the Giants need is an "impact" player in the defensive line. Marshall and Curtis McGriff are adequate as starting defensive ends and have a future with the club. But if the Giants had an all-pro caliber end to complement their linebackers, it would be difficult to top them.

Opposing teams averaged only 18.8 points per game, which ranked first in the NFC East and eighth in the NFL.

Now that defensive coaches have learned to deal with the NFL rules changes of 1978 with "attacking" defenses, the Giants may have the inside track to a division championship.

SPECIAL TEAMS

They called him Ali Haji-Shank, which didn't make Ali Haji-Sheikh too happy.

But one year after a superb rookie season, Haji-Sheikh made only 17 of 33 field-goal attempts and did

Terry Kinard   *Casey Merrill*   *Lawrence Taylor*

not connect on four attempts beyond 50 yards.

"The media started calling me Haji-Shank," Haji-Sheikh said. "I really don't think they knew what they were talking about. I don't know where they got that kind of nickname."

Maybe they were filled with high expectations from his rookie season when Haji-Sheikh was named all-pro and selected to the NFC Pro Bowl team. He made 83.3 percent of his field goals in 1983.

It is almost a sure bet that when the Giants special teams play well, the Giants win. A good example was against the Rams during the regular season when Los Angeles returned a punt for a touchdown and blocked two punts, one of which resulted in a safety. The Giants also fumbled a kickoff in that game and had a record three safeties scored against them.

But against the Rams in the playoffs, the Giants' special teams were almost spotless and the result was a 16-13 victory. Haji-Sheikh may have missed almost half of his field-goal attempts during the regular season, but he was 3 for 3 in the playoff victory.

Punter Dave Jennings, who has played in four Pro Bowls, also had an off-year, averaging 40.1 yards per kick. His net average was only 31.4 yards.

The Giants could use some work on kickoff and punt coverage. Two punts were returned for touchdowns, including one for 83 yards by Henry Ellard of the Rams, longest of the season in the NFC.

New York did not have a player among the NFL's top 10 in either kickoff or punt returns. But there is hope that McConkey will be the Giants' answer to Washington's Mike Nelms.

VETERAN ROSTER

No.	Name	Pos.	Ht.	Wt.	NFL Exp.	Birthdate	College	Games in 1984
67	Ard, Bill	G	6-3	270	5	3/12/59	Wake Forest	15
58	Banks, Carl	LB	6-4	235	2	8/29/62	Michigan State	16
73	Belcher, Kevin	G	6-3	276	3	2/23/61	Texas-El Paso	16
60	Benson, Brad	T	6-3	270	8	11/25/55	Penn State	16
64	Burt, Jim	NT	6-1	260	5	6/7/59	Miami	16
26	Carpenter, Rob	RB	6-1	226	9	4/20/55	Miami, Ohio	16
53	Carson, Harry	LB	6-2	240	10	11/26/53	South Carolina State	16
31	Cephous, Frank	RB	5-10	205	2	7/4/61	UCLA	16
29	Currier, Bill	S	6-0	196	9	1/5/55	South Carolina	9
24	Daniel, Kenny	CB	5-10	180	2	6/1/60	San Jose State	15
37	Flowers, Larry	S	6-1	195	5	4/19/58	Texas Tech	16
30	Galbreath, Tony	RB	6-0	228	10	1/29/54	Missouri	16
61	Godfrey, Chris	G	6-3	265	3	5/17/58	Michigan	10
62	Goode, Conrad	T	6-6	285	2	1/19/62	Missouri	8
83	Gray, Earnest	WR	6-3	191	7	3/2/57	Memphis State	12
6	Haji-Sheikh, Ali	K	6-0	170	3	1/11/61	Michigan	16
79	Hardison, Dee	DE	6-4	274	8	5/2/56	North Carolina	15
36	Haynes, Mark	CB	5-11	195	6	11/6/58	Colorado	15
54	Headen, Andy	LB	6-5	242	3	7/8/60	Clemson	11
48	Hill, Kenny	S	6-0	195	5	7/25/58	Yale	12
15	Hostetler, Jeff	QB	6-3	212	2	4/22/61	West Virginia	0
57	Hunt, Byron	LB	6-5	242	5	12/17/58	Southern Methodist	13
13	Jennings, Dave	P	6-4	200	12	6/8/52	St. Lawrence	16
88	Johnson, Bob	WR	5-11	171	2	12/14/61	Kansas	16
51	Jones, Robbie	LB	6-2	230	2	12/25/59	Alabama	16
69	Jordan, David	G	6-6	276	2	7/14/62	Auburn	14
43	Kinard, Terry	S	6-1	200	3	11/24/59	Clemson	15
72	King, Gordon	T	6-6	275	7	2/3/56	Stanford	0
86	Manuel, Lionel	WR	5-11	175	2	4/13/62	Pacific	16
70	Marshall, Leonard	DE	6-3	285	3	10/22/61	Louisiana State	16
75	Martin, George	DE	6-4	255	11	2/16/53	Oregon	16
80	McConkey, Phil	WR	5-10	170	2	2/24/57	Navy	13
45	McDaniel, LeCharls	CB	5-9	169	5	10/15/58	Cal Poly-SLO	0
76	McGriff, Curtis	DE	6-5	276	6	5/17/58	Alabama	16
52	McLaughlin, Joe	LB	6-1	235	7	7/1/57	Massachusetts	16
71	Merrill, Casey	DE	6-4	260	7	7/16/57	Cal-Davis	16
20	Morris, Joe	RB	5-7	195	4	9/15/60	Syracuse	16
84	Mowatt, Zeke	TE	6-3	240	3	3/5/61	Florida State	16
81	Mullady, Tom	TE	6-3	235	7	1/30/57	Rhodes College	16
63	Nelson, Karl	T	6-6	285	2	6/14/60	Iowa State	16
34	Patterson, Elvis	CB	5-11	188	2	10/21/60	Kansas	15
55	Reasons, Gary	LB	6-4	234	2	2/18/62	N.W. Louisiana State	16
66	Roberts, Bill	T	6-5	280	2	8/5/62	Ohio State	11
17	Rutledge, Jeff	QB	6-1	195	7	1/22/57	Alabama	16
78	Sally, Jerome	NT	6-3	270	4	2/24/59	Missouri	16
44	Shaw, Pete	S	5-10	183	9	8/25/54	Northwestern	16
11	Simms, Phil	QB	6-3	214	7	11/3/56	Morehead State	16
56	Taylor, Lawrence	LB	6-3	243	5	2/4/59	North Carolina	16
38	Tuggle, John	RB	6-1	210	2	1/31/61	California	0
59	Umphrey, Rich	C	6-3	270	4	12/13/58	Colorado	15
87	Williams, Byron	WR	6-2	183	3	10/31/60	Texas-Arlington	16
23	Williams, Perry	CB	6-2	203	2	5/12/61	North Carolina State	16

Coaching Staff

Bill Parcells, head coach; **Bill Belichick,** defensive coordinator; **Romeo Crennell,** special teams; **Ron Erhardt,** offensive coordinator; **Len Fontes,** defensive backfield; **Ray Handley,** running backs; **Fred Hoaglin,** offensive line; **Pat Hodgson,** receivers; **Lamar Leachman,** defensive line; **Johnny Parker,** strength and conditioning; **Mike Pope,** tight ends; **Mike Sweatman,** special teams assistant.

1985 Schedule

Preseason

Aug. 3	Houston at Canton	2:30
Aug. 10	at Denver	7:00
Aug. 17	GREEN BAY	8:00
Aug. 24	N.Y. JETS	8:00
Aug. 30	at Pittsburgh	7:30

Regular Season

Sept. 8	PHILADELPHIA	1:00
Sept. 15	at Green Bay	3:00
Sept. 22	ST. LOUIS	1:00
Sept. 29	at Philadelphia	1:00
Oct. 6	DALLAS	9:00
Oct. 13	at Cincinnati	1:00
Oct. 20	WASHINGTON	1:00
Oct. 27	at New Orleans	3:00
Nov. 3	TAMPA BAY	1:00
Nov. 10	L.A. RAMS	1:00
Nov. 18	at Washington (Mon.)	9:00
Nov. 24	at St. Louis	3:00
Dec. 1	CLEVELAND	1:00
Dec. 8	at Houston	3:00
Dec. 15	at Dallas	12:00
Dec. 21	PITTSBURGH (Sat.)	12:30

1984 Results

Sept. 2	PHILADELPHIA	28-27
Sept. 9	DALLAS	28-7
Sept. 16	at Washington	14-30
Sept. 23	TAMPA BAY	17-14
Sept. 30	at L.A. Rams	12-33
Oct. 8	SAN FRAN. (Mon.)	10-31
Oct. 14	at Atlanta	19-7
Oct. 21	at Philadelphia	10-24
Oct. 28	WASHINGTON	37-13
Nov. 4	at Dallas	19-7
Nov. 11	at Tampa Bay	17-20
Nov. 18	ST. LOUIS	16-10
Nov. 25	KANSAS CITY	28-27
Dec. 2	at N.Y. Jets	20-10
Dec. 9	at St. Louis	21-31
Dec. 15	NEW ORLEANS (Sat.)	3-10
Dec. 23	L.A. Rams	16-13
Dec. 29	San Francisco	10-21

1985 Draft Choices

1. George Adams—19, RB, Kentucky
2. Stacy Robinson—46, WR, North Dakota State
3. Tyrone Davis—58, DB, Clemson, from Houston
3. Brian Johnston—73, C, North Carolina
4. Mark Bavaro—100, TE, Notre Dame
5. Tracy Henderson—132, WR, Iowa State
6. Jack Oliver—159, G, Memphis State
6. Mark Pembrook—165, DB, Cal State-Fullerton, from Seattle
7. Choice to L.A. Raiders
8. Lee Rouson—213, RB, Colorado
9. Frank Wright—240, NT, South Carolina
10. Gregg Dubroc—272, LB, Louisiana State
11. Allen Young—299, DB, Virginia Tech
12. Herb Welch—326, DB, UCLA

PHILADELPHIA EAGLES

Philadelphia played the toughest NFL schedule in 1984, meeting seven playoff-bound teams.

But coach Marion Campbell said his team made a dramatic improvement from the 1983 season despite a record that showed just six victories.

"The difference between the Eagles now and two years ago is like night and day," he said. "A lot of positive things were evident last season that we can build on, not the least of which was character. This team has shown it can battle back from adversity."

Philadelphia played in Super Bowl XV following the 1980 season, but three consecutive losing seasons have left the Eagles with a long way to climb. They were 6-9-1 in 1984, which was slightly better than the 5-11 mark of the previous season.

Philadelphia opened 1984 with a 1-4 record, but finished 5-5-1. A blocked extra point cost the Eagles the Miami game when the Dolphins still were undefeated. The Eagles also lost to St. Louis on a 44-yard field goal with one second to play.

For the first time in their history, the Eagles had three receivers with more than 60 receptions—tight end John Spagnola (65), Pro Bowl receiver Mike Quick (61), and running back Wilbert Montgomery (60).

But Montgomery is no longer the all-pro runner who led the Eagles to Super Bowl XV. The Eagles' offense was too inconsistent in 1984. Quarterback Ron Jaworski again took a beating (34 sacks of a club total of 60) and finished with a 73.5 passer rating and a broken leg in the Cardinals game.

Between the 1983 and 1984 seasons, the Eagles lost 15 players through cuts, trades, and retirements;

Linebacker Jerry Robinson keys the Eagles defense again.

Marion Campbell

Campbell blames last year's losing season on the heavy turnover. Campbell even released all-time leading receiver Harold Carmichael after the 1983 season.

"We aren't going to have that kind of turnover again," Campbell said. "Of course, we're going to be reviewing personnel and preparing for the draft. But I believe the nucleus of our football team is right here."

Wide receiver Kenny Jackson, the club's number-one draft choice from Penn State, missed half of the season with a knee injury. Campbell looks forward to his return.

The year 1984 will be remembered as the year when the Eagles almost moved to Phoenix. Owner Leonard Tose was close to finalizing a partial sale of his team and moving it west when the NFL intervened. Commissioner Pete Rozelle proposed a plan to refinance the team and Mayor W. Wilson Goode of Philadelphia helped so that Tose opted to have the team remain in Philadelphia.

Last spring, Tose sold the team to Miami automobile dealer Norman Braman, a former Philadelphian. Now, after three years of changes in Philadelphia, it is time for the team to settle down and go for that winning season.

OFFENSE

When Quick and Jackson are healthy, the Eagles might have the best receiving tandem in the NFL. Although Quick has compiled two consecutive 1,000-yard seasons, and is the first Eagles player since Tommy McDonald to do so, many coaches believe Jackson is the better all-round receiver.

Jackson was the fourth selection of the 1984 draft and showed much promise with his 26 catches for 398 yards, a 15.3 average for the 11 games he played.

"I am looking forward to seeing how people defense our passing game this year," Campbell said. "People know about Mike Quick. He is a two-time Pro Bowl selection. But Kenny is still a mystery because of his injuries.

Of the 28 NFL teams, the Eagles were twenty-eighth in rushing last season. That is a sad statistic when it is recalled that Montgomery rushed for 1,220 yards in 1978, 1,512 in 1979, and 1,402 in 1981. He missed four games in 1980 because of injury and still ran for 778 yards.

He had only 789 rushing yards last season and one 100-yard game. Even so, that was good news for the Eagles because Montgomery had missed 11 games in 1983 with a knee injury and the fact that he got through 1984 without further damage to the knee gives hope for the future.

Campbell had hoped that running back Michael Haddix, the eighth player selected overall in the 1983 draft, would be the solution to his problems. But Haddix has been too tentative as a runner and has been bothered by fumbles.

The Eagles are now tinkering with the idea of shifting to the one-back offense and using Montgomery more as a receiver and less as a runner.

"Because we couldn't run the ball, we ended up passing too much," Campbell said. "That's why we had so many sacks. History still tells us that it's a balanced attack that gets the job done. We can't rely on just one thing and hope to get our offense in gear."

If Montgomery can somehow return to form, or if Haddix begins to fulfill expectations, the Eagles' running game may have some hope.

The Eagles threw the ball 606 times in 1984, 120 more than the previous year.

When teams chose to double-team Quick, Jaworski and then Joe Pisarcik took advantage of Spagnola, who led NFC tight ends with 65 catches. Spagnola was

Greg Brown

Wes Hopkins

Kenny Jackson

ninth among all receivers in the NFC.

The offensive line improved in 1984 as Leonard Mitchell found a place at right tackle. Mitchell was drafted in the first round three years ago as a defensive tackle, but was switched to offense in 1984. From left to right, the Eagles' starters in the line were tackle Dean Miraldi, guard Steve Kenney, center Mark Dennard, guard Ron Baker, and Mitchell.

Jerry Sisemore, the only starting lineman from Super Bowl XV, retired at the end of last season after 12 years. He had made the Pro Bowl twice—1980 and '82.

"We can't have a lot of injuries and expect to continue to survive," Jaworski said. "We need some good offseason conditioning work and we need a new commitment to the offense. It's time that we stop depending so much on our defense and start getting some points on the board."

DEFENSE

"Defensively, we got our motor running again," Campbell said. "We had more takeaways. Our defense was just a lot more daring. We took our shots."

A year after finishing last in the league in interceptions with eight, the Eagles picked off 20 in 1984. Most of the credit for aggressive defense was given to safeties Wes Hopkins and Ray Ellis, who had a combined 12 interceptions.

Linebacker Jerry Robinson calls Ellis and Hopkins "Frank and Jesse James, the super safeties."

"Those guys are gangsters," Robinson said. "Outlaws. They fly to the ball."

Cornerback Elbert Foules had four interceptions, Herman Edwards had two.

"Our secondary kind of got off to a rough start, but we were rolling by about the sixth week of the season," Campbell said. "Hopkins and Ellis really became a pair who led by example in the secondary. I feel that we have the best safety tandem in football. They are heavy hitters. Wes is one of the best free safeties in football. He is an intimidator, to say the least, and he is a clean hitter all of the way. He's a sure, sharp tackler who just loves to hit people. When Wes hits you, you know that you've been popped."

Three Years at a Glance

Averages NFL Rank	OFFENSE			DEFENSE		
	1984	1983	1982	1984	1983	1982
Points Rank	**17.4** 23	**14.6** 28	**21.2** 11	**20.0** 14	**20.1** 8	**21.7** 18
Yards Rank	**293.6** 26	**283.4** 27	**298.3** 18	**327.4** 12	**340.4** 18	**326.4** 20
Rushing Yards Rank	**83.6** 28	**88.6** 26	**92.1** 25	**136.8** 23	**165.9** 27	**114.6** 15
Passing Yards Rank	**210.0** 11	**194.8** 16	**206.2** 11	**190.6** 6	**174.5** 2	**211.9** 20
Sacks Rank	**3.8** 23T	**3.6** 27	**3.4** 22	**3.8** 4	**2.3** 21	**3.3** 9T
Turnovers Rank	**2.1** 9	**2.3** 8T	**2.6** 14T	**1.9** 20T	**1.4** 28	**3.0** 3T
Punt Returns Rank	**6.3** 26	**5.8** 27	**4.9** 27	**8.4** 13	**9.0** 17	**10.2** 23
Kickoff Returns Rank	**19.6** 14	**18.8** 19	**19.7** 21	**18.8** 7	**17.9** 3	**22.7** 25
Penalty Yards Rank	**39.5** 2	**39.8** 2	**28.1** 2	**56.5** 10	**47.2** 22	**37.9** 26

	W-L Total	Home	Road	Playoffs
1982	3-6	1-4	2-2	None
1983	5-11	1-7	4-4	None
1984	6-9-1	5-3	1-6-1	None

Of the 60 sacks during the regular season, 48½ were delivered by the down linemen. That is especially impressive when you consider that Philadelphia uses a 3-4 alignment.

Kenny Clarke was the league's number-two nose tackle with 10½ sacks and he was removed from the lineup on most passing downs. Defensive end Greg Brown had 15½ sacks. A rejuvenated Dennis Harrison added 12.

Robinson was unhappy about having to play inside linebacker, but he had another solid season. Campbell is considering moving Robinson back to outside linebacker, where he has been named to the NFC Pro Bowl squad three times. In 1984, Robinson led the team with 92 tackles.

Cornerback Herman Edwards should reach a milestone during the 1985 season. He is now second on the club's all-time interception list with 30 and trails only Bill Bradley, who had 34 from 1969 through 1976.

Along with ranking third on the club in tackles with 128, Hopkins led the team in forced fumbles (four) and fumbles recovered (three) in 1984. It is little wonder that he is considered the hardest hitting free safety in the NFL.

But the hit that everyone in Philadelphia will remember from last season was delivered by strong safety Ray Ellis, who knocked Cowboys running back Tony Dorsett unconscious.

Dorsett was swinging around right end and trying to avoid Robinson when Ellis, who was running full speed, met him head-on. Dorsett's head snapped back and he lay motionless for almost two minutes.

To his credit, Dorsett missed only about 10 minutes of the game and was able to return in the second half.

"It was the hardest hit I've ever had in my life," Dorsett said. "And God knows that I've had some hard ones."

Campbell built the Eagles' defense into one of the NFL's leading units while Dick Vermeil was the head coach (1976-1982). After becoming the head coach, however, Campbell admitted that he was not spending enough time with the defense.

Leonard Mitchell   Paul McFadden   Mike Quick

His new commitment to the defensive unit became especially obvious in 1984.

SPECIAL TEAMS

No doubt, Campbell made the right decision in trading placekicker Tony Franklin to New England and rolling the dice with rookie kicker Paul McFadden. Playing for a team that ranked twenty-second in scoring, McFadden was the NFL's fifth-leading scorer in 1984.

He made 30 of 37 attempts and became the first Eagles kicker ever to make two field goals of more than 50 yards in one game (51 and 52 against Detroit). His 30 field goals were the most by an NFL kicker in 1984 and tied him for third on the all-time rookie list.

"I don't know of a kicker who gave his team any more than Paul gave us in 1984," Campbell said. "He did it from everywhere, even from outside 50 yards. And he did it consistently."

Free-agent punter Michael Horan finished second in the NFC with a 35.6 net yardage and his 42.2 gross average was fourth in the conference. The Eagles made good use of Horan, a left-footer. He punted 92 times, the most in the NFC.

Andre Waters's 89-yard kickoff return for a touchdown against Washington was the first scoring return by an Eagles player in six years. But there was some bad news when special teams captain Bill Cowher retired after the season to become special teams coach of the Cleveland Browns.

As the Philadelphia defense became more aggressive, so did the coverage teams. The Eagles did not allow a touchdown via a kickoff or punt return and ranked sixth in the NFC in yardage allowed.

VETERAN ROSTER

No.	Name	Pos.	Ht.	Wt.	NFL Exp.	Birthdate	College	Games in 1984
96	Armstrong, Harvey	NT	6-2	265	4	12/29/59	Southern Methodist	16
63	Baker, Ron	G	6-4	270	8	11/19/54	Oklahoma State	16
98	Brown, Greg	DE	6-5	260	5	1/5/57	Kansas State	16
11	Christensen, Jeff	QB	6-3	200	3	1/8/60	Eastern Illinois	0
71	Clarke, Ken	NT	6-2	255	8	8/28/56	Syracuse	16
21	Cooper, Evan	CB-KR	5-11	180	2	6/28/62	Michigan	16
94	Darby, Byron	DE	6-4	260	3	6/4/60	Southern California	16
65	Dennard, Mark	C	6-1	252	7	11/2/55	Texas A&M	16
46	Edwards, Herman	CB	6-0	190	9	4/27/54	San Diego State	16
24	Ellis, Ray	S	6-1	192	5	4/27/59	Ohio State	16
39	Everett, Major	FB	5-11	215	3	1/4/60	Mississippi College	16
67	Feehery, Gerry	C	6-2	268	3	3/9/60	Syracuse	6
29	Foules, Elbert	CB	5-11	185	3	7/4/61	Alcorn State	16
86	Garrity, Gregg	WR	5-10	171	3	11/24/60	Penn State	10
58	Griggs, Anthony	LB	6-3	230	4	2/12/60	Ohio State	16
26	Haddix, Michael	FB	6-2	225	3	12/27/61	Mississippi State	14
47	Hardy, Andre	RB	6-1	233	2	11/28/61	St. Mary's, Calif.	6
68	Harrison, Dennis	DE	6-8	280	8	7/31/56	Vanderbilt	16
80	Hayes, Joe	WR-KR	5-9	185	2	9/15/60	Central State, Okla.	12
85	Hoover, Melvin	WR	6-0	185	4	8/21/59	Arizona State	12
48	Hopkins, Wes	S	6-1	210	3	9/26/61	Southern Methodist	16
2	Horan, Michael	P	5-11	190	2	2/1/59	Long Beach State	16
81	Jackson, Kenny	WR	6-0	180	2	2/15/62	Penn State	11
7	Jaworski, Ron	QB	6-2	196	12	3/23/51	Youngstown State	13
84	Kab, Vyto	TE	6-5	240	4	12/23/59	Penn State	16
73	Kenney, Steve	G	6-4	270	6	12/26/55	Clemson	11
52	Kraynak, Rich	LB	6-1	225	3	1/20/60	Pittsburgh	14
5	May, Dean	QB	6-5	220	2	5/26/62	Louisville	2
8	McFadden, Paul	K	5-11	155	2	9/24/61	Youngstown State	16
64	Miraldi, Dean	T	6-5	285	3	4/8/58	Utah	16
74	Mitchell, Leonard	T	6-7	285	5	10/12/58	Houston	16
31	Montgomery, Wilbert	RB	5-10	195	9	9/16/54	Abilene Christian	16
34	Oliver, Hubie	FB	5-10	212	4	11/12/57	Arizona	16
9	Pisarcik, Joe	QB	6-4	217	9	7/2/52	New Mexico State	7
82	Quick, Mike	WR	6-2	190	4	5/14/59	North Carolina State	14
55	Reichenbach, Mike	LB	6-2	235	2	9/14/61	East Stroudsburg	12
56	Robinson, Jerry	LB	6-2	225	7	12/18/56	UCLA	15
79	Russell, Rusty	T	6-5	295	2	8/16/63	South Carolina	1
87	Sampleton, Lawrence	TE	6-5	233	4	9/25/59	Texas	16
53	Schulz, Jody	LB	6-4	235	3	8/17/60	East Carolina	15
88	Spagnola, John	TE	6-4	240	6	8/1/57	Yale	16
93	Strauthers, Thomas	DE	6-4	265	3	4/6/61	Jackson State	16
20	Waters, Andre	CB-KR	5-11	182	2	3/10/62	Cheyney State	16
51	Wilkes, Reggie	LB	6-4	235	8	5/27/56	Georgia Tech	14
59	Williams, Joel	LB	6-1	225	7	12/13/56	Wisconsin-La Crosse	16
32	Williams, Michael	RB	6-2	225	3	7/16/61	Mississippi College	16
22	Wilson, Brenard	S-CB	6-0	180	7	8/15/55	Vanderbilt	16
83	Woodruff, Tony	WR	6-0	185	4	11/12/58	Fresno State	16
43	Young, Roynell	CB	6-1	181	6	12/1/57	Alcorn State	7

Coaching Staff

Marion Campbell, head coach; **Tommy Brasher,** defensive line; **Fred Bruney,** assistant head coach, defensive backfield; **Chuck Clausen,** linebackers; **Tom Coughlin,** wide receivers; **Frank Gansz,** tight ends, special teams; **Ken Iman,** offensive line; **Milt Jackson,** wide receivers, running backs; **Ted Marchibroda,** offensive coordinator.

1985 Schedule

Preseason

Aug. 10	at N.Y. Jets	8:30
Aug. 17	at Cleveland	7:30
Aug. 24	L.A. Rams	TBA
Aug. 29	DETROIT	TBA

Regular Season

Sept. 8	at N.Y. Giants	1:00
Sept. 15	L.A. RAMS	1:00
Sept. 22	at Washington	1:00
Sept. 29	N.Y. GIANTS	1:00
Oct. 6	at New Orleans	12:00
Oct. 13	at St. Louis	12:00
Oct. 20	DALLAS	1:00
Oct. 27	BUFFALO	1:00
Nov. 3	at San Francisco	1:00
Nov. 10	ATLANTA	1:00
Nov. 17	ST. LOUIS	1:00
Nov. 24	at Dallas	3:00
Dec. 1	MINNESOTA	1:00
Dec. 8	WASHINGTON	1:00
Dec. 15	at San Diego	1:00
Dec. 22	at Minnesota	12:00

1984 Results

Sept. 2	at N.Y. Giants	27-28
Sept. 9	MINNESOTA	19-17
Sept. 16	at Dallas	17-23
Sept. 23	SAN FRANCISCO	9-21
Sept. 30	at Washington	0-20
Oct. 7	at Buffalo	27-17
Oct. 14	INDIANAPOLIS	16-7
Oct. 21	N.Y. GIANTS	24-10
Oct. 28	ST. LOUIS	14-34
Nov. 4	at Detroit*	23-23
Nov. 11	at Miami	23-24
Nov. 18	WASHINGTON	16-10
Nov. 25	at St. Louis	16-17
Dec. 2	DALLAS	10-26
Dec. 9	NEW ENGLAND	27-17
Dec. 16	at Atlanta	10-26

1985 Draft Choices

1. Kevin Allen—9, T, Indiana
2. Randall Cunningham—37, QB, Nevada-Las Vegas
3. Choice to Miami
4. Greg Naron—93, G, North Carolina
5. Dwayne Jiles—121, LB, Texas Tech
6. Choice to Kansas City
6. Ken Reeves—156, T, Texas A&M, from New England

7. Choice to Washington
8. Tom Polley—205, LB, Nevada-Las Vegas
9. Dave Toub—231, C, Texas-El Paso, from Cleveland
9. Joe Drake—233, DT, Arizona
10. Mark Kelso—261, DB, William & Mary
11. Herman Hunter—289, RB, Tennessee State
12. Todd Russell—317, DB, Boston College

ST. LOUIS CARDINALS

After a near-perfect second half against the Washington Redskins, quarterback Neil Lomax had moved the Cardinals to within a 50-yard field goal of winning the NFC East. But placekicker Neil O'Donoghue was forced to rush his kick from that long distance, and the Cardinals, instead of winning the divisional title, were eliminated from the playoffs with that 29-27 loss. (St. Louis and New York both finished with 9-7 records, but the Giants went to the playoffs under the NFL's tie-breaking procedures.)

Still, St. Louis accomplished some things in 1984 that had not been witnessed in several years—such as defeating Dallas at Texas Stadium, defeating the Washington Redskins once during the regular season, sending a quarterback—Lomax—*and* a wide receiver—Roy Green—to the Pro Bowl, along with linebacker E.J. Junior.

No wonder Dallas Cowboys coach Tom Landry already has made St. Louis the favorite to win the NFC East in 1985.

"They are the team on the come right now, on the roll," Landry said, "and they're hungry because they haven't been on top for a long, long time."

Finishing the season with a 9-7 record in 1984 was a victory in itself. The Cardinals were involved in one of the most exciting games of the season, the loss to Washington.

"It was the first time in a long time that I saw a St. Louis team playing with any guts," said former tight end Jackie Smith, who spent 14 years with the Cardinals. "They had that old fire in their eyes and it kind of reminded you of when [Hall of Fame safety] Larry Wil-

Neil Lomax took charge of Cardinals with 4,619 yards passing.

Jim Hanifan

son was playing. They had a mission."

More than a mission, the Cardinals had the number-two-ranked passer in the NFC. Lomax finished the season with a 92.5 rating. He tied San Francisco's Joe Montana for the most touchdown passes—28—by an NFC quarterback.

Lomax was the biggest story in Cardinals football in nearly a decade. He was transformed from a quarterback with "potential" to one with results. Not only did Lomax demonstrate his accuracy as a passer, he demonstrated his guile.

In planning for the 1985 season, Cardinals fans need only remember the second half of the finale against the Redskins. Lomax completed 25 of 28 passes (one of the incompletions was thrown out of bounds to stop the clock). He finished with a club record 468 passing yards.

"We found out a lot about ourselves that day," said St. Louis center Randy Clark. "We learned that we've got the firepower to win just about any game we're thrown into. Now I think that Neil Lomax is ready to take his place among the top five quarterbacks in the league."

Said guard Joe Bostic, "I'm awfully proud of this team and it's just a shame that the season had to end the way it did for us. We've got a lot to be proud of. I've started looking at our roster. Would you believe that O.J. Anderson and myself are the second-oldest players on the team? We've been here six years. Pat Tilley has been here nine. We've got a lot to look forward to."

Are the Cardinals too young to become a championship team?

"We're young enough to be hungry, but old enough to be mature and to have a sense of direction," coach Jim Hanifan said.

OFFENSE

As recently as 1983, St. Louis fans were booing running back Ottis Anderson for running out of bounds instead of struggling for extra yardage.

"It was a case where I couldn't really please everybody," Anderson says. "I got beat up—battered. I was going to the doctor every Monday morning. It got to the point where I had to take it easy, sit in the whirlpool for awhile."

They didn't boo often in 1984, even though Anderson had to share much of the rushing yardage with Stump Mitchell. Anderson finished with 1,174 yards and six touchdowns.

When the passing game is working, the running game always seems to follow. All parts of the Cardinals' offense clicked in the latter part of the season as they made their bid for the playoffs that came up just short.

Roy Green caught 12 of Lomax's 28 touchdown passes and finished with 78 receptions and a 19.9-yard average.

"Roy Green is a bomb that can go off at any time," Lomax said. "We know that we can score from anyplace on the field with Green in the lineup. Just throw him the ball."

Dallas certainly learned about those long-distance touchdowns. Green caught two touchdown passes of more than 50 yards in a 31-20 defeat of the Cowboys at Texas Stadium.

Typical of any balanced passing attack, the Cardinals have the wily Pat Tilley—to complement Green. Tilley is one of the best route-runners in the league. He finished the season with 52 receptions—26 fewer than Green—but still proved something about himself and the type of receiver he is.

Ottis Anderson

Roy Green

Curtis Greer

"I feel like the game overlooks guys like me," Tilley says. "Some coaches believe that the whole game is speed. That is why guys like me are becoming extinct. It's kind of sad, really. The game is becoming too one-dimensional."

It may take a year or two to develop, but the Cardinals soon may have the league's best offensive line. The Cardinals' starting line includes guard Terry Stieve, center Randy Clark, guard Bostic (brother of Redskins' center Jeff) and tackle Tootie Robbins.

Luis Sharpe, a first-round draft choice from UCLA in 1982, was on his way to becoming one of the NFL's best young linemen, and his unexpected departure to the USFL in April leaves a major-sized void in what was being hailed as the NFL's finest young offensive line. Four-year veteran Art Plunkett will move into Sharpe's spot.

Stieve said the Cardinals line has developed a new togetherness.

"You develop a closeness when you see the guy next to you working his butt off," Stieve said. "You don't get close by going out and having a few beers together. You get close with hard work and sacrifice. When everyone is working hard, respect develops among all of the players."

Hanifan's decision to release 18-year quarterback Jim Hart (who was claimed and signed by Washington) after the 1983 season provided Lomax with needed confidence.

"It told me that I am the quarterback of the Cardinals' future," Lomax said. "I no longer was looking over either shoulder to see where he was coming from."

Reviewing Lomax's season in 1984, Hanifan said, "Obviously, he had an oustanding year because he became one of the few men in the NFL to throw for more than four thousand yards [4,619] in a season and was selected to the Pro Bowl for the first time, which was a great honor for a young man in only his fourth year. He is the type of quarterback that the team can rally around. And believe me, this team really needed that. He has that type of charisma and it bodes well for the future. We would like to see him a little more consistent.

Three Years at a Glance

Averages NFL Rank	OFFENSE			DEFENSE		
	1984	1983	1982	1984	1983	1982
Points Rank	**26.4** 4	**23.4** 9	**15.0** 25	**21.6** 17	**26.8** 25	**18.9** 11
Yards Rank	**396.6** 3	**321.6** 17	**282.4** 23	**318.4** 8	**312.8** 6	**316.4** 14T
Rushing Yards Rank	**130.5** 9	**142.3** 7	**134.3** 7	**120.2** 14	**114.9** 8	**110.6** 12
Passing Yards Rank	**266.1** 3	**179.3** 24	**148.1** 26	**198.2** 9	**197.9** 14	**205.9** 17
Sacks Rank	**3.1** 16T	**3.7** 28	**3.6** 23T	**3.4** 7T	**3.7** 1	**2.6** 14
Turnovers Rank	**2.3** 13T	**3.0** 24	**1.8** 2T	**2.1** 19	**3.0** 4T	**1.7** 26
Punt Returns Rank	**8.5** 13	**7.9** 18	**6.0** 20	**8.9** 15	**6.5** 5	**8.0** 12
Kickoff Returns Rank	**21.1** 5	**20.3** 10	**20.1** 17	**18.2** 5	**19.7** 17	**20.7** 16
Penalty Yards Rank	**56.5** 18	**48.1** 7	**58.7** 21	**36.1** 28	**51.2** 14	**46.7** 18

	W-L Total	Home	Road	Playoffs
1982	5-4	1-3	4-1	0-1, Lost First Round Game
1983	8-7-1	4-3-1	4-4	None
1984	9-7	5-3	4-4	None

But I think the consistency will come with age."
DEFENSE
"A lot of people want to give our offense the full credit for a very good season," Hanifan said. "But there can be no overlooking our defense from last season. We showed aggressivness that we had been lacking. I think that with a few adjustments we might someday have one of the best defenses in the NFL."

Floyd Peters, who developed the "Silver Rush" in Detroit before taking charge of the Cardinals' defense in 1982, continues to do wonders with the defensive line. The defense finished the season in fine form by limiting the Washington Redskins to 96 rushing yards in that final game.

Statistically, the Cardinals had the number-two defense in the NFC East behind the Cowboys. The Cardinals were eighth in the National Football League in overall defense, fourteenth against the run, and ninth against the pass.

Teams had trouble throwing against St. Louis in the second half of the season. The Cardinals held opponents to a third-down efficiency of 27 percent in the final seven games of the season.

Still, injuries in the defensive secondary kept that group in a constant state of flux. Cornerback Lionel Washington led the team with five interceptions, but the key man in the secondary is Benny Perrin. All the deep defenders are known for their ability to deliver a blow. Three of the six leading tacklers on the team, Perrin, Leonard Smith and Wayne Smith, play in the deep secondary.

Now, if the Cardinals can learn to defense the pass as well as they use the weapon on offense, they might have something to look forward to when the 1985 playoffs roll around.

Linebacker E.J. Junior finally was recognized as one of the best at his position. Junior is one of the quickest and most agile linebackers in the NFL, and some have compared him to New York's Lawrence Taylor. He finished the season with a career-best 128 tackles and 9½ sacks and was selected to the NFC Pro Bowl team. Charles Baker adds strength at linebacker.

E.J. Junior

Tootie Robbins

Pat Tilley

Defensive end Curtis Greer, who has averaged almost one sack per game the last two seasons, again was the most consistent member of the defensive line. He had 14 quarterback sacks in a year in which the Cardinals finished with 55. Greer also played in the Pro Bowl. Al (Bubba) Baker, the other defensive end, finished the season with 10 sacks. David Galloway is a strong prospect at defensive end as he enters his fourth season.

SPECIAL TEAMS

Hanifan continues to be patient with kicker Neil O'Donoghue, even though he made only 23 of 35 field-goal attempts. O'Donoghue did make a crucial 27-yarder to beat the Philadelphia Eagles 17-16. But the 6-foot 6-inch O'Donoghue kicks with a low trajectory, and five of his attempts were blocked.

No one can complain about former Pro Bowl punter Carl Birdsong, although his average dropped to 38.1 yards per attempt in 1984.

Linebackers Dave Ahrens and Falaniko Noga, a rookie from American Samoa by way of Hawaii, led the kick-coverage teams with five solo tackles each. The Cardinals allowed only 18.6 yards per kickoff return despite a 96-yard runback for a touchdown by Phil Smith of Indianapolis in the third game of the season.

"We need to do some work with our special teams," Hanifan said. "There is no question about that. That doesn't mean that we're going to do a complete overhaul or anything like that. But we need to do some fine-tuning. Special teams could be the difference between us winning and losing the division championship next season."

VETERAN ROSTER

No.	Name	Pos.	Ht.	Wt.	NFL Exp.	Birthdate	College	Games in 1984
58	Ahrens, Dave	LB	6-3	230	5	12/5/58	Wisconsin	16
51	Allerman, Kurt	LB	6-2	232	9	8/30/50	Penn State	16
32	Anderson, Ottis	RB	6-2	220	7	1/19/57	Miami	15
60	Baker, Al	DE	6-6	270	8	12/9/56	Colorado State	15
52	Baker, Charlie	LB	6-2	234	6	9/26/57	New Mexico	9
18	Birdsong, Carl	P	6-0	192	5	1/1/59	S.W. Oklahoma State	16
71	Bostic, Joe	G	6-3	268	7	4/20/57	Clemson	16
64	Clark, Randy	C	6-3	254	6	7/27/57	Northern Illinois	16
62	Dardar, Ramsey	DT	6-2	264	2	10/3/59	Louisiana State	16
66	Dawson, Doug	G	6-3	267	2	12/27/61	Texas	15
73	Duda, Mark	DT	6-3	263	3	2/4/61	Maryland	8
86	Duncan, Clyde	WR	6-1	192	2	2/5/61	Tennessee	8
31	Ferrell, Earl	RB	6-0	215	4	3/27/58	East Tennessee State	16
65	Galloway, David	DT	6-3	277	4	2/16/59	Florida	14
84	Goode, John	TE	6-2	222	2	11/5/62	Youngstown State	16
81	Green, Roy	WR	6-0	195	7	6/30/57	Henderson State	16
75	Greer, Curtis	DE	6-4	258	6	11/10/57	Michigan	16
35	Griffin, Jeff	CB	6-0	185	5	7/19/58	Utah	8
78	Grooms, Elois	DT	6-4	250	11	5/20/53	Tennessee Tech	11
39	Harrell, Willard	RB	5-9	190	11	9/16/52	Pacific	16
36	Harrington, Perry	RB	5-11	210	6	3/13/58	Jackson State	6
50	Harris, Bob	LB	6-2	215	3	11/11/60	Auburn	16
46	Heflin, Victor	CB	6-0	184	3	7/7/60	Delaware State	16
59	Howard, Thomas	LB	6-2	220	9	8/18/54	Texas Tech	15
54	Junior, E. J.	LB	6-3	235	5	12/8/59	Alabama	16
89	LaFleur, Greg	TE	6-4	236	5	9/16/58	Louisiana State	16
15	Lomax, Neil	QB	6-3	214	5	2/17/59	Portland State	16
40	Love, Randy	RB	6-1	205	7	9/30/56	Houston	16
82	Mack, Cedric	WR-CB	6-0	190	3	9/14/60	Baylor	12
12	Mackey, Kyle	QB	6-2	220	2	3/2/62	East Texas State	0
80	Marsh, Doug	TE	6-3	238	6	6/18/58	Michigan	16
76	Mays, Stafford	DE	6-2	250	6	3/13/58	Washington	16
87	McGill, Eddie	TE	6-6	225	3	7/5/60	Western Carolina	0
14	McIvor, Rick	QB	6-4	210	2	9/26/60	Texas	4
30	Mitchell, Stump	RB	5-9	188	5	3/15/59	Citadel	16
38	Nelson, Lee	S	5-10	185	10	1/30/54	Florida State	16
57	Noga, Niko	LB	6-1	230	2	3/2/62	Hawaii	16
11	O'Donoghue, Neil	K	6-6	210	9	6/18/53	Auburn	16
23	Perrin, Benny	S	6-2	178	4	10/20/59	Alabama	16
85	Pittman, Danny	WR	6-2	205	6	4/3/58	Wyoming	10
70	Plunkett, Art	T	6-7	270	5	3/8/59	Nevada-Las Vegas	16
72	Ralph, Dan	DT	6-4	260	2	3/9/61	Oregon	6
63	Robbins, Tootie	T	6-4	278	4	6/2/58	East Carolina	16
56	Scott, Carlos	C	6-4	300	3	7/2/60	Texas-El Paso	16
45	Smith, Leonard	S	5-11	190	3	9/2/60	McNeese State	12
44	Smith, Wayne	CB	6-0	175	6	5/9/57	Purdue	16
68	Stieve, Terry	G	6-2	265	9	3/10/54	Wisconsin	14
83	Tilley, Pat	WR	5-10	178	10	2/15/53	Louisiana Tech	16
33	Walker, Quentin	WR	6-1	200	2	8/27/61	Virginia	3
48	Washington, Lionel	CB	6-0	184	3	10/21/60	Tulane	15
42	Whitaker, Bill	S	6-0	182	5	11/18/59	Missouri	7

Coaching Staff

Jim Hanifan, head coach; **Chuck Banker,** offensive backs; **Rudy Feldman,** linebackers; **Pete Hoerner,** strength and flexibility; **Dick Jamieson,** offensive coordinator; **Leon McLaughlin,** special assistant; **Ernie McMillan,** offensive line; **Floyd Peters,** assistant head coach-defense; **Jerry Smith,** defensive line; **Emmitt Thomas,** receivers; **Lance Van Zandt,** defensive backfield.

1985 Schedule

Preseason

Aug. 9	CHICAGO	7:30
Aug. 15	at L.A. Rams	7:00
Aug. 23	PITTSBURGH	7:30
Aug. 31	at Kansas City	7:30

Regular Season

Sept. 8	at Cleveland	1:00
Sept. 15	CINCINNATI	12:00
Sept. 22	at N.Y. Giants	1:00
Sept. 29	GREEN BAY	12:00
Oct. 7	at Washington (Mon.)	9:00
Oct. 13	PHILADELPHIA	12:00
Oct. 20	at Pittsburgh	1:00
Oct. 27	HOUSTON	12:00
Nov. 4	DALLAS (Mon.)	8:00
Nov. 10	at Tampa Bay	1:00
Nov. 17	at Philadelphia	1:00
Nov. 24	N.Y. GIANTS	3:00
Nov. 28	at Dallas (Thanks.)	3:00
Dec. 8	NEW ORLEANS	12:00
Dec. 15	at L.A. Rams	1:00
Dec. 21	WASHINGTON (Sat.)	3:00

1984 Results

Sept. 2	at Green Bay	23-24
Sept. 9	BUFFALO	37-7
Sept. 16	at Indianapolis	34-33
Sept. 23	at New Orleans	24-34
Sept. 30	MIAMI	28-36
Oct. 7	at Dallas	31-20
Oct. 14	CHICAGO	38-21
Oct. 21	WASHINGTON	26-24
Oct. 28	at Philadelphia	34-14
Nov. 4	L.A. RAMS	13-16
Nov. 11	DALLAS	17-24
Nov. 18	at N.Y. Giants	10-16
Nov. 25	PHILADELPHIA	17-16
Dec. 2	at New England	33-10
Dec. 9	N.Y. GIANTS	31-21
Dec. 16	at Washington	27-29

1985 Draft Choices

1. Freddie Nunn—18, LB, Mississippi
2. Choice to Atlanta
2. Scott Bergold—51, T, Wisconsin, from Washington through Atlanta
3. Lance Smith—72, T, Louisiana State
4. Ron Wolfley—104, RB, West Virginia
5. K.D. Dunn—116, TE, Clemson, from Atlanta
5. Louis Wong—131, G, Brigham Young
6. Jay Novacek—158, WR, Wyoming
7. Choice to Washington through Kansas City
8. Rob Monaco—212, G, Vanderbilt
9. Scott Williams—244, TE, Georgia
10. Dennis Williams—271, RB, Furman
11. Ricky Anderson—298, K, Vanderbilt
12. Lonnie Young—325, DB, Michigan State

WASHINGTON REDSKINS

In Washington, they called it the All-Injured Reserve Team and it included players such as Charlie Brown, Jeff Bostic, Joe Washington, and Mark Murphy. During the regular season, 16 players were placed on the injured-reserve list.

But the Redskins still managed to defeat Dallas twice and won the division title for the second year in a row.

Washington's season ended as it had begun, with guard Ken Huff going down with an injury in the divisional-playoff round against Chicago. Huff's fractured right ankle virtually ended Washington's chances of moving the ball on the ground as Chicago won 23-19.

Washington still was true to its trademark, winning its last four games of the regular season for the third consecutive year. The Redskins have developed into a late-season team, one that generates the proper intensity once money and the playoffs are on the line.

What the Redskins could not do was handle the Bears' fierce pass rush in the playoffs. Quarterback Joe Theismann was sacked seven times in that game, and a total of 21 times in the final three regular-season games. Theismann's passing game was not the same after injuries that sidelined center Bostic and tackle George Starke.

"It was a frustrating way to end it all," coach Joe Gibbs said. "We just ran out of what we had left. The season was a good test of our fortitude. I thought we were going to have a late surge and do something great, but....

"I characterize this team as one that played with a lot of guts. We didn't always have a lot going for us, but we did have a lot of guts."

Redskins' Art Monk set an NFL record of 106 receptions.

Joe Gibbs

When Washington opened the season with losses to San Francisco and Miami, there were doubts about Gibbs's team. Back-to-back losses to St. Louis and the Giants at midseason created more doubts.

But the Redskins still finished with an 11-5 record and a two-game lead in the NFC East.

Three years ago, Gibbs won a Super Bowl with a team that was considered relatively young. No more. John Riggins will turn 36 before the 1985 season and his future is in doubt because of a chronic back problem. The Redskins canvassed every NFL team in search of another running back and finally came up with a powerful choice in George Rogers from the New Orleans Saints, who became expendable after the Saints acquired Earl Campbell from Houston last season. Rogers is just 26 years old.

Fifteen Redskins will be over 30 when the 1985 season begins. Joe Theismann will turn 36 in September.

Like the Dallas Cowboys, the Redskins needed some "impact" players from the draft. They will not be able to depend on Riggins and Theismann much longer.

"I don't care what anybody says about our age," Theismann said. "I still consider this a young team. And I fully intend to grow old with this football team. You will see me around for awhile. You can be certain of that. I just think that we had a lot of problems with injuries last season. But that is not the sign of a team getting old. It's just a team without much luck."

Gibbs and general manager Bobby Beathard built the Redskins from the ground floor beginning in 1981, and they maintained that success through last season. But Gibbs now faces the task of adjusting the gauges on a team that has participated in two of the last three Super Bowls.

Can the Redskins be fine-tuned in time for Super Bowl XX? Or will an upstart team such as the St. Louis Cardinals assume control of the NFC East?

"Thinking positively is one thing that we've got to continue to do," guard Russ Grimm said. "This team can stay near the top for a long time if we can only remain positive in our thoughts."

OFFENSE

"Art Monk could catch a BB in the dark if he heard the gun go off," said Charley Taylor, the second-leading receiver of all time. "That's how much confidence I have in the man."

Taylor, who was inducted into the Pro Football Hall of Fame in 1984, also happens to be the Redskins' receivers coach. He had a first-hand view of Monk's record season of 106 receptions.

"Art was unstoppable, just unstoppable," Taylor said. "Those are the kind of seasons you need to have from a guy every once in awhile."

In 1984, Monk had 8 or more catches in six games, twice caught 11 passes, and was named to the NFC Pro Bowl squad. For Washington, Monk's timing was perfect. His landmark season helped the Redskins overcome some crippling injuries. John Riggins had a bad back, Joe Washington was limping with a sore knee, and Charlie Brown missed almost half the season with a severely sprained ankle.

Still, only two NFL teams—the Miami Dolphins and San Francisco 49ers—topped the Redskins' 426 points. Washington has scored in double figures in the last 55 games.

The Redskins' 142-yard rushing average was fourth in the NFC. When the Redskins can control the ball via the rush, they rarely are beaten. They have compiled a 38-4 record the last three years when running the ball more than 30 times. With 40 rushes, they are 20-1.

Darrell Green

Russ Grimm

Dexter Manley

Riggins also became the oldest running back to gain more than 1,000 yards in a season. He was admitted to the hospital twice with back problems, but still finished the year with 1,239 yards.

What happens to the Redskins if the 240-pound Riggins is forced to retire? Why, Gibbs will just go to the 229-pound Rogers, who had two 1,000-plus yard seasons in four years with the Saints, but fell off to 914 yards last year. He's a strong runner though not as powerful as Riggins. But he possesses more speed.

Theismann finished fourth among NFC passers last season with an 86.6 rating. His 283 completions in 477 attempts were good for 3,391 yards and 24 touchdowns. He was intercepted only 13 times. However, the Redskins need back-up help for Theismann now that Jim Hart has retired. Jay Schroeder and Babe Laufenberg are the reserves and neither has had much playing time nor showed the ability to take charge.

Because of the injuries, the Redskins were forced to make eight trades in 1984. No doubt, the acquisition of wide receiver Calvin Muhammad was the most significant. Playing in the last 12 games, Muhammad caught 42 passes for 729 yards. He also provided speed at wide receiver that complemented Monk.

In return for Muhammad, Washington sent a fourth-round draft choice to the Los Angeles Raiders.

After two seasons as a reserve, Clint Didier brought his speed to a starting job at tight end and nearly tripled his career receptions with 30 for 350 yards and 5 touchdowns (he caught 11 passes his first two years). The Redskins' other tight ends are Don Warren and Rick Walker, both of whom have started.

If healthy, the Redskins still have one of the best offensive lines in the NFL. The Hogs were represented in the AFC-NFC Pro Bowl by tackle Joe Jacoby and guard Russ Grimm.

The absence of Bostic (eight games) and Starke (seven games) did not help the offensive line. Bostic was replaced by Rick Donnalley while both Huff and Mark May subbed for Starke.

"You've got to hand it to Joe," Gibbs said. "He didn't have all the guys around to help him. But he still got the

Three Years at a Glance

Averages NFL Rank	OFFENSE			DEFENSE		
	1984	1983	1982	1984	1983	1982
Points	**26.6**	**33.8**	**21.1**	**19.4**	**20.8**	**14.2**
Rank	3	1	12	11T	11	1
Yards	**334.4**	**383.7**	**331.7**	**335.1**	**329.0**	**284.4**
Rank	9	3	7	18	12	4
Rushing Yards	**142.1**	**164.1**	**126.7**	**99.3**	**80.6**	**105.1**
Rank	4	3	10	2	1	8
Passing Yards	**192.3**	**219.6**	**205.0**	**235.8**	**248.4**	**179.3**
Rank	19	7	12T	25	28	7
Sacks	**3.0**	**2.2**	**3.3**	**4.1**	**3.2**	**3.6**
Rank	14T	6T	20T	2	6T	3T
Turnovers	**1.8**	**1.1**	**1.8**	**2.7**	**3.8**	**2.7**
Rank	3T	1	2T	4	1	11
Punt Returns	**8.6**	**7.9**	**7.8**	**4.9**	**9.9**	**3.5**
Rank	12	19	16	2	22	2
Kickoff Returns	**19.6**	**20.7**	**21.6**	**19.2**	**19.5**	**17.3**
Rank	15	6	4	9	15	2
Penalty Yards	**45.2**	**48.5**	**44.9**	**50.2**	**44.4**	**46.6**
Rank	7	8	8	18	24T	19

	W-L Total	Home	Road	Playoffs
1982	8-1	3-1	5-0	4-0, Won Super Bowl XVII
1983	14-2	7-1	7-1	2-1, Lost Super Bowl XVIII
1984	11-5	7-1	4-4	0-1, Lost Divisional Playoff Game

job done in the same fashion. I'm proud of the way he handled himself and the team throughout the season."

DEFENSE

Stopping the run the last few seasons has been the forte of the Redskins. Again, they were second in the NFL in rushing defense, allowing only 99.3 yards per game. Eight opponents were held to fewer than 100 yards. In the last 30 Redskins regular-season games, only one running back—Gerald Riggs of Atlanta—has gained more than 100 yards.

Washington finished sixth in the NFC in points-allowed with 310.

After an incredible takeaway ratio of plus-43 during the 1983 season, the Redskins dropped to plus-15, but still led the NFC East in that category.

With Dexter Manley leading the way, Washington finished second in the NFL with 66 sacks. The defense now has a streak of 15 games with three or more sacks.

Manley, who spent a brief time in Gibbs's doghouse in 1984, finished the season with 13½ sacks. Linebacker Monte Coleman had 10½.

The Redskins certainly missed safety Murphy, who is considered the brains of the Washington secondary. Murphy missed nine games. In his place, Curtis Jordan had two interceptions and 79 solo tackles.

Cornerback Vernon Dean, who had his best season, led the team with seven interceptions; Darrell Green added five. Green was the defense's lone representative as a starter in the AFC-NFC Pro Bowl. After only two seasons in the NFL, Green already is considered one of the league's best cornerbacks. Some scouts thought he was too small for the NFL, but the Redskins drafted him in the first round and haven't regretted it.

Strong safety Tony Peters returned to the Redskins after a one-year suspension, but missed nine games with an injury.

Only two defensive players—linebacker Neal Olkewicz and Green—were able to start all 16 regular-season games.

The linebackers are a veteran group, with Coleman, Olkewicz, and Rich Milot all going into their seventh seasons and Mel Kaufman starting his fifth. When

Mike Nelms   *John Riggins*   *Joe Theismann*

healthy, it's a solid group.

Tackle Dave Butz made every all-pro team in 1983, but had only 4½ sacks in 1984. Two of those were in one game against Dallas.

"We weren't the best defense in the league," Gibbs said. "But we weren't that far behind the pack. I think that if everyone is able to come back from injuries we're going to be one of the best again."

SPECIAL TEAMS

Mark Moseley, the last straight-on kicker in the NFL, made his fifteenth career "clutch" kick from 37 yards away to beat the St. Louis Cardinals in the final regular-season game to win the NFC East title. In 1984, he also made his twelfth kick of 50 or more yards during his 13-year career.

Moseley now ranks sixth on the all-time field-goal list with 266. There is little hope, however, of his ever becoming number-one. The leader with 351 field goals is Jan Stenerud and he still is kicking with Minnesota.

Mike Nelms, who might be the bravest kick returner in the NFL, put together his fourth consecutive 1,000-yard season (not counting the 1982 strike year) in both punt and kickoff returns.

The NFL may have changed its rule to require a kick returner to wave his arm for a fair catch. But it probably will not matter to Nelms, who doesn't know the definition of a fair catch.

Not only did Nelms have another good season, the Redskins were second in the NFL in punt coverage with a 4.9-yard average. The longest punt return of the year against them was only 14 yards, by Ken Johnson of Atlanta.

VETERAN ROSTER

No.	Name	Pos.	Ht.	Wt.	NFL Exp.	Birthdate	College	Games in 1984
67	Beasley, Tom	DE	6-5	248	8	8/11/54	Virginia Tech	13
53	Bostic, Jeff	C	6-2	258	6	9/18/58	Clemson	8
69	Brooks, Perry	DT	6-3	270	8	12/4/54	Southern	16
87	Brown, Charlie	WR	5-10	179	4	10/29/58	South Carolina State	9
65	Butz, Dave	DT	6-7	295	13	6/23/50	Purdue	15
48	Coffey, Ken	S	6-0	190	3	11/7/60	Southwest Texas State	12
51	Coleman, Monte	LB	6-2	230	7	11/4/57	Central Arkansas	16
54	Cronan, Peter	LB	6-2	238	8	1/13/55	Boston College	3
32	Dean, Vernon	CB	5-11	178	4	5/5/59	San Diego State	16
86	Didier, Clint	TE	6-5	240	4	4/4/59	Portland State	11
76	Donnalley, Rick	C-G	6-2	257	4	12/11/58	North Carolina	15
77	Grant, Darryl	DT	6-1	275	5	11/22/59	Rice	15
28	Green, Darrell	CB	5-8	170	3	2/15/60	Texas A&I	16
35	Griffin, Keith	RB	5-8	185	2	10/26/61	Miami	16
68	Grimm, Russ	G	6-3	275	5	5/2/59	Pittsburgh	16
5	Hayes, Jeff	P	5-11	175	4	8/19/59	North Carolina	16
61	Huff, Ken	G	6-4	265	11	2/21/53	North Carolina	15
66	Jacoby, Joe	T	6-7	305	5	7/6/59	Louisville	16
82	Jones, Anthony	TE	6-3	248	2	5/16/60	Wichita State	16
22	Jordan, Curtis	S	6-2	205	9	1/25/54	Texas Tech	16
40	Kane, Rick	RB	6-0	200	9	11/12/54	San Jose State	12
55	Kaufman, Mel	LB	6-2	218	5	2/24/58	Cal Poly-SLO	15
63	Kimball, Bruce	G	6-2	260	3	8/19/56	Massachusetts	8
50	Kubin, Larry	LB	6-2	234	4	2/26/59	Penn State	16
12	Laufenberg, Babe	QB	6-2	195	2	12/5/59	Indiana	0
79	Liebenstein, Todd	DE	6-6	255	3	1/9/60	Nevada-Las Vegas	1
72	Manley, Dexter	DE	6-3	250	5	2/2/59	Oklahoma State	15
71	Mann, Charles	DE	6-6	260	3	4/12/61	Nevada-Reno	16
84	Mauti, Rich	WR	6-0	195	8	5/24/54	Penn State	16
73	May, Mark	T	6-6	295	5	11/2/59	Pittsburgh	16
78	McGee, Tony	DE	6-3	249	15	1/18/49	Bishop, Tex.	16
83	McGrath, Mark	WR	5-11	175	4	12/17/57	Montana State	13
57	Milot, Rich	LB	6-4	237	7	5/28/57	Penn State	14
81	Monk, Art	WR	6-3	209	6	12/5/57	Syracuse	16
30	Moore, Jeff	RB	6-0	196	6	8/20/56	Jackson State	7
3	Moseley, Mark	K	6-0	204	14	3/12/48	Stephen F. Austin	16
89	Muhammad, Calvin	WR	6-0	190	4	12/10/58	Texas Southern	10
29	Murphy, Mark	S	6-4	210	9	7/13/55	Colgate	7
21	Nelms, Mike	KR-WR	6-1	202	6	4/8/55	Baylor	16
52	Olkewicz, Neal	LB	6-0	233	7	1/30/57	Maryland	16
23	Peters, Tony	S	6-1	190	10	4/28/53	Oklahoma	8
44	Riggins, John	RB	6-2	240	14	8/4/49	Kansas	14
38	Rogers, George	RB	6-2	225	6	12/8/58	South Carolina	16
10	Schroeder, Jay	QB	6-4	215	2	6/28/61	UCLA	0
26	Smith, Ricky	CB	6-0	182	4	7/20/60	Alabama State	12
74	Starke, George	T	6-5	260	13	7/18/48	Columbia	9
	Sverchek, Paul	DT	6-3	256	2	5/9/61	Cal Poly-SLO	3
7	Theismann, Joe	QB	6-0	198	12	9/9/49	Notre Dame	16
62	Towns, Morris	T	6-4	263	9	1/10/54	Missouri	4
88	Walker, Rick	TE	6-4	235	9	5/28/55	UCLA	16
85	Warren, Don	TE	6-4	242	7	5/5/56	San Diego State	16
24	Washington, Anthony	CB	6-1	204	5	2/4/58	Fresno State	16
47	Williams, Greg	S	5-11	185	4	8/1/59	Mississippi State	16
	Williams, Mike	TE	6-4	251	3	8/27/59	Alabama A&M	1
39	Wonsley, Otis	RB	5-10	214	5	8/13/57	Alcorn State	16

Coaching Staff

Joe Gibbs, head coach; **Don Breaux,** offensive backs; **Joe Bugel,** assistant head coach-offense; **Bill Hickman,** administrative assistant; **Larry Peccatiello,** defensive coordinator; **Richie Petitbon,** assistant head coach-defense; **Jerry Rhome,** quarterbacks; **Dan Riley,** conditioning; **Wayne Sevier,** special teams; **Warren Simmons,** tight ends; **Charley Taylor,** wide receivers; **LaVern Torgeson,** defensive line.

1985 Schedule

Preseason

Aug. 10	at Atlanta	8:00
Aug. 18	at L.A. Raiders	1:00
Aug. 23	NEW ENGLAND	8:00
Aug. 30	at Tampa Bay	8:00

Regular Season

Sept. 9	at Dallas (Mon.)	8:00
Sept. 15	HOUSTON	1:00
Sept. 22	PHILADELPHIA	1:00
Sept. 29	at Chicago	12:00
Oct. 7	ST. LOUIS (Mon.)	9:00
Oct. 13	DETROIT	1:00
Oct. 20	at N.Y. Giants	1:00
Oct. 27	at Cleveland	1:00
Nov. 3	at Atlanta	1:00
Nov. 10	DALLAS	4:00
Nov. 18	N.Y. GIANTS (Mon.)	9:00
Nov. 24	at Pittsburgh	1:00
Dec. 1	SAN FRANCISCO	4:00
Dec. 8	at Philadelphia	1:00
Dec. 15	CINCINNATI	1:00
Dec. 21	at St. Louis (Sat.)	3:00

1984 Results

Sept. 2	MIAMI	17-35
Sept. 10	at San Francisco (Mon.)	31-37
Sept. 16	N.Y. GIANTS	30-14
Sept. 23	at New England	26-10
Sept. 30	PHILADELPHIA	20-0
Oct. 7	at Indianapolis	35-7
Oct. 14	DALLAS	34-14
Oct. 21	at St. Louis	24-26
Oct. 28	at N.Y. Giants	13-37
Nov. 5	ATLANTA (Mon.)	27-14
Nov. 11	DETROIT	28-14
Nov. 18	at Philadelphia	10-16
Nov. 25	BUFFALO	41-14
Nov. 29	at Minnesota (Thurs.)	31-17
Dec. 9	at Dallas	30-28
Dec. 16	ST. LOUIS	29-27
Dec. 30	CHICAGO	19-23

1985 Draft Choices

1. Choice to New Orleans
2. Tory Nixon—33, DB, San Diego State, from Atlanta
2. Choice to St. Louis through Atlanta
3. Choice to L.A. Raiders through Houston
4. Choice to L.A. Raiders
5. Raphel Cherry—122, RB, Hawaii, from New Orleans
5. Choice to Pittsburgh
6. Danzell Lee—163, TE, Lamar
7. Jamie Harris—177, KR, Oklahoma State, from Philadelphia
7. Lionel Vital—185, RB, Nicholls State, from St. Louis through Kansas City
7. Choice to L.A. Raiders through New England
8. Barry Wilburn—219, DB, Mississippi
9. Mitch Geier—247, G, Troy State
10. Terry Orr—263, RB, Texas, from New Orleans
10. Choice to L.A. Raiders
11. Raleigh McKenzie—290, G, Tennessee, from New Orleans
11. Garry Kimble—304, DB, Sam Houston State
12. Dean Hamel—309, DT, Tulsa, from Buffalo
12. Bryant Winn—331, LB, Houston

CHICAGO BEARS

One of the first things the Bears' offensive coaches did after last season was to visit Mississippi Valley State University, where coach Archie (Gunslinger) Cooley had wowed the country with his high-scoring passing game. The passing game is the last piece in Chicago's puzzle. The Bears' defense was the best in the NFL last year by nearly every measurement. They have led the league in rushing yardage two seasons in a row. That was enough to get them to the NFC Championship Game, but they know they'll need a stronger passing game to go further.

The Bears impressed 49ers coach Bill Walsh enough that he called them "the team to beat" this year after his team ended their season last year. Whether or not Walsh was just diverting attention from his own team, the Bears no longer will be able to sneak up on people.

But there's reason to expect improvement, based simply on the reasonable assumption that the Bears will be able to keep their regular quarterback—or even their second one—healthy for more than three games in a row. That was the limit last season, when they must have become the only team ever to play for a conference championship after starting five quarterbacks.

First-stringer Jim McMahon has recovered fully from the kidney lacerations that kept him out of the last six games and the playoffs. He started nine games, but he played four of those with a painful broken hand. The Bears won the other five. They also won two of the three full games back-up Steve Fuller played. McMahon had the NFC's best passer rating before his second injury. He had just two interceptions in 143 attempts, and Fuller threw 78 passes with no interceptions.

Bears' defensive end Richard Dent led NFC in sacks with 17½.

Mike Ditka

Caution was the first priority on offense. If the Bears had to punt, so what? Their defense would get them the ball in about the same place four plays later. The Bears' pattern was to get ahead early. In their first 12 games, they scored in the first quarter, and only San Francisco did better than their 91-33 point advantage in first quarters. Chicago protected its leads by rushing the passer and playing mistake-free offense.

The Bears' 72 sacks were an NFL record. They controlled the ball more than all 18 of their opponents, with a league-leading average of 35:08 minutes a game. Their ratio of 22 touchdown runs to 14 touchdown passes was highest in the league.

Chicago's 10-6 record was the best in the division since the Bears and the Buccaneers both went 10-6 in 1979. Chicago won seven of eight against division opponents and two of four against playoff teams, shutting out the Broncos and drubbing the Raiders. Then they became the first team to beat the Redskins in a playoff game at RFK Stadium.

OFFENSE

The offensive burden Walter Payton carries is getting lighter, if only because he is carrying it farther. When Payton was breaking Jim Brown's all-time rushing record early last season, he said the best part about it was that the Bears were winning. When their season ended one game short of the Super Bowl, Payton was clearly the most devastated Bear.

Payton goes into this season surrounded by the best talent of his 11-year career, but he remains the centerpiece of the offense. Even if McMahon rises to expectations, it is Payton who will make it possible to throw long play-action passes on the first play of the game.

Payton, 31, even played quarterback for six downs last season. He threw two touchdown passes from halfback. He led the team with 45 catches. His blocking leveled defensive linemen and cartwheeled blitzers. But most impressive was his running. He has played 142 consecutive games, the most recent at an age when most running backs are ex-running backs. In 1984, Payton had his most carries (381) and second-most yards (1,684).

Payton goes into this season with 13,309 rushing yards—997 ahead of Brown and 2,200 behind the admittedly outrageous goal he had set for the end of next season. He also has 17,511 combined yards, 3,047 carries, eight 1,000-yard rushing seasons, three seasons with 2,000 yards from scrimmage, and 63 100-yard games. Those are all NFL records.

The Bears played best last season when they spread the rushing workload to their above-average fullback types, Matt Suhey and Calvin Thomas. They were 7-1 in games when the fullbacks carried at least 10 times. Suhey's per-carry average slipped from 4.6 to 3.4 in a 424-yard season, but his blocking and 41 catches kept him valuable. Thomas, strictly a runner, ran for 186 yards and averaged 4.7.

Ditka believes deeply in Dallas's philosophy of a diversified attack. A team must pass well to score points.

McMahon has shown flashes of brilliance as a passer. In three seasons, he has completed 58.6 percent of his passes and thrown for 28 touchdowns with 23 interceptions. His strength has been turning broken plays into big plays. But that has been a liability, too. He tends to be injured often.

Fuller is one of the league's best back-up quarterbacks, but he is fairly fragile, too. He separated his throwing shoulder twice last year.

Of all the young players Ditka has added to the

Todd Bell

Jim Covert

Dan Hampton

Bears, the most pleasant offensive surprise has been Dennis McKinnon, an undrafted wide receiver in 1983 who has become the team's most reliable pass-catcher. McKinnon caught 30 passes before needing arthroscopic knee surgery 12 games into last season.

Willie Gault has been mildly disappointing because of some questionable work habits and passive catching style, especially when the ball is in traffic. But Gault also is one of the fastest men in football. His 74 catches in two seasons have averaged 19.2 yards and produced 14 touchdowns.

The Bears need better depth at wide receiver. Ken Margerum is returning from serious knee surgery, Brian Baschnagel is in his tenth season, and Brad Anderson and Jack Cameron (a college cornerback), were seldom-used rookies last year. Ditka has been trying to find a tight end who would remind him of himself, the standard for Bears tight ends. He keeps coming back to Emery Moorehead, an overgrown wide receiver who averaged 17.1 yards on his 29 catches last year and has 101 catches and nine touchdowns in 2½ seasons. Ditka thought he had his mirror image when he drafted Tim Wrightman on the third round three years ago, and he'll have the former UCLA All-America on the roster for the first time this season after his injury-plagued USFL career.

The best offensive lineman is Jim Covert, whom Payton calls, "the best tackle in the league." Covert and center Jay Hilgenberg were AFC-NFC Pro Bowl alternates, and Ditka said the voters wouldn't have embarrassed themselves by including Keith Van Horne, who began fulfilling first-round expectations in his fourth season. Defensive players say powerful Mark Bortz, the third-year left guard who played defense in college, could turn out to be the best of them all when he learns the position. Right guard Kurt Becker is the embodiment of exuberance overcoming aesthetics.

DEFENSE

The Bears' defense still has some unattained goals. The players wanted to lead the league in fewest yards allowed for all 16 weeks, which they did last year, and they wanted to lead against both the run and the pass,

Three Years at a Glance

Averages NFL Rank	OFFENSE			DEFENSE		
	1984	1983	1982	1984	1983	1982
Points Rank	**20.3** 16	**19.4** 20	**15.7** 22	**15.5** 3	**18.8** 5	**19.3** 12
Yards Rank	**339.8** 7	**364.4** 6	**277.0** 26	**241.4** 1	**320.8** 8	**316.8** 16
Rushing Yards Rank	**185.9** 1	**170.4** 1	**109.8** 18	**86.1** 1	**125.0** 11T	**100.2** 5
Passing Yards Rank	**153.9** 26	**193.9** 17	**167.2** 23	**155.4** 2	**195.8** 12	**216.6** 21
Sacks Rank	**2.3** 7T	**3.3** 23	**3.7** 25	**4.5** 1	**3.2** 6T	**3.3** 9T
Turnovers Rank	**1.9** 7T	**2.3** 8T	**2.1** 8T	**2.1** 16T	**2.4** 15	**2.2** 20T
Punt Returns Rank	**8.9** 11	**8.0** 16	**5.9** 21	**6.1** 4	**7.3** 8	**9.2** 22
Kickoff Returns Rank	**18.3** 26	**16.4** 28	**18.3** 25	**21.2** 21	**18.6** 8	**17.9** 5
Penalty Yards Rank	**53.2** 15	**54.3** 18	**46.9** 10	**43.6** 27	**42.9** 26	**50.1** 15

	W-L Total	Home	Road	Playoffs
1982	3-6	2-2	1-4	None
1983	8-8	5-3	3-5	None
1984	10-6	6-2	4-4	1-1, Lost NFC Championship Game

which they did until the last two minutes of their last game. Then they gave up a meaningless touchdown drive that dropped them three yards per game behind New Orleans in pass defense.

Then there's the matter of first downs. The Bears allowed 216 last year. It was the fewest in the league, both against the run and the pass.

Defensive coordinator Buddy Ryan calls the Bears' defensive philosophy "putting pressure on everybody." It requires some risks, and Ditka wondered whether they were worth the results until last season. But the more he thought about it, the more he saw the defense applying pressure the same way he wanted to do on offense. Ryan's multiple coverages and alignments made opponents think fast, and the players' all-out abandon made them move fast.

The trademark for the Bears' defense last season became the blitz, although Ryan prefers not to use it. He doesn't use it if the opponent has a blocking scheme that can render it useless. But if the opponent is vulnerable to the blitz, the Bears apply it in heavy doses.

The Bears finished the season tied with San Francisco for the fewest touchdown passes allowed, 14. Not counting touchdowns scored on returns, the Bears' defense allowed 214 points, also the NFL's fewest.

A weak point for the defense was the relative lack of turnovers—21 interceptions and 13 fumble recoveries.

But they have players who can make big plays. Linebacker Mike Singletary, defensive tackle Dan Hampton, defensive end Richard Dent, and strong safety Todd Bell started in the AFC-NFC Pro Bowl, and Ryan said Gary Fencik and linebackers Otis Wilson and Al Harris belonged there, too.

Singletary, that rare middle linebacker who plays every down, was the NFC's defensive player of the year.

Bell is the player Ryan calls most indispensible to the defense because his assignments range from linebacker to cornerback.

Dent led the NFC with 17½ sacks despite starting only the last nine games. An eighth-round draft choice in 1983, he has bulked up from 224 pounds to 253. Hampton and defensive tackle Steve McMichael had

Jay Hilgenberg

Walter Payton

Mike Singletary

11½ and 10 sacks, respectively. Left end Mike Hartenstine is a run-stuffer who also can cover receivers.

The Bears considered themselves weak at linebacker before last season, so they drafted Wilber Marshall and Ron Rivera in the first two rounds. They tried to trade Wilson, who responded with his best season. Harris kept improving in his first linebacker season after five as a 255-pound defensive end; he'll face a stiff challenge from Marshall this year.

In Leslie Frazier and Mike Richardson, Ryan says he has "safeties playing cornerback." He is loaded at safety. Behind Bell and Fencik, Dave Duerson would start for most teams. The Bears discovered a true cornerback in Shaun Gayle, their tenth-round pick last year.

SPECIAL TEAMS

Bob Thomas had six challengers for his placekicking job in training camp. He not only won the job, he had the best of his nine seasons. Thomas made 22 of 28 field-goal tries, was 8 for 12 beyond 40 yards, and finished with a streak of 11 in a row.

Punter Dave Finzer also finished his rookie season strong. His 26 punts inside the 20 were a league high, and were tainted by only four touchbacks. Finzer's 40.1 average was adequate for windy Soldier Field.

Return and coverage teams improved markedly for the Bears. Duerson led a punt-coverage team that allowed 6.1 yards per return, fourth best in the league. McKinnon and steady Jeff Fisher were above ordinary with an 8.7-yard average on Bear returns.

Kickoffs were not such a bright story. With Cameron and Dennis Gentry handling most of the chances, the Bears' 18.3-yard average ranked third from the bottom.

VETERAN ROSTER

No.	Name	Pos.	Ht.	Wt.	NFL Exp.	Birthdate	College	Games in 1984
86	Anderson, Brad	WR	6-2	196	2	1/21/61	Arizona	13
60	Andrews, Tom	C	6-4	261	2	1/11/62	Louisville	7
84	Baschnagel, Brian	WR	5-11	185	10	1/8/54	Ohio State	16
79	Becker, Kurt	G	6-5	270	4	12/22/58	Michigan	16
25	Bell, Todd	S	6-1	205	5	11/28/58	Ohio State	16
62	Bortz, Mark	G	6-6	271	3	2/12/61	Iowa	15
54	Cabral, Brian	LB	6-1	227	7	6/23/56	Colorado	16
30	Cameron, Jack	WR	6-0	182	2	11/5/61	Winston-Salem State	16
74	Covert, Jim	T	6-4	283	3	3/22/60	Pittsburgh	16
95	Dent, Richard	DE	6-5	253	3	12/13/60	Tennessee State	16
22	Duerson, Dave	S	6-1	205	3	11/28/60	Notre Dame	16
88	Dunsmore, Pat	TE	6-3	237	3	10/2/59	Drake	11
64	Fada, Rob	G	6-2	272	3	5/7/61	Pittsburgh	14
45	Fencik, Gary	S	6-1	197	10	6/11/54	Yale	16
15	Finzer, Dave	P	6-0	195	2	2/3/59	DePauw	16
24	Fisher, Jeff	CB	5-10	195	5	2/25/58	Southern California	16
21	Frazier, Leslie	CB	6-0	189	5	4/3/59	Alcorn State	11
71	Frederick, Andy	T	6-6	265	9	7/25/54	New Mexico	16
4	Fuller, Steve	QB	6-4	195	7	1/5/57	Clemson	6
83	Gault, Willie	WR	6-0	178	3	9/5/60	Tennessee	16
23	Gayle, Shaun	CB	5-11	191	2	3/8/62	Ohio State	15
29	Gentry, Dennis	RB	5-8	184	4	2/10/59	Baylor	16
99	Hampton, Dan	DT	6-5	266	7	9/19/57	Arkansas	15
90	Harris, Al	LB	6-5	253	7	12/31/56	Arizona State	16
73	Hartenstine, Mike	DE	6-3	258	11	7/27/53	Penn State	16
63	Hilgenberg, Jay	C	6-3	255	5	3/21/59	Iowa	16
75	Humphries, Stefan	G	6-3	265	2	1/20/62	Michigan	10
32	Hutchison, Anthony	RB	5-10	186	3	2/4/61	Texas Tech	12
49	Jordan, Donald	RB	6-0	210	2	2/9/62	Houston	13
98	Keys, Tyrone	DE	6-7	267	3	10/24/59	Mississippi State	14
89	Krenk, Mitch	TE	6-2	225	2	11/19/59	Nebraska	8
12	Lisch, Rusty	QB	6-4	215	6	12/21/56	Notre Dame	7
82	Margerum, Ken	WR	6-0	180	4	10/5/58	Stanford	0
58	Marshall, Wilber	LB	6-1	225	2	4/18/62	Florida	15
85	McKinnon, Dennis	WR	6-1	185	3	8/22/61	Florida	12
9	McMahon, Jim	QB	6-1	185	4	8/21/59	Brigham Young	9
76	McMichael, Steve	DT	6-2	263	6	10/17/57	Texas	16
87	Moorehead, Emery	TE	6-2	225	9	3/22/54	Colorado	16
34	Payton, Walter	RB	5-10	202	11	7/25/54	Jackson State	16
53	Rains, Dan	LB	6-1	222	3	4/26/56	Cincinnati	16
27	Richardson, Mike	CB	6-0	188	3	5/23/61	Arizona State	15
59	Rivera, Ron	LB	6-3	244	2	1/7/62	California	15
81	Saldi, Jay	TE	6-3	227	10	10/8/54	South Carolina	15
50	Singletary, Mike	LB	6-0	228	5	10/9/58	Baylor	16
26	Suhey, Matt	RB	5-11	216	6	7/7/58	Penn State	16
16	Thomas, Bob	K	5-10	177	10	8/7/52	Notre Dame	16
33	Thomas, Calvin	RB	5-11	235	4	1/7/60	Illinois	16
78	Van Horne, Keith	T	6-6	265	5	11/6/57	Southern California	14
70	Waechter, Henry	DT	6-5	270	4	2/13/59	Nebraska	3
55	Wilson, Otis	LB	6-2	231	6	9/15/57	Louisville	15

Coaching Staff

Mike Ditka, head coach; **Jim Dooley,** research and quality control; **Dale Haupt,** defensive line; **Ed Hughes,** offensive coordinator; **Steve Kazor,** special teams; **Jim LaRue,** defensive backfield; **Ted Plumb,** receivers; **Johnny Roland,** offensive backs; **Buddy Ryan,** defensive coordinator; **Dick Stanfel,** offensive line.

1985 Schedule

Preseason

Aug. 9	at St. Louis	7:30
Aug. 17	INDIANAPOLIS	6:00
Aug. 26	at Dallas	7:00
Aug. 31	BUFFALO	6:00

Regular Season

Sept. 8	TAMPA BAY	12:00
Sept. 15	NEW ENGLAND	12:00
Sept. 19	at Minnesota (Thurs.)	7:00
Sept. 29	WASHINGTON	12:00
Oct. 6	at Tampa Bay	1:00
Oct. 13	at San Francisco	1:00
Oct. 21	GREEN BAY (Mon.)	8:00
Oct. 27	MINNESOTA	12:00
Nov. 3	at Green Bay	12:00
Nov. 10	DETROIT	12:00
Nov. 17	at Dallas	12:00
Nov. 24	ATLANTA	12:00
Dec. 1	at Miami (Mon.)	9:00
Dec. 8	INDIANAPOLIS	12:00
Dec. 14	at N.Y. Jets (Sat.)	12:30
Dec. 22	at Detroit	1:00

1984 Results

Sept. 2	TAMPA BAY	34-14
Sept. 9	DENVER	27-0
Sept. 16	at Green Bay	9-7
Sept. 23	at Seattle	9-38
Sept. 30	DALLAS	14-23
Oct. 7	NEW ORLEANS	20-7
Oct. 14	at St. Louis	21-38
Oct. 21	at Tampa Bay	44-9
Oct. 28	MINNESOTA	16-7
Nov. 4	L.A. RAIDERS	17-6
Nov. 11	at L.A. Rams	13-29
Nov. 18	DETROIT	16-14
Nov. 25	at Minnesota	34-3
Dec. 3	at San Diego (Mon.)	7-20
Dec. 9	GREEN BAY	14-20
Dec. 16	at Detroit	30-13
Dec. 30	Washington	23-19
Jan. 6	San Francisco	0-23

1985 Draft Choices

1. William Perry—22, DT, Clemson
2. Reggie Phillips—49, DB, Southern Methodist
3. James Maness—78, WR, Texas Christian
4. Kevin Butler—105, K, Georgia
5. Choice to N.Y. Jets
6. Choice to L.A. Rams
7. Charles Bennett—190, DE, S.W. Louisiana
8. Steve Buxton—217, T, Indiana State
9. Thomas Sanders—250, RB, Texas A&M
10. Pat Coryatt—273, DT, Baylor
11. James Morrissey—302, LB, Michigan State
12. Choice to San Diego

DETROIT LIONS

The Detroit Lions had the closest thing possible in the offseason to a personality change. They enter the 1985 season with a new coach (Darryl Rogers, formerly of Arizona State), a new quarterback (former Buffalo starter Joe Ferguson), and a new defense (a 3-4 instead of a 4-3). All of those changes make a team that traditionally has been difficult to figure even more difficult.

The Lions entered last season as clear-cut favorites to win the NFC Central Division. They had won 8 of their last 11 games in 1983 and had come within a missed field goal of beating San Francisco in the final seconds in the playoffs.

One year later, they won one of their last eight games for a 4-11-1 finish. They were the only NFC team without a Pro Bowl player, and their coach of seven years, Monte Clark, was fired with two years left on his contract. The Lions will begin this season, once again, as a long shot, scrambling behind the new clear-cut favorites, Chicago and Green Bay.

Billy Sims's return from a serious knee injury would help, certainly; the Lions were 1-6-1 without him. But the root of their problems was much harder to pinpoint, as Clark lamented all season. He tried various ways to motivate them, but the Lions made costly mistakes, causing turnovers or penalties when big plays could have won games. Their 138 penalties were a team record, and the second-most in the NFL. In a three-point loss to San Diego, penalties nullified two touchdowns on the same drive.

Maybe Detroit is a team in need of a college coach's rah-rah attitude. If so, Rogers, who was at Michigan State before Arizona State, could shake the blahs out of

Keith Dorney, one of the bright spots in Lions' offensive line.

Darryl Rogers

a team that seems to have playoff-caliber talent but a layoff attitude.

The opening game, a 30-27 loss to the 49ers on a last-gasp field goal, was a harbinger of the season which went from the ridiculous to the disastrous. Reese McCall became the first NFL player penalized for spiking the ball after a touchdown. Tackle Rich Strenger tore knee ligaments and had to be replaced by overweight guard Homer Elias, who pulled a groin muscle. The Lions went on to lose five games by four points or less. In a 1-5 start, their first four defeats were by 3, 4, 1, and 3 points.

OFFENSE

Detroit does have some good players. Despite the loss of Sims and having to use four left tackles, three left guards, and three centers, the Lions still ranked third in the NFL last year in average gain per rush. Trouble was, they weren't able to run the ball as often as most teams because they spent so much of the season trying to come from behind.

The questions about the Lions' offense still focus on their passing game. Detroit hasn't had a truly stable situation at quarterback for several years, with Gary Danielson and Eric Hipple usually fighting it out for the starting position. Last season, Danielson was solid, beating out Hipple and two other challengers for the starting position and then passing for 3,076 yards, 17 touchdowns, and a 61.5 completion percentage. But Rogers was unimpressed. He traded Danielson to Cleveland in the offseason after bringing in Joe Ferguson as the new starter. Ferguson is a 12-year veteran who has been starting for the Bills since his rookie year. Although 1984 was a down year for Ferguson (he passed for only 1,991 yards and 12 touchdowns and finished ranked twenty-sixth in the NFL), the former Arkansas star has career totals of 2,188 completions, 27,950 yards, and 181 touchdown passes.

The Lions carried four quarterbacks last season, although Hipple spent several weeks on injured reserve.

Mike Machurek had the strongest arm of the bunch, but he wound up fourth-string. John Witkowski, a sixth-round rookie, improved steadily.

Mark Nichols finally showed glimpses of brilliance with 34 catches for a whopping 21.9-yard average. He had only 35 catches in his first three seasons. Leonard Thompson, the other starting wide receiver, had the best season of his 10-year career with 50 catches and 773 yards despite missing three games because of a broken jaw suffered in a game against Green Bay. Jeff Chadwick has caught 77 passes in his two seasons.

The Lions' passing game could become downright explosive with help from their first two 1984 draft choices, both of whom were disappointing as rookies. Danielson called first-round tight end David Lewis a "stiff" after he lost his starting job in midseason to Rob Rubick, a twelfth-rounder in 1982 from Grand Valley State. Lewis caught two touchdown passes in the Thanksgiving game, but he was shut out in the last three weeks and finished with just 16 catches, two more than Rubick. Pete Mandley seldom played except as a kickoff returner.

The Lions' most prolific receiver the last two years has been fullback James Jones, who had 46 catches as a rookie and a team record 77 last season. Sims always has been a receiving threat out of the backfield, and Ken Jenkins, Sims' replacement last season, averaged 11.7 yards on 21 catches.

Jenkins took some of the sting out of Sims's injury. Overlooked in the 1982 draft, the 5-8 Bucknell alumnus joined the Lions in 1983 as a kick returner. He replaced

Doug English

Ken Fantetti

Joe Ferguson

Sims with 358 yards and a 4.6-yard average.

But not many men can replace a healthy, motivated Sims. In five NFL seasons, he has averaged 85 yards rushing and 35 receiving per game. He was off to a sensational start—with 687 rushing yards, a 5.4-yard average and five touchdowns— before he tore knee ligaments and cartilage in the eighth game.

If Sims returns at anywhere near full-speed, the Lions could have the league's best group of running backs. Jones was the team's offensive MVP last season, adding 532 rushing yards to his 662 on receptions. Besides Jenkins, the Lions' bench features Dave D'Addio, a 235-pound fullback who can block and catch and averaged 6.6 yards on seven carries as a rookie. Dexter Bussey, the club career-yardage leader retired.

Injuries also resulted in pleasant discoveries on the offensive line. Don Laster played left tackle capably, and Chris Dieterich made a smooth transition from left tackle to left guard. Don Greco is a solid, tough right guard. Keith Dorney remains consistently masterful at right tackle. The Lions would have an above-average line if center Steve Mott recovers from injuries.

DEFENSE

Ken Fantetti is one of those underrated players who probably would be thinking of the Pro Bowl as an annual obligation if he played on a perennial playoff team. He can bury the run. He led the Lions in tackles four straight seasons before last year, when he missed the opening game because of a contract holdout and a later game because his shoulder was bleeding. A screw in his shoulder from the previous year had come loose.

Right defensive tackle Doug English has been to four Pro Bowls. William Gay replaced Al Baker at right end in 1983 and got to the quarterback just like Baker did, making the Pro Bowl with English. Gay moved to the left side and the quarterback became out of reach. Last year, Gay moved back to right end in time to lead the team with 10 sacks. English has been known to land on some quarterbacks himself. He was second to Baker and then Gay for three straight seasons until last year, when he had just five and missed the Pro Bowl assign-

Three Years at a Glance

Averages NFL Rank	OFFENSE			DEFENSE		
	1984	1983	1982	1984	1983	1982
Points	**17.7**	**21.7**	**20.1**	**25.5**	**17.9**	**19.6**
Rank	21	15	15	23	2	13
Yards	**332.4**	**321.0**	**281.6**	**332.4**	**326.0**	**302.4**
Rank	12	18	24	17	11	9
Rushing Yards	**126.1**	**136.3**	**113.6**	**113.0**	**131.5**	**94.9**
Rank	14	12	16	8	16	4
Passing Yards	**206.3**	**184.7**	**168.0**	**219.4**	**194.5**	**207.6**
Rank	13T	22	22	21	11	18
Sacks	**3.8**	**2.8**	**3.3**	**2.3**	**2.7**	**3.6**
Rank	25	14T	20T	23	13T	3T
Turnovers	**2.3**	**2.4**	**2.9**	**1.6**	**2.3**	**2.9**
Rank	13T	15T	23T	23T	16	5T
Punt Returns	**6.7**	**11.3**	**10.6**	**10.5**	**7.7**	**9.1**
Rank	22	2	7	24	12	21
Kickoff Returns	**18.2**	**19.5**	**20.8**	**20.8**	**16.1**	**19.9**
Rank	27	13	9	18	2	15
Penalty Yards	**72.8**	**61.8**	**60.9**	**61.1**	**66.4**	**67.2**
Rank	26	23	24	6	3	3

	W-L Total	Home	Road	Playoffs
1982	4-5	2-3	2-2	0-1, Lost First Round Game
1983	9-7	6-2	3-5	0-1, Lost Divisional Playoff Game
1984	4-11-1	2-5-1	2-6	None

ment. And like Fantetti, English stuffs the run.

Fantetti and English will be at new positions this year, inside linebacker and nose tackle instead of middle linebacker and defensive tackle. New defensive coordinator Wayne Fontes, from Tampa Bay, will replace one of the few remaining 4-3 defenses with a 3-4. Fantetti, English, and most of the other Lion defenders will have to get used to seeing plays develop from different angles.

However they line up, the Lions have the players to give opposing offenses a rugged road. But the sum was less than the parts last season. With virtually the same people who allowed the fewest points in the NFC in 1983, the Lions gave up 122 more points last year and ranked thirteenth in the NFC, twenty-fifth overall. Their pass rush slowed down early, when Gay was positioned briefly at left end. They had only six interceptions in the first 12 games before finishing with 14, still fewer than all but four teams.

The Lions did stop the run. Their yield of 3.5 yards per carry was the league's lowest. Fantetti was the team's defensive MVP. Alvin Hall and William Graham asserted themselves at safety, Hall leading in tackles. Jimmy Williams, a speedy right linebacker in his third season, continued to blossom.

The key to restoring the Lions' pass rush may be Fontes's plan for Michael Cofer, a 245-pound defensive end his first two seasons. Fontes will try him as a roving linebacker, looking for blitz openings. Cofer could be a load if the Lions can take advantage of his instinctive pass-rushing ability without making him take on 270-pound blockers or cover fast backs on pass routes, and the 3-4 is the vehicle for that. It also might be a help to reserve middle linebackers Steve Doig and August Curley, who would battle 1984 starter Garry Cobb for the inside spot next to Fantetti.

On the line, the eventual nose tackle might be second-year man Eric Williams, who shows great quickness coming off the ball. Curtis Green, the left tackle last season, probably would become an end.

The Lions seemed to have the league's best pair of young cornerbacks when they won the division. Bobby

William Gay

James Jones

Billy Sims

Watkins and Bruce McNorton are in their fourth seasons. But while Watkins played acceptably last year, intercepting six passes, McNorton has to persuade opponents again that he is not an inviting target.

SPECIAL TEAMS

Two years ago, the Lions ranked in the top five in both kickoff-return differential and punt-return differential, the simplest barometers of a team's success on coverage and returns. Last year, they were the only NFL team in the bottom five in both categories.

The Lions have plenty of capable return men. That's the primary job for Robbie Martin, as it was for Jenkins before Sims's injury. It also was the way Mandley earned his keep while learning at wide receiver. But they need blockers. Martin's 8.4-yard punt-return average was far below his 11.2 for the previous two seasons, and Mandley averaged a pedestrian 17.7 on kickoffs. Jenkins, at 22.0, would have ranked eleventh among NFL kickoff returners if he had had enough attempts.

Ed Murray summed up a placekicker's lot insightfully, if not happily, when he said, "Your teammates are the blood and sweat. You're the tears." Although he maintained the NFL's second-best all-time field-goal percentage, Murray missed last-minute field goals that would have beaten Minnesota and Philadelphia. Murray's string of 153 consecutive extra points is the league's longest.

Mike Black is an acceptable punter who improved his average from 41.0 to 41.6 in his second season. He needs to put more distance between his eight touchbacks and 13 kicks downed inside the 20 last year.

VETERAN ROSTER

No.	Name	Pos.	Ht.	Wt.	NFL Exp.	Birthdate	College	Games in 1984
68	Baack, Steve	T	6-3	260	2	11/16/60	Oregon	16
54	Barnes, Roosevelt	LB	6-2	228	4	8/3/58	Purdue	16
11	Black, Michael	P	6-1	197	3	1/18/61	Arizona State	16
80	Bland, Carl	WR	5-11	182	2	8/17/61	Virginia Union	3
89	Chadwick, Jeff	WR	6-3	190	3	12/16/60	Grand Valley State	16
53	Cobb, Garry	LB	6-2	227	7	3/16/57	Southern California	16
66	Cofer, Michael	DE	6-4	245	3	4/7/60	Tennessee	16
50	Curley, August	LB	6-2	226	3	1/24/60	Southern California	8
44	D'Addio, Dave	FB	6-1	229	2	7/13/61	Maryland	16
72	Dieterich, Chris	G	6-3	260	6	7/27/58	North Carolina State	16
93	Dodge, Kirk	LB	6-1	231	2	6/4/62	Nevada-Las Vegas	11
58	Doig, Steve	LB	6-2	245	4	3/28/60	New Hampshire	16
70	Dorney, Keith	T	6-5	265	7	12/3/57	Penn State	16
61	Elias, Homer	G	6-2	255	8	5/1/55	Tennessee State	12
78	English, Doug	DT	6-5	258	10	8/25/53	Texas	16
57	Fantetti, Ken	LB	6-1	232	7	4/7/57	Wyoming	14
12	Ferguson, Joe	QB	6-1	195	13	4/30/50	Arkansas	12
65	Fowler, Amos	C	6-2	253	8	2/11/56	Southern Mississippi	15
26	Frizzell, William	CB	6-2	198	2	9/8/62	North Carolina Central	16
79	Gay, William	DE	6-4	257	8	5/28/55	Southern California	16
33	Graham, William	S	5-11	191	4	9/27/59	Texas	14
67	Greco, Don	G	6-2	265	4	4/1/59	Western Illinois	16
62	Green, Curtis	DT	6-3	258	5	6/3/57	Alabama State	16
35	Hall, Alvin	S	5-10	184	5	8/12/58	Miami, Ohio	16
17	Hipple, Eric	QB	6-2	198	6	9/16/57	Utah State	8
31	Jenkins, Kenneth	RB	5-8	185	3	5/8/59	Bucknell	14
21	Johnson, Demetrious	S	5-11	190	3	7/21/61	Missouri	16
51	Jones, David	C	6-2	257	2	10/25/61	Texas	10
30	Jones, James	FB	6-2	229	3	3/21/61	Florida	16
92	King, Angelo	LB	6-0	222	5	2/10/58	South Carolina State	16
73	Laster, Don	T	6-4	278	3	12/13/58	Tennessee State	14
43	Latimer, Albert	S	5-11	181	5	10/14/57	Clemson	15
64	Lee, Larry	G	6-2	263	5	9/10/59	UCLA	15
87	Lewis, David	TE	6-3	235	2	6/8/61	California	16
14	Machurek, Mike	QB	6-0	205	4	7/22/60	Idaho State	4
82	Mandley, Pete	WR	5-9	191	2	7/29/61	Northern Arizona	15
83	Martin, Robbie	WR	5-8	178	5	12/3/58	Cal Poly-SLO	14
81	McCall, Reese	TE	6-6	245	8	6/15/56	Auburn	16
29	McNorton, Bruce	S-CB	5-10	175	4	2/28/59	Georgetown College	16
36	Meade, Mike	FB	5-10	227	4	2/12/60	Penn State	15
63	Moss, Martin	DE	6-3	255	4	12/16/58	UCLA	16
52	Mott, Steve	C	6-2	265	3	3/24/61	Alabama	6
3	Murray, Ed	K	5-9	175	6	8/29/56	Tulane	16
86	Nichols, Mark	WR	6-1	208	5	10/29/59	San Jose State	15
84	Rubick, Rob	TE	6-2	234	4	9/27/60	Grand Valley State	16
20	Sims, Billy	RB	5-11	212	6	9/18/55	Oklahoma	8
71	Strenger, Rich	T	6-7	276	2	3/10/60	Michigan	1
39	Thompson, Leonard	WR	5-11	192	11	7/28/52	Oklahoma State	16
27	Watkins, Bobby	S-CB	5-10	184	4	5/31/60	Southwest Texas State	16
76	Williams, Eric	DT	6-4	260	2	2/24/62	Washington State	12
59	Williams, Jimmy	LB	6-2	230	4	11/15/60	Nebraska	16
18	Witkowski, John	QB	6-1	205	2	6/18/62	Columbia	3

Coaching Staff

Darryl Rogers, head coach; **Bob Baker,** offensive coordinator; **Carl Battershell,** special teams, tight ends; **Don Doll,** special assignments; **Wayne Fontes,** defensive coordinator; **Paul Lanham,** receivers; **Bill Muir,** offensive line; **Mike Murphy,** linebackers; **Rex Norris,** defensive line; **Willie Shaw,** defensive backs; **Ivy Williams,** offensive backs.

1985 Schedule

Preseason

Aug. 9	BUFFALO	8:00
Aug. 16	at Seattle	7:30
Aug. 25	CINCINNATI	8:00
Aug. 29	at Philadelphia	TBA

Regular Season

Sept. 8	at Atlanta	1:00
Sept. 15	DALLAS	1:00
Sept. 22	at Indianapolis	12:00
Sept. 29	TAMPA BAY	1:00
Oct. 6	at Green Bay	12:00
Oct. 13	at Washington	1:00
Oct. 20	SAN FRANCISCO	1:00
Oct. 27	MIAMI	1:00
Nov. 3	at Minnesota	12:00
Nov. 10	at Chicago	12:00
Nov. 17	MINNESOTA	4:00
Nov. 24	at Tampa Bay	1:00
Nov. 28	N.Y. JETS (Thanks.)	12:30
Dec. 8	at New England	1:00
Dec. 15	GREEN BAY	1:00
Dec. 22	CHICAGO	1:00

1984 Results

Sept. 2	SAN FRANCISCO	27-30
Sept. 9	at Atlanta*	27-24
Sept. 16	at Tampa Bay	17-21
Sept. 23	MINNESOTA	28-29
Sept. 30	at San Diego	24-27
Oct. 7	DENVER	7-28
Oct. 14	TAMPA BAY*	13-7
Oct. 21	at Minnesota	16-14
Oct. 28	at Green Bay	9-41
Nov. 4	PHILADELPHIA*	23-23
Nov. 11	at Washington	14-28
Nov. 18	at Chicago	14-16
Nov. 22	GREEN BAY (Thanks.)	31-28
Dec. 2	at Seattle	17-38
Dec. 10	L.A. RAIDERS (Mon.)	3-24
Dec. 16	CHICAGO	13-30

1985 Draft Choices

1. Lomas Brown—6, T, Florida
2. Kevin Glover—34, C, Maryland
3. James Johnson—62, LB, San Diego State
4. Kevin Hancock—90, LB, Baylor
5. Joe McIntosh—118, RB, North Carolina State
6. Stan Short—146, G, Penn State
7. Tony Staten—174, DB, Angelo State
8. Scotty Caldwell—202, RB, Texas-Arlington
9. June James—230, LB, Texas
10. Clayton Beauford—258, WR, Auburn
11. Kevin Harris—286, DB, Georgia
12. Mike Weaver—314, G, Georgia

GREEN BAY PACKERS

Forrest Gregg wanted to start this season as soon as the last one ended. He had just finished his first year as the Green Bay Packers' coach. The transition difficulties, the miserable 1-7 start, were well behind him. Gregg was riding high on the crest of the 7-1 second half that he expected to carry the Packers back to their rightful NFL prominence this season.

Instead, he told the players to watch every playoff game they could. "I know how I feel watching the playoff games—a little sick in my stomach," Gregg said. "I wanted them to think about what they would give to be there. What sacrifice would they make to be there? I think that could make an impression about what it's worth—more than the money. People like recognition, and the sheer joy of being involved in those playoffs is hard to put into words. It's a great feeling. I would not want them to start another one without me."

The way the Packers plodded through their first several games under Gregg, they seemed prepared to take a blindfold and cigarette from opponents. After winning their opener, they scored 20 points in losing the next three. But the next four losses were within a touchdown, and the last two were impressive showings against playoff-bound Denver and Seattle. From there, the Packers won seven of their last eight and finished with an 8-8 record.

The schedule was softer in the second half, but two of the victories were against playoff teams. Four victories, including one against the Rams, were by 24 points or more. After averaging 17 points in their first eight games, the Packers averaged 32 in their last eight.

"The first thing was to get this team headed back in

Wide receiver James Lofton puts speed into Packers' attack.

Forrest Gregg

the right direction," Gregg said. "I think we've done that."

The Packers no longer are just an offensive team racing opponents up and down the field. They can play defense, too. Their defense improved from last in NFL total yardage to sixteenth.

They didn't patch all their holes in Gregg's first season. They still need a breakaway running back. Their pass rush still is sporadic. Of their 44 sacks, defensive linemen made only 24. But as Gregg said, "Our needs are more subtle than they were a year ago."

"Under Forrest," said tight end Paul Coffman, "the Packers will be a championship team again."

OFFENSE

Aside from quarterback Lynn Dickey's continuing health, the most important thing for the Packers' offense could be for running back Eddie Lee Ivery to play his first full season since 1980. It wasn't a coincidence that Ivery got his first starting call in the ninth game, when the Packers began turning their season around. Ivery isn't the speed back he was before two knee operations, but he may be quicker off the ball. He had all of his 552 rushing yards in the last eight games. The Packers' rushing average improved from 94 yards a game in the first half-season to 159 in the second half.

Since a knee injury to Ivery in the opening game of 1981, the Packers were a team that looked at the run as a device to give their receivers a rest. Dickey kept them competitive by throwing, but he did it out of necessity, which is not as effective as doing it out of choice.

"I'd gladly trade all my yards passing for yards rushing," Dickey said after a 4,000-yard season in 1983. "If we had all those yards rushing, we still would have been playing at the end of the year. You get a back running for a hundred yards and you keep the ball away from the other team, and your risk of turnover is much less."

Lacking the breakaway threat, the Packers' running game makes do with a volume backfield. Four different backs averaged at least 4.1 yards per carry last year, including Ivery's 5.6. Gerry Ellis led the team with 581 yards (4.7 per carry), playing both running back positions. Jessie Clark had 331 of his 375 yards in the first eight games, before his elbow injury. Harlan Huckleby was effective in sporadic use. The disappointment was Del Rodgers, going into his third year with perhaps his last chance to show he can be the one to inject some speed into the Packers' ground game.

Line coach Jerry Wampfler didn't make many friends early in the season. He was downright dogmatic about which techniques Packers blockers would use. He also didn't care whose backside he blistered in the course of critically changing habits. "After you've done something a certain way for a long time, it's tough to unlearn it and learn a different way," said 1984 Pro Bowl center Larry McCarren, whose streak of 162 straight games ended with a neck injury. After the linemen adjusted to Wampfler, McCarren said they played as well as they ever had in his 12 seasons. Besides opening running lanes, the linemen allowed only 11 sacks in the last eight games, compared to 31 in the first eight.

Gregg, a Pro Football Hall of Fame tackle, spent much of the season collecting castoff linemen to set up a competitive free-for-all at most positions this summer. The safest bet to retain his starting job is right guard Ron Hallstrom, whom Gregg says has the size and speed to be all-pro. Hallstrom, 6-6 and 283 pounds, was a first-round choice in 1982 who washed out at tackle and nearly was cut in 1984 training camp. Gregg started him with 6-5, 282-pound Tim Huffman at guard in

Alphonso Carreker   *Lynn Dickey*   *Mike Douglass*

the fourth game in an effort to put some bulk in the line.

Other aspiring inside linemen include 6-5, 270-pound guard Keith Uecker, a midseason waiver acquisition; 6-5, 272-pound Blake Moore, who's expected to give McCarren a stern run for his starting job, and holdover guards Leotis Harris and Dave Drechsler. Huffman also could challenge Karl Swanke at left tackle. Greg Koch is reasonably secure at right tackle.

Pass protection is especially important to the Packers because of both Dickey's immobility and history of injuries. The team's steady improvement toward the middle of last season coincided with the healing of Dickey's back. But the quarterback situation is not as desperate now that Randy Wright, a sixth-round rookie, has proved himself a capable reserve. Third-stringer Rich Campbell is doubtful in the Packers' plans.

James Lofton remains one of those few legitimate sprinters at wide receiver who has the route-running skills slower players must master. His 1,361 yards on 62 catches last year were a career high, and his 22.0-yard average per catch led all NFL regulars. "He's the only receiver I know who fights for the ball like a defensive back," Bears cornerback Leslie Frazier said.

Phillip Epps finished last season at flanker ahead of John Jefferson, who cleaned out his locker to demonstrate his desire to be traded. They both wound up with 26 catches, but Epps led in yardage 435-339 and in touchdowns 3-0. Beyond that, the outside receiving corps is thin.

The Packers could relieve that problem through judicious use of tight ends if Gary Lewis recovers from a lung disorder. Ed West replaced him creditably last year as the number-two tight end, scoring four touchdowns with his six catches. The starter is Coffman, one of the league's best tight ends and a resourceful receiver who has become a Pro Bowl regular despite ordinary speed.

DEFENSE

The Packers' defense doesn't try to outfox other teams anymore. It doesn't try to run around and guess with them, which often resulted in running ball carriers down from behind. Instead of angling away from

Three Years at a Glance

Averages NFL Rank	OFFENSE			DEFENSE		
	1984	1983	1982	1984	1983	1982
Points Rank	**24.4** 7	**26.8** 5	**25.1** 5T	**19.3** 10	**27.4** 26	**18.8** 10
Yards Rank	**340.6** 6	**385.8** 2	**323.3** 12	**330.7** 16	**400.2** 28	**300.8** 8
Rushing Yards Rank	**126.2** 13	**112.9** 21	**120.1** 12	**134.1** 20	**165.1** 26	**103.6** 6
Passing Yards Rank	**214.4** 9	**272.8** 12	**203.2** 14	**196.6** 8	**235.1** 24	**197.2** 12
Sacks Rank	**2.6** 9T	**2.6** 11	**3.6** 23T	**2.8** 15T	**2.6** 16T	**2.2** 17T
Turnovers Rank	**2.3** 15T	**3.1** 26	**2.9** 23T	**2.6** 5T	**1.9** 24T	**2.6** 12T
Punt Returns Rank	**7.3** 20	**8.0** 15	**7.6** 18	**8.0** 10	**8.9** 16	**10.6** 24
Kickoff Returns Rank	**20.3** 9	**16.9** 27	**19.5** 22	**16.0** 1	**18.3** 7	**19.4** 13
Penalty Yards Rank	**57.2** 19	**40.5** 3	**38.1** 5	**70.6** 1	**60.3** 4	**69.9** 1

	W-L Total	**Home**	**Road**	**Playoffs**
1982	5-3-1	3-1	2-2-1	1-1, Lost Second Round Game
1983	8-8	5-3	3-5	None
1984	8-8	5-3	3-5	None

blockers to fill holes, Packers linemen and linebackers take on blockers nose-to-nose.

The new defensive style helped lower the Packers' opponents' per-game averages last year by 49 passing yards, 21 rushing yards, three first downs, six plays, and eight points. The Packers jumped from twenty-fourth in the league to eighth in pass defense. Against the run, they cut their touchdowns allowed from 28 to 14. Total touchdowns were down from 55 to 34.

Defensive linemen Alphonso Carreker and Donnie Humphrey and free safety Tom Flynn started as rookies. Inside linebacker Randy Scott, cornerback Tim Lewis, and strong safety Mark Murphy were full-season starters for the first time. Between the fresh blood in the lineup and the aggressive instructions on the chalkboard, the Packers were attacking offenses.

Linebackers still are the strength of the unit. Mike Douglass is the quick, big-play man on the right side who led the team with nine sacks. John Anderson, on the other side, is skillful in pass coverage and heavy-duty against the run. George Cumby and Scott plug up the middle. Cliff Lewis and Rich Wingo are reserves who could start for other teams, and second-year man John Dorsey reminded Gregg of Ray Nitschke with his abandon in training camp practices.

The pass rush will improve if Ezra Johnson recovers from his second back operation in two offseasons. The nine-year veteran has averaged 15 sacks in his three full seasons, including 14½ in 1983, but his bad back limited him to sporadic action and seven sacks last season.

At left end, Carreker came to the NFL with a pass-rushing reputation but played the run well enough to lead Packers linemen in tackles. Humphrey started at the other end and moved inside on passing downs, but his play at nose tackle in the final game encouraged the coaches to consider moving him there permanently. Terry Jones and ex-Giant Bill Neill alternated quarters there last season. Humphrey's right end spot most likely would be filled by Robert Brown, whose five sacks were second among linemen.

Flynn led the conference with nine interceptions and

Tom Flynn

Ron Hallstrom

Larry McCarren

the team with three fumble recoveries; Lewis's seven interceptions included a 99-yard return; Murphy led the team in tackles, and Mark Lee had his best season at left corner. All that happened with veteran safeties on injured reserve, Johnnie Gray most of the season, and Mike McCoy all season.

SPECIAL TEAMS

Al Del Greco has turned out to be everything the Packers had hoped for Eddie Garcia, which was to be a worthy replacement for Jan Stenerud. Garcia was the sad story of the season in Green Bay, missing six of nine field-goal tries as the pressure of filling Stenerud's shoes squeezed him out of the league. Del Greco replaced him and made his first eight attempts. He finished 9 for 12, including 4 for 6 beyond 40 yards.

Bucky Scribner's 42.3-yard punting average was eighth in the NFL and third among punters on cold-weather fields. His good hang time helped the Packers limit opponents to an 8.0-yard average on punt returns, tenth lowest in the league.

The bad news was that the Packers' punt returners averaged only 7.3 yards. Epps, the primary man, managed just 6.9, with Flynn giving it a try, too.

Kickoffs were more pleasant. The coverage team limited opponents to a league-low average of 16.0 yards, and Rodgers averaged 21.6 for the Packers, including a 97-yard touchdown. "I take kickoff returns three yards at a time," says Rodgers, who ranked thirteenth but was just one yard away from eighth. "Once I get three yards, I look for three more." Epps and Huckleby chipped in with return averages around 19 yards. The team average of 20.3 yards ranked ninth in the NFL.

VETERAN ROSTER

No.	Name	Pos.	Ht.	Wt.	NFL Exp.	Birthdate	College	Games in 1984
59	Anderson, John	LB	6-3	229	8	2/14/56	Michigan	16
93	Brown, Robert	DE	6-2	250	4	5/21/60	Virginia Tech	16
	Brunner, Scott	QB	6-5	200	6	3/24/57	Delaware	0
19	Campbell, Rich	QB	6-4	219	5	12/21/58	California	3
58	Cannon, Mark	C	6-3	258	2	6/14/52	Texas-Arlington	16
76	Carreker, Alphonso	DE	6-6	260	2	5/25/62	Florida State	14
88	Cassidy, Ron	WR	6-0	180	6	7/23/57	Utah State	15
33	Clark, Jessie	FB	6-0	233	3	1/3/60	Arkansas	11
82	Coffman, Paul	TE	6-3	225	7	3/29/56	Kansas State	14
21	Crouse, Ray	RB	5-11	214	2	3/16/59	Nevada-Las Vegas	16
52	Cumby, George	LB	6-0	224	6	7/5/56	Oklahoma	16
10	Del Greco, Al	K	5-10	195	2	3/2/62	Auburn	9
98	DeLuca, Tony	NT	6-4	250	2	11/16/60	Rhode Island	1
12	Dickey, Lynn	QB	6-4	203	15	10/19/49	Kansas State	15
99	Dorsey, John	LB	6-2	235	2	8/31/60	Connecticut	16
53	Douglass, Mike	LB	6-0	214	8	3/15/55	San Diego State	16
61	Drechsler, Dave	G	6-3	264	3	7/18/60	North Carolina	16
31	Ellis, Gerry	FB	5-11	225	6	11/12/57	Missouri	16
85	Epps, Phillip	WR	5-10	155	4	11/11/59	Texas Christian	16
41	Flynn, Tom	S	6-0	195	2	3/24/62	Pittsburgh	15
65	Hallstrom, Ron	T	6-6	283	4	6/11/59	Iowa	16
69	Harris, Leotis	G	6-1	265	7	6/28/55	Arkansas	0
27	Hayes, Gary	CB	5-10	180	2	8/19/57	Fresno State	16
78	Hoffman, Gary	T	6-7	282	2	9/28/61	Santa Clara	1
38	Hood, Estus	CB	5-11	189	8	11/14/55	Illinois	16
25	Huckleby, Harlan	RB	6-1	201	6	12/30/57	Michigan	16
74	Huffman, Tim	T	6-5	282	5	8/31/59	Notre Dame	16
79	Humphrey, Donnie	DE	6-3	275	2	4/20/61	Auburn	16
40	Ivery, Eddie Lee	RB	6-0	214	6	7/30/57	Georgia Tech	10
83	Jefferson, John	WR	6-1	204	8	2/3/56	Arizona State	13
90	Johnson, Ezra	DE	6-4	259	9	10/2/55	Morris Brown	13
43	Jones, Daryll	S	6-0	190	2	3/23/62	Georgia	16
63	Jones, Terry	NT	6-2	253	8	11/8/56	Alabama	16
68	Koch, Greg	T	6-4	276	9	6/14/55	Arkansas	15
22	Lee, Mark	CB	5-11	188	6	3/20/58	Washington	16
56	Lewis, Cliff	LB	6-1	224	5	11/9/59	Southern Mississippi	16
81	Lewis, Gary	TE	6-5	234	5	12/30/58	Texas-Arlington	3
26	Lewis, Tim	CB	5-11	191	3	12/18/61	Pittsburgh	16
80	Lofton, James	WR	6-3	197	8	7/5/56	Stanford	16
94	Martin, Charles	DE	6-4	270	2	8/31/59	Livingston	16
54	McCarren, Larry	C	6-3	251	13	11/9/51	Illinois	12
29	McCoy, Mike	S	5-11	190	9	8/16/53	Colorado	0
28	McLeod, Mike	S	6-0	180	2	5/4/58	Montana State	11
60	Moore, Blake	C-G	6-5	272	6	5/8/58	Wooster	11
37	Murphy, Mark	S	6-2	201	5	4/22/58	West Liberty State	16
77	Neill, Bill	NT	6-4	267	5	3/15/59	Pittsburgh	16
51	Prather, Guy	LB	6-2	229	5	3/28/58	Grambling	16
35	Rodgers, Del	RB	5-10	202	3	6/22/60	Utah	14
55	Scott, Randy	LB	6-1	222	5	1/31/59	Alabama	16
13	Scribner, Bucky	P	6-0	202	3	7/11/60	Kansas	16
67	Swanke, Karl	T	6-6	262	6	12/29/57	Boston College	15
84	Taylor, Lenny	WR	5-10	179	2	2/15/61	Tennessee	2
70	Uecker, Keith	G-T	6-5	270	4	6/29/60	Auburn	6
86	West, Ed	TE	6-1	242	2	8/2/61	Auburn	16
50	Wingo, Rich	LB	6-1	227	6	7/16/56	Alabama	16
16	Wright, Randy	QB	6-2	194	2	1/12/61	Wisconsin	8

Coaching Staff

Forrest Gregg, head coach; **Lew Carpenter,** receivers; **Virgil Knight,** strength and conditioning; **Dick Modzelewski,** defensive coordinator, defensive line; **Herb Paterra,** linebackers, special teams; **George Priefer,** special teams, defensive assistant; **Ken Riley,** secondary; **George Sefcik,** offensive backfield; **Bob Schnelker,** offensive coordinator; **Jerry Wampfler,** offensive line.

1985 Schedule

Preaseason

Aug. 10	at Dallas	8:00
Aug. 17	at N. Y. Giants	8:00
Aug. 24	ATLANTA at Milwaukee	7:00
Aug. 31	N.Y. JETS	7:00

Regular Season

Sept. 8	at New England	1:00
Sept. 15	N.Y. GIANTS	3:00
Sept. 22	N.Y. JETS at Milw.	3:00
Sept. 29	at St. Louis	12:00
Oct. 6	DETROIT	12:00
Oct. 13	MINNESOTA at Milw.	12:00
Oct. 21	at Chicago (Mon.)	8:00
Oct. 27	at Indianapolis	1:00
Nov. 3	CHICAGO	12:00
Nov. 10	at Minnesota	12:00
Nov. 17	NEW ORLEANS at Milw.	12:00
Nov. 24	at L.A. Rams	1:00
Dec. 1	TAMPA BAY	12:00
Dec. 8	MIAMI	12:00
Dec. 15	at Detroit	1:00
Dec. 22	at Tampa Bay	1:00

1984 Results

Sept. 2	ST. LOUIS	24-23
Sept. 9	at L.A. Raiders	7-28
Sept. 16	CHICAGO	7-9
Sept. 23	at Dallas	6-20
Sept. 30	at Tampa Bay*	27-30
Oct. 7	SAN DIEGO	28-34
Oct. 15	at Denver (Mon.)	14-17
Oct. 21	SEATTLE at Milw	24-30
Oct. 28	DETROIT	41-9
Nov. 4	at New Orleans	23-13
Nov. 11	MINNESOTA at Milw	45-17
Nov. 18	L.A. RAMS at Milw	31-6
Nov. 22	at Detroit (Thanks.)	28-31
Dec. 2	TAMPA BAY	27-14
Dec. 9	at Chicago	20-14
Dec. 16	at Minnesota	38-14

1985 Draft Choices

1. Ken Ruettgers—7, T, Southern California, from Cleveland through Buffalo
1. Choice to Buffalo
2. Choice to Buffalo
3. Rich Moran—71, G, San Diego State
4. Walter Stanley—98, WR, Mesa, Colo.
5. Brian Noble—125, LB, Arizona State
6. Mark Lewis—155, TE, Texas A&M
7. Eric Wilson—171, LB, Maryland, from Minnesota
7. Gary Ellerson—182, RB, Wisconsin
8. Ken Stills—209, DB, Wisconsin
9. Morris Johnson—239, G, Alabama A&M
10. Ronnie Burgess—266, DB, Wake Forest
11. Joe Shield—294, QB, Trinity, Conn.
12. Jim Meyer—323, P, Arizona State

MINNESOTA VIKINGS

By the end of last season, outdoorsman Bud Grant's new way of life away from football was looking better and better. Hunting and fishing had to seem like pretty good ways for Vikings fans to spend autumn Sunday afternoons. Anything but watching another team stuff and mount their beloved Vikings.

It was an ugly season, especially at the end. Instead of improving under first-year head coach Les Steckel, Minnesota lost its last six games by an average score of 40-13. Its last three opponents had 31 points by halftime. The Vikings' 3-13 record was their poorest since 1962, their second season. They gave up 484 points and 59 touchdowns, both team records and league highs.

Now it's Bud Grant to the rescue, and he might as well have ridden into town on a white horse, so joyous was the relief over his rehiring as Vikings coach.

Grant had gotten 12 of his 17 Vikings teams into the playoffs, retiring with a 151-87-5 record and four Super Bowl appearances.

But things were different then. Today's Vikings are not the kind of team a coach takes over to pad his won-lost record. The team did not fall apart overnight because Steckel shook it too hard. Even Grant won't be able to make everything all right just by shortening training camp and sharpening his glare.

In Grant's last six seasons, the Vikings went 44-44-1, without a season better than 9-7. Early-round drafting mistakes and tight salary budgets had kept them from replacing the players who won four conference championships in eight years through 1976.

Steckel was best known for his harsh training camp, which began with two injuries in an obstacle-course

Jan Stenerud, 42, gives Vikings a scoring weapon.

Bud Grant

competition and intensified at a dizzying pace. When the season ended, linebacker Scott Studwell said, "I believe this team burned out six weeks ago, physically and mentally ran out of gas. Six weeks of full pads in training camp and full pads every day in the season wears on you."

Grant has rejoined an uncommonly young Vikings team that had 18 new players at the end of last season. The 1984 team also was hampered by injuries that cost 27 players full games and allowed only four to start every game.

OFFENSE

Quarterback Tommy Kramer will be back. That sounds nice to Vikings fans. It also sounds familiar. He was back last year, too, after a serious 1983 knee injury, but he missed seven of the last eight games with a shoulder injury. The Vikings also lacked an above-average receiver and the manpower to withstand injuries in a thin offensive line. They wound up using tackles at guard and guards at center. They scored more than 20 points only five times last season, twice in their last 10 games.

Kramer was one of the league's most feared clutch performers when he was healthy. His rehabilitation in the offseason is an encouraging sign for his return at full-strength, but it's a fact of NFL life that a team is lucky if it doesn't have to call on its second-string quarterback to win some games.

The Vikings thought they had such a reserve in Archie Manning, one of the league's most likable players. Chicago Bears defenders spoke of him with compassion and admiration after sacking him 11 times in one game. But Manning is an old 36. He took untold beatings as a young quarterback in New Orleans, and trips to Houston and Minnesota put him through more adversity. Steckel eventually replaced him with Wade Wilson, who could better avoid the pass rushes that flowed through Vikings linemen. But Wilson, an eighth-round draft choice in 1981, had never been projected as more than emergency help. He threw 11 interceptions and only five touchdowns while building just a 52.7 rating.

Only Atlanta and New England allowed their quarterbacks to be sacked more times than Minnesota's 64. Starting linemen missed 28 games because of injuries, but guard Terry Tausch and tackles Steve Riley and Tim Irwin each started all 16. Tausch, a natural tackle, played guard in place of Brent Boyd, who missed the entire season. Curtis Rouse, a 318-pound tackle, played guard for Wes Hamilton when Hamilton missed five games. Two other guards, Jim Hough and then Ron Sams, had to play center because Dennis Swilley retired.

Center was a problem in particular. Sams hadn't played the position since junior high school. Against the Bears, he contributed to the 11 sacks by frequently rolling the ball to Manning in Shotgun formation.

At the other line positions, the Vikings have enough players. The question is, how many good players? The one bright spot in the Vikings' passing game was 5-foot 8-inch wide receiver Leo Lewis, who led the team with four touchdowns. Lewis averaged 17.7 yards on his 47 catches, two more team-leading figures. He had caught only 22 passes in his previous three seasons, but he became a mainstay after Steckel cut Terry LeCount and inexplicably ignored Sammy White. Mike Jones had 38 catches as the starting flanker, but Dwight Collins beat him out at the end of the season.

This season is a crossroads for White, a 10-year veteran. He finished last season with 21 catches. He had only 9 receptions in his last seven games before missing the last three with a lacerated tongue. Steckel

Charlie Johnson

Tommy Kramer

Doug Martin

switched him from flanker to split end so Jones could start, then phased him out after Lewis emerged.

Tight end Steve Jordan was another Viking who tripled his career-reception total, with 38 in his third season. Jordan, who won Steckel's pre-training "Iron Man" competition on the obstacle course, figures to be at one of the team's most competitive positions this summer. Joe Senser, Bob Bruer, Don Hasselbeck, and Mike Mularkey all have been NFL starters.

The Vikings' running game could be the best since Chuck Foreman's heyday in the mid-1970s, even though they had just 10 rushing touchdowns last year—from no fewer than seven individuals. Alfred Anderson ran for 773 yards as a rookie. Darrin Nelson and Ted Brown contributed another combined 848 in an unusually diverse attack. Anderson will have to improve on his 17 receptions in Grant's offense; Nelson's 3.1-yard average was unbecoming for a former sprinter.

DEFENSE

Most of all, the Vikings need a pass rush. They need a lot of things, but a pass rush is essential these days, when quarterbacks are routinely passing for 300 yards. If receivers have time to run around until they're open, you lose by 45-17, 34-3, and 51-7, as the Vikings did in November and December. Minnesota had 25 sacks last season, fewest in the NFL and barely half their total of 47 the previous year.

Professional quarterbacks can play catch with their targets if they have time. Vikings opponents completed 65.1 percent of their passes, a league high. And the Vikings' 11 interceptions were the fewest in the NFL. Their defense dropped from sixth to twenty-sixth in passing yards allowed (236 per game) and it ranked last overall by allowing 397 yards per game and 6.0 yards per play.

From 1975 through 1980, four of the Vikings' top six draft choices were defensive linemen. So why are the Vikings no longer convening over fallen quarterbacks?

As it turns out, those four choices were not all inspired ones. Steckel cut James (Duck) White, with an eight-year average of 3.6 sacks, in training camp last

Three Years at a Glance

Averages NFL Rank	OFFENSE			DEFENSE		
	1984	1983	1982	1984	1983	1982
Points Rank	**17.3** 24	**19.8** 18	**20.8** 13	**30.3** 28	**21.8** 17	**22.0** 19
Yards Rank	**294.8** 25	**313.7** 20	**319.9** 14	**397.0** 28	**342.9** 19	**321.7** 19
Rushing Yards Rank	**115.3** 18	**113.0** 20	**101.3** 22	**160.8** 27	**161.5** 25	**113.3** 14
Passing Yards Rank	**179.5** 22	**200.7** 13	**218.6** 5	**236.2** 26	**181.4** 6	**208.3** 19
Sacks Rank	**4.0** 26	**2.7** 12T	**2.4** 11	**1.6** 28	**2.9** 11	**3.3** 9T
Turnovers Rank	**2.6** 23T	**2.0** 5	**1.9** 5T	**1.8** 22	**3.0** 4T	**2.3** 17T
Punt Returns Rank	**7.0** 21	**8.8** 12	**8.2** 13	**8.9** 16	**7.4** 9	**5.9** 8
Kickoff Returns Rank	**20.6** 7	**21.6** 3	**21.2** 6	**21.7** 24	**19.9** 18	**17.4** 3
Penalty Yards Rank	**47.6** 8	**46.8** 5T	**55.1** 17	**65.4** 4	**47.4** 21	**44.3** 22

	W-L Total	Home	Road	Playoffs
1982	5-4	4-1	1-3	1-1, Lost Second Round Game
1983	8-8	3-5	5-3	None
1984	3-13	2-6	1-7	None

year. Then Randy Holloway was dismissed after eight games. Holloway had 5 of the Vikings' 14 sacks at the time, easily leading the team. The Cardinals vouched for Steckel's decision, though, picking Holloway up but cutting him a few weeks later. The other once-bright prospects, Mark Mullaney and Doug Martin, limped through injury seasons with three sacks between them.

Mullaney has had a good career—unspectacular and usually under-appreciated—but he is going into his eleventh season and has been able to play in only 14 of 32 games in the last two years. On the other hand, Martin should be entering his prime. He has played just five seasons. He began two of them with extended holdouts, and the one last year segued into ankle and knee injuries. In his other three seasons, Martin led the Vikings in sacks.

Nose tackle Charlie Johnson, always considered primarily a run-stuffer, had five sacks for the Vikings in 1984. He is dependable, having missed only two of 105 games since his rookie year, 1977.

Neil Elshire, going into in his fifth season, showed promise at Mullaney's right end spot. Otherwise, the Vikings' defensive line consisted of Tampa Bay castoff Hasson Arbubakrr and rookies Greg Smith and John Haines, the player Steckel was accommodating when he cut Holloway.

Behind the linemen, the Vikings are much better off inside than outside. Scott Studwell is their best linebacker. Walker Lee Ashley, the other inside backer, began blossoming last season while the overall defense was wilting. The safeties are solid, with John Swain on the weakside and Tommy Hannon on the strongside. Hannon was the only defender to start every game.

But the starting outside linebackers were Robin Sendlein, who hasn't played up to his second-round expectations of the 1981 draft, and veteran Matt Blair, who is in his twelfth year and on the downside of a great career. At cornerback, the Vikings had to start second-year safety Joey Browner on the left side, where he was no match for the fastest wide receivers. Rufus Bess led the team in interceptions at right corner, but he had only three. It would help two positions if Willie Teal can

Darrin Nelson

Steve Riley

Scott Studwell

return to cornerback after a disappointing season that was interrupted by a knee injury. That would free Browner for safety. The Vikings allowed a league-high 35 touchdown passes.

SPECIAL TEAMS

Jan Stenerud will be 42 in November, but Stenerud has given quite a boot to age prejudice. He has made 82.3 percent of his field-goal attempts since Kansas City cut him in 1980. He solved the problem of chronic pain in his left ankle with a special brace last year. Already the NFL's all-time field-goal leader, Stenerud is 389 points away from George Blanda's career scoring record.

He was the trade steal of last season, but the Vikings couldn't take full advantage of him. He tried only two field goals in the last five games. He made them both, of course; he made all but 3 of his 23 tries.

Stenerud did beat Detroit almost single-footedly when he kicked five field goals in a 29-28 victory. He didn't miss any tries closer than 46 yards, and his field goal from 54 yards away was the NFL's second-longest of the season.

With Greg Coleman punting, the Vikings have an excellent kicking pair. Coleman's net average of 36.6 yards led the NFC.

Despite the influx of young players, traditionally special-teams hustlers, the Vikings ranked sixteenth in punt coverage and twenty-fourth in kickoff coverage. Nelson was a kickoff-return threat, ranking sixth in the league with a 22.8-yard average, but Steckel's decision to use him on punt returns was not a success. Nelson averaged a substandard 7.8 yards returning punts, while Lewis added a 7.6 average.

VETERAN ROSTER

No.	Name	Pos.	Ht.	Wt.	NFL Exp.	Birthdate	College	Games in 1984
46	Anderson, Alfred	RB	6-1	213	2	8/4/61	Baylor	16
69	Arbubakrr, Hasson	DE	6-4	250	3	12/9/60	Texas Tech	4
58	Ashley, Walker Lee	LB	6-0	240	3	7/28/60	Penn State	15
21	Bess, Rufus	CB	5-9	185	7	3/13/56	South Carolina State	16
59	Blair, Matt	LB	6-5	235	12	9/20/50	Iowa State	11
62	Boyd, Brent	G	6-3	275	5	3/23/57	UCLA	0
23	Brown, Ted	RB	5-10	210	7	2/2/57	North Carolina State	13
47	Browner, Joey	S	6-2	205	3	5/15/60	Southern California	16
82	Bruer, Bob	TE	6-5	240	6	5/22/54	Mankato State	0
8	Coleman, Greg	P	6-0	185	9	9/9/54	Florida A&M	16
84	Collins, Dwight	WR	6-1	208	2	8/23/61	Pittsburgh	16
43	Colter, Jeff	CB	5-10	171	2	4/23/61	Kansas	16
73	Elshire, Neil	DE	6-6	260	5	3/8/58	Oregon	12
64	Feasel, Grant	C-T	6-8	278	3	6/28/60	Abilene Christian	15
50	Fowlkes, Dennis	LB	6-2	230	3	3/11/61	West Virginia	14
25	Greene, Marcellus	CB	6-0	184	2	12/12/57	Arizona	14
90	Haines, John	NT	6-6	260	2	12/16/61	Texas	8
61	Hamilton, Wes	G	6-3	270	10	4/24/53	Tulsa	4
45	Hannon, Tom	S	5-11	195	9	3/5/55	Michigan State	16
60	Hernandez, Matt	T	6-6	262	3	10/16/61	Purdue	13
51	Hough, Jim	G	6-2	275	8	8/4/56	Utah State	9
76	Irwin, Tim	T	6-6	285	5	12/13/58	Tennessee	16
65	Johnson, Charlie	NT	6-3	275	9	2/17/52	Colorado	16
52	Johnson, Dennis	LB	6-3	235	6	6/19/58	Southern California	16
89	Jones, Mike	WR	5-11	176	3	4/14/60	Tennessee State	16
83	Jordan, Steve	TE	6-3	230	4	1/10/61	Brown	14
9	Kramer, Tommy	QB	6-2	205	9	3/7/55	Rice	9
39	Lee, Carl	CB-S	5-11	185	3	4/6/61	Marshall	16
87	Lewis, Leo	WR	5-8	170	5	9/17/56	Missouri	16
4	Manning, Archie	QB	6-3	211	15	5/9/49	Mississippi	6
56	Martin, Chris	LB	6-2	230	3	12/19/60	Auburn	16
79	Martin, Doug	DE	6-3	255	6	5/22/57	Washington	13
54	McNeill, Fred	LB	6-2	230	12	5/6/52	UCLA	13
86	Mularkey, Mike	TE	6-4	245	3	11/19/61	Florida	16
77	Mullaney, Mark	DE	6-6	245	11	4/30/53	Colorado State	7
20	Nelson, Darrin	RB	5-9	180	4	1/2/59	Stanford	15
49	Nord, Keith	S	6-0	195	6	3/13/57	St. Cloud State	0
36	Rice, Allen	RB-S	5-10	198	2	4/5/62	Baylor	14
78	Riley, Steve	T	6-6	260	12	11/23/52	Southern California	16
68	Rouse, Curtis	G	6-3	305	4	7/13/60	Tenn.-Chattanooga	16
67	Sams, Ron	G	6-3	255	2	4/12/61	Pittsburgh	12
57	Sendlein, Robin	LB	6-3	225	5	12/1/58	Texas	15
81	Senser, Joe	TE	6-4	235	6	8/18/56	West Chester State	8
91	Smith, Gregory	NT	6-3	261	2	10/22/59	Kansas	16
3	Stenerud, Jan	K	6-2	190	19	11/26/42	Montana State	16
55	Studwell, Scott	LB	6-2	230	9	8/27/54	Illinois	16
29	Swain, John	CB	6-1	195	5	9/4/59	Miami	15
66	Tausch, Terry	T	6-5	275	4	2/5/59	Texas	16
37	Teal, Willie	CB	5-10	195	6	12/20/57	Louisiana State	11
24	Turner, Maurice	RB	5-11	199	2	9/10/60	Utah State	13
34	Wagoner, Dan	S	5-10	180	3	12/12/59	Kansas	5
85	White, Sammy	WR	5-11	195	10	3/16/54	Grambling	13
11	Wilson, Wade	QB	6-3	210	5	2/1/59	East Texas State	8

Coaching Staff

Bud Grant, head coach; **Tom Batta,** defensive assistant; **Jerry Burns,** assistant head coach, offensive coordinator; **Pete Carroll,** defensive backs; **Bob Hollway,** defensive coordinator; **Andy MacDonald,** receivers; **John Michels,** offensive line; **Floyd Reese,** linebackers; **Dick Rehbein,** kicking teams, tight ends; **Marc Trestman,** running backs; **Paul Wiggin,** defensive line.

1985 Schedule

Preseason

Aug. 10	at Miami	8:00
Aug. 17	PITTSBURGH	7:00
Aug. 24	SEATTLE	7:00
Aug. 30	at Denver	7:00

Regular Season

Sept. 8	SAN FRANCISCO	12:00
Sept. 15	at Tampa Bay	4:00
Sept. 19	CHICAGO (Thurs.)	7:00
Sept. 29	at Buffalo	1:00
Oct. 6	at L.A. Rams	1:00
Oct. 13	Green Bay at Milw.	12:00
Oct. 20	SAN DIEGO	12:00
Oct. 27	at Chicago	12:00
Nov. 3	DETROIT	12:00
Nov. 10	GREEN BAY	12:00
Nov. 17	at Detroit	4:00
Nov. 24	NEW ORLEANS	12:00
Dec. 1	at Philadelphia	1:00
Dec. 8	TAMPA BAY	3:00
Dec. 15	at Atlanta	1:00
Dec. 22	PHILADELPHIA	12:00

1984 Results

Sept. 2	SAN DIEGO	13-42
Sept. 9	at Philadelphia	17-19
Sept. 16	ATLANTA	27-20
Sept. 23	at Detroit	29-28
Sept. 30	SEATTLE	12-20
Oct. 7	at Tampa Bay	31-35
Oct. 14	at L.A. Raiders	20-23
Oct. 21	DETROIT	14-16
Oct. 28	at Chicago	7-16
Nov. 4	TAMPA BAY	27-24
Nov. 11	vs. Green Bay at Milw.	17-45
Nov. 18	at Denver	21-42
Nov. 25	CHICAGO	3-34
Nov. 29	WASHINGTON (Thurs.)	17-31
Dec. 8	at San Francisco (Sat.)	7-51
Dec. 16	GREEN BAY	14-38

1985 Draft Choices

1. Choice to Houston
1. Chris Doleman—4, LB, Pittsburgh, from Atlanta
2. Issiac Holt—30, DB, Alcorn State
3. Kirk Lowdermilk—59, C, Ohio State
3. Tim Meamber—60, LB, Washington, from Atlanta
3. Tim Long—66, T, Memphis State, from San Diego
4. Buster Rhymes—85, WR, Oklahoma
4. Kyle Morrell—106, DB, Brigham Young, from L.A. Rams
5. Mark MacDonald—115, G, Boston College
6. Steve Bono—142, QB, UCLA
6. Tim Newton—164, NT, Florida, from L.A. Raiders
7. Choice to Green Bay
8. Nikita Blair—198, LB, Texas-El Paso
9. Jaime Covington—227, RB, Syracuse
10. Juan Johnson—254, WR, Langston, Oklahoma
11. Tim Williams—283, DB, North Carolina A&T
12. Byron Jones—310, NT, Tulsa

TAMPA BAY BUCCANEERS

Tampa Bay owner Hugh Culverhouse had other interviews scheduled when he talked to Leeman Bennett. He canceled them. Culverhouse had found his man. Bennett would be the Buccaneers' head coach.

Bennett came highly recommended by the man who had fired him two seasons earlier, Atlanta Falcons owner Rankin Smith, Sr. Smith called firing Bennett his biggest mistake in 19 years of owning the team. Bennett's Falcons had gone 46-41 from 1977-1982, and 1-3 in the only three playoff appearances in their history. In Tampa Bay, Bennett says he is taking over a "much better" team than the one he assumed in Atlanta.

Although they were 6-10 last year, the Buccaneers were within a touchdown in seven of their defeats. After a 3-3 start, they lost seven of eight, then won their last two by 17 and 20 points.

The Buccaneers' perennial downfall has been injuries. Last season was an improvement on the previous year's M*A*S*H unit, but the loss of linebackers Hugh Green and Cecil Johnson, safety Cedric Brown, and cornerback Mike Washington fairly gutted the defense.

Bennett will coach the Buccaneers much as he coached the Falcons. Former Falcons lieutenants Jimmy Raye and Doug Shively will coordinate the offense and defense, respectively. Bennett's tactics are most similar to Seattle coach Chuck Knox, for whom he worked with the Los Angeles Rams in the mid-1970s.

Shively's most recent job was at San Diego, where he was defensive line coach under former Tampa Bay defensive coordinator Tom Bass. He is well-versed on the 3-4 defense that has been so effective in Tampa. From his Atlanta background, Shively could be ex-

James Wilder is Buccaneers' all-purpose running back.

Leeman Bennett

pected to add more aggressive risk-taking to the Buccaneers, who for years were the extreme example of a basic defense that laid back to stop the big play.

Raye's latest job was offensive coordinator for the Rams. He won't have Eric Dickerson at Tampa Bay, but he'll have James Wilder, another Pro Bowl workhorse from a one-back offense. Wilder set an NFL record with 407 carries, 90.6 percent of the Buccaneers' workload at running back. Counting runs and catches, Wilder had 13 games in triple figures and 2,229 total yards.

The Rams' one-man offense doesn't entirely reflect Raye's ideas about moving the ball. He prefers spicing a ball-control ground game with frequent long passes, as the Falcons had done under Bennett and the Rams tried last season until their personnel dictated otherwise. In tight end Jimmie Giles and wide receivers Kevin House and Gerald Carter, the Buccaneers have receivers who can go long in a hurry.

Bennett and Knox are the NFL's pre-eminent disciples of statistician Bud Goode, who gorges a computer on statistics to determine the ones that correlate most with winning or losing. That means tailoring a club for excellent special teams, high turnover differentials, and a ground game and play-action passes that set each other up. Emphasis on special teams will be something new for the Buccaneers. They lost more turnovers last year than all but three teams, with a minus-11 differential.

OFFENSE

Tampa Bay is coming off its best offensive season ever. Last year the Buccaneers found a quarterback, a downfield running mate for House, a steady combination of offensive linemen, and an offense to take full advantage of Wilder. They set team records with 335 points, 40 touchdowns, 17 rushing touchdowns, 20 passing touchdowns, 344 first downs, 332.6 yards per game, 221.6 passing yards per game, 334 pass completions, and a .593 completion percentage. They needed only

68 punts, 14 fewer than their previous low. From last in the league in 1983, the Buccaneers improved their total offense ranking to tenth.

The search for a quarterback to replace departed Doug Williams was costly. First, Tampa Bay tried Jack Thompson. He cost them the first pick in the 1984 draft, which they might have used to keep Steve Young out of the USFL. (Tampa Bay owns the rights to the former BYU All-America quarterback.) Then they traded last offseason for Steve DeBerg, who cost them a fourth-round choice last year and a number-two this year. DeBerg won the starting job early in the season and had a passer rating of 79.3, the Buccaneers' highest ever. He threw more touchdowns than interceptions, 19-18, completing 60.5 percent of his passes for 3,554 yards.

Young still is on the horizon. Tampa Bay secured his rights in last year's supplemental draft. DeBerg, who has been replaced by Joe Montana in San Francisco and John Elway in Denver, says, "I just kind of prepared these teams for the savior to come."

For now, the savior in Tampa Bay is DeBerg, whose background is 49ers coach Bill Walsh's short passing game, the airborne off-tackle play. "You throw little flares and dump passes to James Wilder and you can almost eliminate the defensive linemen," DeBerg said. "He can get six or seven yards, and that's an excellent running play."

Wilder averaged a respectable 8.0 yards on his 85 catches, which were the most by an NFL back. He also ran for 1,544 yards and 13 touchdowns. Counting his four 1983 starts at tailback, Wilder has averaged 101

Keith Browner

Steve DeBerg

Hugh Green

rushing yards, 26 carries, five catches, and 41 receiving yards per game in the 20 games he has played since moving from fullback.

But Wilder is virtually the extent of the Tampa Bay running game. DeBerg was the second-leading rusher last year with 59 yards. Adger Armstrong, the fullback in the two-back alignment, caught 22 passes. The rest of the backs are in the fine print on the team's statistics sheet. The annual intriguing possibility is running back James Owens, but he is coming off a knee injury and has gone six seasons without making his Olympic-hurdler speed conspicuous.

House's 13.2-yards-per-catch average was the best indication that the Buccaneers' passing game tightened its reins under DeBerg. His previous four-year career average had been 18.8, with single-season averages ranging from 15.6 to 22.1.

The Buccaneers had three receivers with 60 catches or more, just like Miami. Carter's 60 were one more than his previous four-year total.

At tight end, Giles's production has slipped each of the last two seasons, to the point that the nine-year veteran of three Pro Bowls may be going into a put-up-or-shut-up year. He had just 24 catches, a 12.9-yard average, and two touchdowns. Jerry Bell's numbers were 29 receptions for a 13.6 average and 4 touchdowns at the motion tight end in his first season as a regular. But Bennett always has made good use of speedy tight ends, and Giles still is fast.

A pleasant suprise on offense was right tackle Ron Heller, a fourth-round draft choice out of Penn State who made most all-rookie teams. Heller's play helped make up for the disappointments of Kelly Thomas and Gene Sanders, who ultimately lost his left tackle job to Ken Kaplan.

At guard and center, the Buccaneers are overflowing. Randy Grimes, who could start at either position finished last season at center after Steve Wilson's injury. Sean Farrell may be a season away from the Pro Bowl at right guard, ex-Steeler Steve Courson still is a reliable left guard, and ex-Bengals guard Glenn Bujnoch is more than capable in reserve.

Three Years at a Glance

Averages NFL Rank	OFFENSE			DEFENSE		
	1984	1983	1982	1984	1983	1982
Points	**20.9**	**15.1**	**17.6**	**23.8**	**23.8**	**19.8**
Rank	14	27	18	21	22	15
Yards	**332.6**	**279.8**	**321.7**	**342.1**	**337.3**	**271.3**
Rank	10	28	13	20	16	3
Rushing Yards	**111.0**	**84.6**	**105.8**	**139.6**	**130.1**	**117.6**
Rank	19	27	19	25	15	18
Passing Yards	**221.6**	**195.3**	**215.9**	**202.6**	**207.2**	**153.8**
Rank	8	15	6	13	19	4
Sacks	**2.8**	**3.1**	**1.2**	**2.0**	**2.6**	**2.8**
Rank	11T	19T	1T	25T	15	13
Turnovers	**2.7**	**2.3**	**2.6**	**2.0**	**2.6**	**2.3**
Rank	26T	10	14T	27T	12	17T
Punt Returns	**6.1**	**7.1**	**5.7**	**8.6**	**10.2**	**8.3**
Rank	27	22	23	14	23	16
Kickoff Returns	**19.9**	**19.3**	**16.6**	**19.9**	**20.8**	**21.8**
Rank	11	14	28	12	22	23
Penalty Yards	**54.7**	**52.0**	**33.0**	**67.4**	**49.9**	**36.1**
Rank	16	14	3	2	17	27

	W-L Total	Home	Road	Playoffs
1982	5-4	4-1	1-3	0-1, Lost First Round Game
1983	2-14	1-7	1-7	None
1984	6-10	6-2	0-8	None

DEFENSE

Any defense with Hugh Green and Lee Roy Selmon can be dangerous. Selmon, a Pro Bowl starter the last six years, has been such a force at right end that the Buccaneers have been able to put eight men in pass coverage and still make quarterbacks scurry for cover. Green, a Pro Bowl starter in two of his four seasons, has a knack for showing up where the ball is.

In the eight games Green missed because of his car accident last season, the Buccaneers won twice. They were 4-4 with Green behind Selmon at right linebacker. "When we had both of them on the same side, we were able to do things to help the other side," said former defensive coordinator Wayne Fontes. "We blitzed more, put more pressure on the quarterback, and did more slanting."

Selmon didn't have his usual double figures in sacks, but the tackles who had to block him said it wasn't because his play was tapering off in his ninth season. It was because offenses were willing to do whatever it took to seal him away from the quarterback. The only other threat was nose tackle David Logan, who ranked second in tackles and probably would have been to some Pro Bowls by now if he had played for a winning team. Selmon led the team with eight sacks, as its total fell from 42 to 32, fewer than all but two teams.

John Cannon started at left end last season after the Buccaneers gave up on Booker Reese, who had cost them their first-round pick in 1983. Cannon is adequate, but he doesn't divert attention from Logan and Selmon.

The injuries to Green and Johnson forced Tampa Bay to go much of the season with two rookies at outside linebacker. Chris Washington and Keith Browner both showed promise amid their youthful mistakes. They make linebacker by far the team's deepest area, with Danny Spradlin, Richard Wood, and Robert Thompson. The incumbent starters inside are Scot Brantley and leading tackler Jeff Davis.

Brown's return from a knee injury would restore some flexibility. Beasley Reece and Brown both can play left and right safety, alternating the free-safety po-

Ron Heller *Kevin House* *Lee Roy Selmon*

sition to confuse defenses. Mark Cotney, a former starter, replaced Brown capably but is purely a strong safety. He is most effective against the run, although he led the team with five interceptions.

Jeremiah Castille, the Buccaneers' first truly fast cornerback in years, continued to progress last year in his second season. John Holt has been capable on the right side, but Tampa Bay is looking for fleet second-year man Fred Acorn to make his presence felt this season. Beyond them, the veteran depth is limited to retreads Norris Thomas and Maurice Harvey.

SPECIAL TEAMS

The Buccaneers may have their first reliable place-kicker since Garo Yepremian. Obed Ariri was 19 for 26 on field goals and scored a team-record 95 points. He started shakily, but that was largely because Tampa Bay went eight games before letting him try a field goal shorter than 40 yards. In the last eight games, Ariri was 13 for 15, including 12 for 13 inside 40 yards.

Frank Garcia led NFC punters with a 42.2-yard average in 1983, when he was a 26-year-old rookie who had been cut five times in the NFL and once in the USFL. His falloff to 41.9 last year dropped him to sixth in the conference, nineteenth overall. Worse was his nine touchbacks, almost equaling the 12 he landed inside the 20. But nearly half his 68 punts—32—were not returned.

Leon Bright's 7.5-yard punt return average can't be tolerated again. But it was better than the sub-3.0 averages of the other returners who tried. The problem might be with the blockers. Michael Morton's 22.0-yard average on kickoff returns was acceptable, and Owens is always a threat, although he averaged just 21.0.

VETERAN ROSTER

No.	Name	Pos.	Ht.	Wt.	NFL Exp.	Birthdate	College	Games in 1984
27	Acorn, Fred	CB	5-10	180	2	3/17/61	Texas	16
2	Ariri, Obed	K	5-8	170	2	4/7/56	Clemson	16
46	Armstrong, Adger	RB	6-0	225	6	6/21/57	Texas A&M	15
82	Bell, Jerry	TE	6-5	230	4	3/7/59	Arizona State	16
83	Bell, Theo	WR	6-0	195	9	12/21/53	Arizona	15
71	Braggs, Byron	DE	6-4	270	5	10/10/59	Alabama	14
52	Brantley, Scot	LB	6-1	230	6	3/7/59	Florida	16
29	Bright, Leon	RB	5-9	190	5	5/19/55	Florida State	12
34	Brown, Cedric	S	6-2	200	9	5/6/54	Kent State	9
57	Browner, Keith	LB	6-5	240	2	1/24/62	Southern California	16
77	Bujnoch, Glenn	G	6-6	265	10	12/20/53	Texas A&M	8
78	Cannon, John	DE	6-5	260	4	7/30/60	William & Mary	16
86	Carroll, Jay	TE	6-4	230	2	11/8/61	Minnesota	16
87	Carter, Gerald	WR	6-1	190	6	6/19/57	Texas A&M	16
28	Carver, Melvin	RB	5-11	225	4	7/14/59	Nevada-Las Vegas	5
23	Castille, Jeremiah	CB	5-10	175	3	1/15/61	Alabama	16
33	Cotney, Mark	S	6-0	205	10	6/26/52	Cameron State	16
72	Courson, Steve	G	6-1	270	8	10/1/55	South Carolina	14
31	Curry, Craig	S	6-0	190	2	7/20/61	Texas	5
75	Darns, Phil	DE	6-3	245	2	7/27/59	Mississippi Valley	2
58	Davis, Jeff	LB	6-0	230	4	1/26/60	Clemson	16
17	DeBerg, Steve	QB	6-3	205	9	1/19/54	San Jose State	16
25	Dierking, Scott	RB	5-11	225	9	5/24/55	Purdue	8
81	Dixon, Dwayne	WR	6-1	205	2	8/2/62	Florida	10
62	Farrell, Sean	G	6-3	260	4	5/25/60	Penn State	15
44	Ferguson, Vagas	RB	6-0	205	4	3/6/57	Notre Dame	0
5	Garcia, Frank	P	6-0	205	3	6/5/57	Arizona	16
88	Giles, Jimmie	TE	6-3	240	9	11/8/54	Alcorn State	14
53	Green, Hugh	LB	6-2	225	5	7/27/59	Pittsburgh	8
60	Grimes, Randy	C-G	6-4	265	3	7/20/60	Baylor	10
73	Heller, Ron	T	6-6	270	2	8/25/62	Penn State	14
21	Holt, John	CB	5-11	180	5	5/14/59	West Texas State	15
89	House, Kevin	WR	6-1	185	6	12/20/57	Southern Illinois	16
91	Janatta, John	T	6-7	275	2	4/10/61	Illinois	0
56	Johnson, Cecil	LB	6-2	235	9	8/9/55	Pittsburgh	8
79	Kaplan, Ken	T	6-4	270	2	1/12/60	New Hampshire	16
16	Kiel, Blair	QB	6-0	200	2	11/29/61	Notre Dame	10
76	Logan, David	NT	6-2	250	7	10/25/56	Pittsburgh	16
67	Morgan, Karl	NT	6-1	255	2	2/23/61	UCLA	13
20	Morton, Michael	RB	5-8	180	4	2/6/60	Nevada-Las Vegas	16
26	Owens, James	RB	5-11	200	7	7/5/55	UCLA	4
38	Peoples, George	RB	6-0	215	4	8/25/60	Auburn	6
43	Reece, Beasley	S	6-1	195	10	3/18/54	North Texas State	16
74	Sanders, Gene	T	6-3	285	7	11/10/56	Texas A&M	16
63	Selmon, Lee Roy	DE	6-3	250	10	10/20/54	Oklahoma	16
55	Spradlin, Danny	LB	6-1	235	5	3/3/59	Tennessee	15
70	Thomas, Kelly	T	6-6	270	3	9/9/60	Southern California	10
41	Thomas, Norris	CB	6-0	180	9	5/3/54	Southern Mississippi	15
84	Thomas, Zach	WR	6-0	185	3	9/8/60	South Carolina State	14
14	Thompson, Jack	QB	6-3	220	6	5/18/56	Washington State	5
59	Thompson, Robert	LB	6-3	230	3	2/4/60	Michigan	9
51	Washington, Chris	LB	6-4	225	2	3/6/62	Iowa State	16
32	Wilder, James	RB	6-3	220	5	5/12/58	Missouri	16
50	Wilson, Steve	C	6-4	270	10	5/19/54	Georgia	16
85	Witte, Mark	TE	6-3	235	3	12/3/59	North Texas State	16

Coaching Staff

Leeman Bennett, head coach; **Greg Brown,** offensive-film assistant; **Joe Dinge,** strength; **Kim Helton,** offensive line; **Don Lawrence,** defensive line; **Vic Rapp,** running backs; **Jimmy Raye,** offensive coordinator-quarterbacks; **Dick Roach,** defensive backs; **Larry Seiple,** receivers; **Doug Shively,** defensive coordinator-linebackers; **Howard Tippett,** special teams-linebackers.

1985 Schedule

Preseason

Aug. 10	PITTSBURGH	8:00
Aug. 17	ATLANTA	8:00
Aug. 24	at New Orleans	7:00
Aug. 30	WASHINGTON	8:00

Regular Season

Sept. 8	at Chicago	12:00
Sept. 15	MINNESOTA	4:00
Sept. 22	at New Orleans	12:00
Sept. 29	at Detroit	1:00
Oct. 6	CHICAGO	1:00
Oct. 13	L.A. RAMS	1:00
Oct. 20	at Miami	4:00
Oct. 27	NEW ENGLAND	1:00
Nov. 3	at N.Y. Giants	1:00
Nov. 10	ST. LOUIS	1:00
Nov. 17	at N.Y. Jets	1:00
Nov. 24	DETROIT	1:00
Dec. 1	at Green Bay	12:00
Dec. 8	at Minnesota	3:00
Dec. 15	INDIANAPOLIS	1:00
Dec. 22	GREEN BAY	1:00

1984 Results

Sept. 2	at Chicago	14-34
Sept. 9	at New Orleans	13-17
Sept. 16	DETROIT	21-17
Sept. 23	at N.Y. Giants*	14-17
Sept. 30	GREEN BAY*	30-27
Oct. 7	MINNESOTA	35-31
Oct. 14	at Detroit*	7-13
Oct. 21	CHICAGO	9-44
Oct. 28	at Kansas City	20-24
Nov. 4	at Minnesota	24-27
Nov. 11	N.Y. GIANTS	20-17
Nov. 18	at San Francisco	17-24
Nov. 25	L.A. RAMS	33-34
Dec. 2	at Green Bay	14-27
Dec. 9	ATLANTA	23-6
Dec. 16	N.Y. JETS	41-21

1985 Draft Choices

1. Ron Holmes—8. DE. Washington
2. Choice to Houston through Denver
3. Ervin Randle—64. LB. Baylor
4. Mike Heaven—92. DB. Illinois
5. Choice to N.Y. Jets
6. Choice to Cincinnati
7. Mike Prior—176. DB. Illinois State
8. Phil Freeman—204. WR. Arizona
9. Steve Calabria—232. QB. Colgate
10. Donald Igwebuike—260. K. Clemson
11. James Williams—288. RB. Memphis State
12. Jim Rockford—316. DB. Oklahoma
12. Jim Melka—330. LB. Wisconsin. from L.A. Rams

ATLANTA FALCONS

It was five years ago, if memory serves correctly, that a prominent national weekly sports magazine took a grand leap of faith and named the Falcons as the team of the 1980s, pro football's next dynasty. No one in the Falcons' front office ever made that same claim, so they can't be held accountable for failing to land on the same mantel as the Pittsburgh Steelers.

On the other hand, nobody expected the 1980s to treat the Falcons so rudely, either. Halfway through a decade of what could modestly be described as frustrating, Atlanta now will settle for being included in pro football's next playoff pool.

Just a winning record might suffice, because the team that Leeman Bennett took to a 12-4 record and a division title in 1980 slipped to 7-9, 5-4, 7-9, and finally 4-12 a year ago. Having fired Bennett after the 1982 season, the Falcons coaxed assistant head coach Dan Henning, from the Washington Redskins' Super Bowl coaching staff, the following year.

Now, entering his third year in Atlanta, Henning and the Falcons are looking for something that reminds them of the Redskins' success. They certainly didn't find it last year. Trouble started when all-pro running back William Andrews tore up his knee in training camp. It escalated when Billy (White Shoes) Johnson crumpled to the ground in week 6 of the season when the Falcons still were a respectable 3-3. Then came the crescendo—nine consecutive losses by an average margin of 15 points.

An offense that had been one of the NFL's most balanced, wheezed to its sick bed during 1984 as injuries mounted. The Falcons scored more than 14 points just

Gerald Riggs gives Falcons a double-edged running game.

Dan Henning

once in nine consecutive losses. And the gripes that filled half-empty Atlanta Fulton County Stadium reached an unprecedented decibel level. Wasn't Dan Henning hired because he had a great reputation as an offensive coach?

Yes, but he wasn't a faith healer. Without Johnson and Andrews and with quarterback Steve Bartkowski growing more immobile with every sack, the Falcons' offense ranked nineteenth in the league.

The defense showed signs of improving and finished fifteenth overall in the league. There were, nonetheless, signs of failure: a 35-10 loss at Pittsburgh, a 35-14 loss at Cincinnati. In week 16, the Falcons finally won a game. But only 15,582 fans came to see them beat Philadelphia 26-10.

"You look back at last season," Henning said, "and the key—discounting the loss of William Andrews, which we knew going into the season—was that we only had all our people healthy for only one game."

And the key in 1985?

"Getting all our people healthy," Henning said. And keeping them that way.

OFFENSE

This is where the improvement must start, as quickly as possible. Bartkowski is coming off a knee injury, sustained on the last of 10 sacks against Cleveland in week 12 of the 1984 season. As a free agent, he may not fit into the Falcons' plans or vice versa, no matter how healthy he is.

When Bartkowski was injured, Atlanta had high hopes for back-up quarterback Mike Moroski, who had been Bartkowski's understudy since 1979. But Moroski was less than inspiring when he got his chance, finishing the season with just two touchdown passes and nine interceptions, though passing for 784 yards in his four games as a starter.

By the final game of the season, the ball was in the hands of free agent David Archer, who took over in relief of Moroski against Philadelphia, and completed 11 of 18 passes for 181 yards. Archer at least earned more careful study for himself in training camp this year. As insurance, the Falcons signed former Duke star Ben Bennett, their sixth-round pick in 1984 who originally had opted for the USFL.

Even without Andrews, the Falcons found a legitimate ball carrier in Gerald Riggs (353 carries, 1,486 yards, 13 touchdowns). "He filled William Andrews's basic role," Henning said, "and should be better with experience." The Falcons picked up more insurance in case Andrews can't come back by obtaining all-purpose back Joe Washington from the Redskins.

More bad news will follow if Billy Johnson can't make it back from knee surgery. Without Johnson as the big-play Nickel receiver, the Falcons converted only 35 percent of their third-down situations and lost a genuine team leader.

Wide receiver Stacey Bailey, a fourth-year Falcon, became the prime target. His 67 catches for 1,138 yards made him only the third receiver in Falcons history to surpass 1,000 yards receiving. Alfred Jackson, Bailey's bookend, had his best year ever with 52 receptions and 731 yards.

So why did the Falcons struggle so much offensively? The answer lies primarily in pass protection. Bartkowski was sacked 40 times before going down for the count against Cleveland. In all, the Falcons allowed 67 sacks for losses of 496 yards.

Injuries sidelined guard R.C. Thielemann and Pro Bowl tackle Mike Kenn. Right tackle, a spot that veteran Warren Bryant once owned, became a void of in-

Stacey Bailey

Rick Bryan

Billy Johnson

experience after he was waived. Center Jeff Van Note, playing in what seemed like his hundredth NFL season (it really was his sixteenth), was a rock. But just in case Van Note can't make it through another year, the Falcons signed former University of Georgia center Wayne Radloff, who was all-USFL in 1984.

Henning didn't point any fingers during the Falcons' offensive demise. Not even when the team scored no more than two touchdowns in any of those nine consecutive losses. But there was some fallout when the season finally ended.

The Falcons offered offensive line coach Bob Fry a job in the front office, while also indicating he was free to pursue other coaching opportunities. Henning then hired Larry Beightol, who had been offensive coordinator at the University of Missouri. Steve Crosby, the Falcons' quarterback and receivers' coach in 1984, left Atlanta to join the Cleveland Browns. Henning said he will spend more time on the field coaching the Falcons' quarterbacks in 1985.

"More like I did in 1983," Henning said of a year when the Falcons had a legitimate two-prong attack. If the Falcons can land a starter at offensive tackle or wide receiver with the fourth pick in the draft, on-the-field coaching should be a little more fun for all the coaches than it was in 1984.

DEFENSE

The Falcons think they might have learned something from the Chicago Bears' defense in 1984. And if the new trend is toward multiple defensive fronts and a guess-who's-blitzing-now approach, Atlanta seems ready to embrace it.

"We're going to try to be a more pressure-type defense," said defensive coordinator John Marshall. "That doesn't always mean you're blitzing one or two guys. But it does mean more of an attacking defense."

The Falcons improved more defensively in 1984 than a 4-12 record would indicate. First-round draft pick Rick Bryan found a spot at tackle and stayed there for 16 games. James Britt moved from safety to corner and played competently.

A defense that was ranked twenty-fifth in the league

Three Years at a Glance

Averages NFL Rank	OFFENSE			DEFENSE		
	1984	1983	1982	1984	1983	1982
Points Rank	**17.6** 22	**23.1** 10	**20.3** 14	**23.9** 22	**24.3** 23	**22.1** 20
Yards Rank	**315.3** 19	**351.8** 8	**329.2** 9	**329.9** 15	**364.1** 25	**316.4** 14T
Rushing Yards Rank	**124.6** 15	**139.0** 11	**131.2** 9	**134.6** 21	**144.3** 22	**116.0** 17
Passing Yards Rank	**190.6** 20	**212.8** 11	**198.0** 18	**195.4** 7	**219.8** 20	**200.4** 13
Sacks Rank	**4.2** 28	**3.4** 24T	**2.8** 16T	**2.4** 22	**1.9** 26T	**2.0** 21T
Turnovers Rank	**2.6** 23T	**1.8** 3	**2.3** 11T	**2.0** 27T	**1.9** 26	**2.8** 7T
Punt Returns Rank	**6.4** 24	**10.6** 6	**11.4** 3	**10.7** 25	**5.3** 2	**8.2** 13
Kickoff Returns Rank	**19.5** 16	**18.8** 20	**17.7** 27	**21.9** 27	**20.2** 19	**22.6** 24
Penalty Yards Rank	**63.2** 24	**50.4** 12	**72.8** 27	**51.3** 16	**44.4** 24T	**61.0** 7

	W-L Total	**Home**	**Road**	**Playoffs**
1982	5-4	2-3	3-1	0-1, Lost First Round Game
1983	7-9	4-4	3-5	None
1984	4-12	2-6	2-6	None

in 1983 soared to fifteenth. A modest improvement, but improvement nevertheless. But the defense was only twenty-first against the run, which had much to do with opponents jumping to early leads and playing safe in the second half of games.

The problem was that the Falcons rarely mounted a strong pass rush, sacking opposing quarterbacks only 38 times. Also, they made only 12 interceptions. The Falcons' starting cornerbacks totaled just three. Still, their pass defense ranked seventh in the NFL.

One training camp experiment this year will be to flop Bryan to defensive end and move Mike Pitts to Bryan's tackle spot. Pitts is the more physical player; Bryan has better quickness. Any move that can improve the pass rush, and thus the Falcons' secondary coverage, will be welcome.

While Britt played well at one corner, former number-one pick Bobby Butler didn't quite live up to expectations. Fighting the reputation as a big-hit-no-cover defense, the Falcons will open the free safety job for competition between incumbent Tom Pridemore and second-year man Scott Case. At strong safety, Kenny Johnson led the Falcons with five interceptions. No one else had more than two.

The Falcons survived some injuries at linebacker and should be better in 1985 if only because of experience. The problems of the 1984 season allowed them to look at young linebackers such as Jeff Jackson and Thomas Benson.

"Somewhere along the line, you have to quit shooting for gaining experience," Marshall said. "This is a critical year for us. It usually takes five years to say, 'We're solid.' But in the third year, now, is when you should start to see some positive trends.

"We've improved. If you took our 1983 offense and combined it with our 1984 defense you'd have a playoff team. A heckuva playoff team."

SPECIAL TEAMS

Injuries had a domino effect on the Falcons' special teams in 1984. The lack of depth in the offense became even thinner when the football exchanged hands.

The grand plan was for Billy Johnson to use 1984 as a

Kenny Johnson   *Mike Kenn*   *Mick Luckhurst*

platform to assault the all-time punt return yardage record, but his knee injury stopped that. The next candidate was Sylvester Stamps, who ended up with a pulled hamstring. The Falcons averaged 6.4 yards per punt return, third poorest in the league. Their punt coverage team allowed 10.7 yards per return, fourth highest in the league. The Rams returned one for a touchdown on a Monday night ("A coach's nightmare," said special teams' coach Ted Fritsch).

Other statistics were more favorable. Placekicker Mick Luckhurst hit 20 of 27 field goal tries and beat the Rams in Anaheim with a last-second field goal. Punter Ralph Giacomarro had a 42.0 average and put 13 of his 68 punts out of bounds inside the 20.

"When you get key people hurt, it forces your back-up people to take on extra duties," Fritsch said. "As a result that took away from our special teams. We had to simplify things but still stay sophisticated enough so that it wasn't so easy to scout us.

The biggest concern for the Falcons is getting Billy Johnson back from knee surgery. Johnson was averaging 10.1 yards per return before his season ended on a punt return against the Rams. If Johnson is out of the picture, the Falcons will have to choose from among Floyd Hodge, wide receiver Willie Curran, and former Washington Redskins Smurf Virgil Seay.

Last season, at a time when the Falcons' approach was all-out pressure on the punter, Seay returned seven punts for a total of 12 yards.

"He almost got his head taken off a few times," Fritsch said. "I had to sit down with him to tell him it wasn't always going to be like that."

VETERAN ROSTER

No.	Name	Pos.	Ht.	Wt.	NFL Exp.	Birthdate	College	Games in 1984
31	Andrews, Wiliam	RB	6-0	213	6	12/25/55	Auburn	0
16	Archer, Dave	QB	6-2	203	2	2/15/62	Iowa State	2
39	Austin, Cliff	RB	6-0	190	3	3/2/60	Clemson	15
82	Bailey, Stacey	WR	6-0	157	4	2/10/60	San Jose State	16
10	Bartkowski, Steve	QB	6-4	218	11	11/12/52	California	11
69	Benish, Dan	DT	6-5	265	3	11/21/61	Clemson	15
87	Benson, Cliff	TE	6-4	234	2	8/28/61	Purdue	16
53	Benson, Thomas	LB	6-2	235	2	9/6/61	Oklahoma	16
26	Britt, James	CB	6-0	185	3	9/12/60	Louisiana State	16
77	Bryan, Rick	DE	6-4	260	2	3/20/62	Oklahoma	16
73	Burley, Gary	DT	6-3	290	10	12/8/52	Pittsburgh	12
23	Butler, Bobby	CB	5-11	175	5	5/28/59	Florida State	15
21	Cain, Lynn	RB	6-1	205	7	10/16/55	Southern California	15
25	Case, Scott	S	6-0	178	2	5/17/62	Oklahoma	16
70	Chapman, Mike	C-G	6-4	250	2	2/10/61	Texas	4
88	Cox, Arthur	TE	6-2	255	3	2/5/61	Texas Southern	16
89	Curran, William	WR	5-11	175	4	12/30/59	UCLA	14
50	Curry, Buddy	LB	6-4	228	6	6/4/58	North Carolina	16
71	Dufour, Dan	T-C	6-5	280	3	10/18/60	UCLA	6
58	Frye, David	LB	6-2	213	3	6/21/61	Purdue	16
34	Gaison, Blane	S	6-1	188	5	5/13/58	Hawaii	15
1	Giacomarro, Ralph	P	6-1	194	3	1/17/61	Penn State	16
75	Harris, Roy	DT	6-2	266	2	3/26/61	Florida	15
30	Haworth, Steve	S	6-0	188	3	9/16/61	Oklahoma	5
83	Hodge, Floyd	WR	6-0	195	4	7/18/59	Utah	12
8	Holly, Bob	QB	6-2	205	4	6/1/60	Princeton	0
85	Jackson, Alfred	WR	6-0	190	8	8/3/55	Texas	16
51	Jackson, Jeff	LB	6-1	228	2	10/9/61	Auburn	16
81	Johnson, Billy	WR	5-9	177	10	1/27/52	Widener	6
37	Johnson, Kenny	S	5-11	172	6	1/7/58	Mississippi State	16
78	Kenn, Mike	T	6-7	266	8	2/9/56	Michigan	14
54	Kuykendall, Fulton	LB	6-4	228	11	6/10/53	UCLA	16
80	Landrum, Mike	TE	6-2	231	2	11/6/61	Southern Mississippi	15
55	Levenick, Dave	LB	6-3	220	3	5/29/59	Wisconsin	8
18	Luckhurst, Mick	K	6-2	183	5	3/31/58	California	16
52	Malancon, Rydell	LB	6-1	219	2	1/10/62	Louisiana State	7
49	Matthews, Allama	TE	6-2	230	3	8/24/61	Vanderbilt	6
62	Miller, Brett	T	6-7	285	3	10/2/58	Iowa	15
15	Moroski, Mike	QB	6-4	203	7	9/4/57	Cal-Davis	16
64	Pellegrini, Joe	G-C	6-4	258	4	4/8/57	Harvard	15
74	Pitts, Mike	DT	6-5	270	3	9/25/60	Alabama	14
27	Pridemore, Tom	S	5-11	186	8	4/29/56	West Virginia	16
72	Provence, Andrew	DE	6-3	260	3	3/8/61	South Carolina	16
59	Rade, John	LB	6-1	225	3	8/31/60	Boise State	7
56	Richardson, Al	LB	6-3	222	6	9/23/57	Georgia Tech	16
42	Riggs, Gerald	RB	6-1	230	4	11/6/60	Arizona State	15
67	Sanders, Eric	T	6-7	280	5	10/22/58	Nevada-Reno	10
61	Scully, John	G	6-6	255	5	8/2/58	Notre Dame	16
41	Seay, Virgil	WR	5-8	180	5	1/1/58	Troy State	14
48	Small, Gerald	CB	5-11	192	8	8/10/56	San Jose State	16
65	Smith, Don	DE	6-5	270	7	5/9/57	Miami	16
84	Stamps, Sylvester	RB	5-7	166	2	2/24/61	Jackson State	10
68	Thielemann, R. C.	G	6-4	262	9	8/12/55	Arkansas	16
86	Tuttle, Perry	WR	6-0	180	4	8/2/59	Clemson	8
32	Tyrrell, Tim	RB	6-1	201	2	2/19/61	Northern Illinois	11
57	Van Note, Jeff	C	6-2	250	17	2/7/46	Kentucky	16
	Washington, Joe	RB	5-10	179	10	9/24/53	Oklahoma	7

Coaching Staff

Dan Henning, head coach; **Larry Beightol,** offensive line; **George Dostal,** strength and conditioning; **Sam Elliott,** running backs; **Ted Fritsch,** special teams; **Bob Harrison,** receivers; **Bobby Jackson,** linebackers; **Joe Madden,** defensive assistant, research and development; **John Marshall,** defensive coordinator; **Garry Puetz,** assistant offensive line; **Dan Sekanovich,** assistant head coach, defensive line; **Jack Stanton,** defensive backfield.

1985 Schedule

Preseason

Aug. 10	WASHINGTON	8:00
Aug. 17	at Tampa Bay	8:00
Aug. 24	Green Bay at Milw.	7:00
Aug. 30	MIAMI	8:00

Regular Season

Sept. 8	DETROIT	1:00
Sept. 15	at San Francisco	1:00
Sept. 22	DENVER	1:00
Sept. 29	at L.A. Rams	1:00
Oct. 6	SAN FRANCISCO	1:00
Oct. 13	at Seattle	1:00
Oct. 20	NEW ORLEANS	1:00
Oct. 27	at Dallas	12:00
Nov. 3	WASHINGTON	1:00
Nov. 10	at Philadelphia	1:00
Nov. 17	L.A. RAMS	1:00
Nov. 24	at Chicago	12:00
Dec. 1	L.A. RAIDERS	4:00
Dec. 8	at Kansas City	12:00
Dec. 15	MINNESOTA	1:00
Dec. 22	at New Orleans	12:00

1984 Results

Sept. 2	at New Orleans	36-28
Sept. 9	DETROIT*	24-27
Sept. 16	at Minnesota	20-27
Sept. 23	HOUSTON	42-10
Sept. 30	at San Francisco	5-14
Oct. 7	at L.A. Rams	30-28
Oct. 14	N.Y. GIANTS	7-19
Oct. 22	L.A. RAMS (Mon.)	10-24
Oct. 28	at Pittsburgh	10-35
Nov. 5	at Washington (Mon.)	14-27
Nov. 11	NEW ORLEANS	13-17
Nov. 18	CLEVELAND	7-23
Nov. 25	at Cincinnati	14-35
Dec. 2	SAN FRANCISCO	17-35
Dec. 9	at Tampa Bay	6-23
Dec. 16	PHILADELPHIA	26-10

1985 Draft Choices

1. Bill Fralic—2. T. Pittsburgh
   from Houston through Minnesota
2. Choice to Washington
2. Mike Gann—45. DE. Notre Dame. from St. Louis
3. Choice to Minnesota
4. Emile Harry—89. WR Stanford
5. Choice to St. Louis
6. Choice to Miami
6. Reggie Pleasant—152. DB. Clemson. from New Orleans
7. Choice to Cincinnati
8. Ashley Lee—201. DB. Virginia Tech
8. Ronnie Washington—215. LB. N.E. Louisiana from New England
9. Micah Moon—228. LB. North Carolina
10. Brent Martin—257. C. Stanford
11. John Ayres—284. DB. Illinois
12. Ken Whisenhunt—313. TE. Georgia Tech

LOS ANGELES RAMS

For the fans in Anaheim, the ones who swallowed hard at the Rams' 16-13 loss in a wild-card playoff game against the New York Giants, this might be even harder to swallow:

The 1984 Rams went about as far as they could have hoped to go under the circumstances. Forget that they had Eric Dickerson's 2,105 yards and an offensive line that resembled a Panzer division. Forget that after losing to San Francisco 33-0, they later proved they belonged in the playoffs in a tough 19-16 loss to the same team. Forget all that, and listen to John Robinson, who should know.

"No doubt about it," said the Rams' head coach. "We botched up the Giants game, I know. But last season we had pulled in our horns and were doing our best just to survive.

"People would say, 'You can't go to the Super Bowl without passing more. You just have to open the offense more to make it to the Super Bowl.' I'd think to myself, 'No kidding.' What we proved is that you can take an inexperienced back-up quarterback and still win some games, enough to go to the playoffs. I just can't imagine what we did not being the right approach."

The Rams didn't go to the Super Bowl with Jeff Kemp at quarterback, but he didn't take them to the bottom of the heap either. In a sense, what the 10-6 Rams did, is row into the NFL waters in a survival boat.

Los Angeles was 9-4 in Kemp's 13 starts. Generally speaking, Kemp did nothing much more flashy than pitch the ball to Eric Dickerson. Surely, there was more to Kemp's season. But it was that no-risk offensive approach that earned the Rams a spot in the playoffs.

Eric Dickerson aims at new rushing records after 2,105.

John Robinson

Kemp, who started 1984 as a reserve to Vince Ferragamo and was forced to take over when Ferragamo broke a bone in his hand, probably will find himself a reserve again this season. On March 26, the Rams signed 34-year-old Dieter Brock, an 11-year veteran of the Canadian Football League who twice was named most valuable player.

Defensively, the Rams got the most of what they had after injuries hurt the pass rush (Gary Jeter and Jack Youngblood) and the secondary (Johnnie Johnson, Nolan Cromwell, and Eric Harris). Los Angeles finished fourteenth in defense, third against the run. They were solid, if not spectacular.

Looking past the glitter of Dickerson's assault on O.J. Simpson's single-season rushing record, the Rams were, as Robinson says, a pretty good team building toward a championship. There was no playoff success to match the 1983 victory over Dallas. Just a 16-13 loss to a team they had beaten 33-12 earlier in the season.

One change will be obvious in 1985: the evolution of Robinson's job as head coach.

"When you come in as a head coach, you have to familiarize yourself with the overall environment," Robinson said. "After you do that for a few years, you have a chance to zero in and be more specific. I think that's the way it has to work."

So, in 1985, Robinson will get more specific by coaching his quarterbacks on a daily basis, while remembering his offensive staple. The exclamation point on the 1984 season was a 1985 March news conference at which Dickerson awarded rings to his blockers. "This year, hopefully, we'll do more with our passing game," Robinson says. "But every once in a while, we'll still say, 'Eric, here, you take the ball this time.'"

OFFENSE

The Rams will try to add an exclamation point to the simple declarative sentence that defined their season a year ago.

As long as Dickerson's legs will carry him, the story

always will be "See Eric run." But the reason the Rams are seeking more balance is an offense that last year ranked twenty-seventh in passing.

No matter what the Rams design for 1985, there is one certainty. The architect will not be Jimmy Raye, who left the offensive coordinator's job with the Rams to assume the same duties at Tampa Bay.

Robinson will in effect become a quarterback's guru for a team that made it to the playoffs in 1984 without a multi-faceted offensive scheme.

Not to detract from Kemp, who completed 143 of 284 passes for 2,021 yards and 13 touchdowns. Kemp did what was asked of him. He threw only seven interceptions after taking over for Ferragamo, who was injured in week 3.

This time, Kemp will be dealing with Brock, who reminded the media when he signed his contract that he didn't intend to sit on the bench. Brock threw for nearly 35,000 yards during his Canadian League career which included 9½ years at Winnipeg and 1½ more with Hamilton. He is a stocky 6-1 and 195 pounds and he possesses a strong arm.

If he can displace Kemp, Brock will be the Rams' seventh starting quarterback since 1980, following in the footsteps of Pat Haden, Ferragamo, Jeff Rutledge, Dan Pastorini, Bert Jones, and Kemp.

More important, Kemp handed off to Dickerson enough that Dickerson accumulated more yards on the ground than Kemp did through the air.

But this year, well, this year is when Robinson would like to see balance really come to pass in Anaheim. Rob-

Bill Bain

Dieter Brock

Ron Brown

inson swears there will be no quarterback controversy. With Kemp, Brock, Ferragamo, and veteran Steve Dils on hand, Robinson may not have a controversy but he will have a decision to make.

"A major decision," Robinson says. "And we'll have made the decision by training camp. At majority of the work will be going to one guy when we get to camp."

Whoever the quarterback is, he won't need directions to find Dickerson, who rushed for 14 touchdowns in 1984. Barry Redden, the Rams' number-one draft pick the year before they drafted Dickerson, is a strong back-up. Dwayne Crutchfield adds beef on short-yardage plays.

Somehow, the Rams managed to rank twenty-first offensively with a running game that rated second-best in the league. So the move in 1985 will be to a passing offense based on timing to take advantage of the speed of world-class sprinter Ron Brown. Brown stands to become a full-time player after a season of learning, replacing veteran wide receiver Drew Hill (who will continue to return kickoffs). With Brown and Henry Ellard, the Rams' won't lack for big-play capacity.

Robinson can afford to dream big on offense with a line that has talent up to its chin straps. When the Rams lost 1984 Pro Bowl tackle Jackie Slater to knee surgery, they were able to flop veteran Bill Bain to Slater's spot and plug Irv Pankey in at left tackle.

Center Doug Smith and guard Kent Hill accompanied Dickerson to the Pro Bowl. There also is youth in waiting. A former USC All-America, Tony Slaton, who was cut by Buffalo, spent last year on the Rams' injured-reserve list and could figure in their plans for 1985.

If the offense is now going to be John Robinson's baby, he'll have more than enough help. Former USC offensive coordinator Norval Turner now is the Rams' tight end coach. Lew Erber, an offensive coordinator at New England under Ron Meyer, will be on hand to coach the wide receivers.

DEFENSE

No coaching changes here. Fritz Shurmur still has the job of finding a pass rush brawny enough to make his zone coverages work. "I think we're in a situation now

Three Years at a Glance

Averages NFL Rank	OFFENSE			DEFENSE		
	1984	1983	1982	1984	1983	1982
Points Rank	**21.6** 12	**22.6** 11	**22.2** 9	**19.8** 13	**21.5** 15	**27.8** 28
Yards Rank	**312.9** 21	**342.1** 12	**336.0** 6	**329.1** 14	**337.0** 15	**370.3** 27
Rushing Yards Rank	**179.0** 2	**140.8** 9	**113.9** 15	**100.0** 3	**111.3** 6	**133.6** 22
Passing Yards Rank	**133.9** 27	**201.3** 12	**222.1** 4	**229.1** 24	**225.7** 22	**236.8** 24
Sacks Rank	**2.0** 3	**1.4** 1T	**1.7** 5T	**2.7** 17T	**2.1** 23	**2.0** 21T
Turnovers Rank	**2.2** 12	**2.9** 20T	**2.7** 17T	**2.4** 9	**2.8** 9	**2.0** 23T
Punt Returns Rank	**12.2** 2	**9.8** 9	**11.0** 5	**5.6** 3	**6.4** 4	**12.9** 27
Kickoff Returns Rank	**21.4** 4	**18.2** 24	**19.3** 23	**17.4** 3	**18.7** 10	**23.4** 28
Penalty Yards Rank	**51.9** 13	**46.8** 5T	**61.1** 25	**54.4** 14	**50.3** 16	**59.0** 9

	W-L Total	Home	Road	Playoffs
1982	2-7	1-4	1-3	None
1983	9-7	5-3	4-4	1-1, Lost Divisional Playoff Game
1984	10-6	5-3	5-3	0-1, Lost First Round Game

where we're getting what we can out of what we got,"
Shurmur says. "Not that we don't have some very good
players. But we could always use that dominant pass
rusher, whether it's a defensive end or an outside linebacker. We played the run pretty well."

The Rams ranked third in the league against the rush
last year, twenty-fourth against the pass. It was a defense short on thrills, but effective nonetheless. After a
1-2 start, the Rams' defense allowed an average of 12
points in the team's next six victories, primarily by
crunching opponents' running games. But Los Angeles
gave up a ton of passing yards.

Defensive end Reggie Doss is a good run defender,
as is nose tackle Greg Meisner. The bulk of the pass
rush in 1984 came from Jack Youngblood, who has
been slowed by a sciatic nerve condition in his back.

The Rams' 3-4 scheme is demanding on the 35-year-
old Youngblood, a lightweight (240 pounds) by modern
defensive end standards. The Rams could get some
help in the pass-rush department if Gary Jeter (bad
back) can return to form.

The Rams' defensive scheme also plays to one of the
team's strengths—linebackers. Jim Collins led the
Rams with 186 tackles and had a Pro Bowl year even
though he didn't have the votes to prove it. Carl Ekern,
George Andrews (who was injured part of 1984), Mel
Owens, and Mike Wilcher are steady, even if they're
not exactly marquee names.

In 1984, the Rams obtained all-pro cornerback Gary
Green in a trade. Los Angeles might have a terrific secondary one of these years if it can avoid the injuries it in-
curred in 1984. First, Johnnie Johnson broke his leg in
training camp; the Rams filled his spot by moving Eric
Harris to strong safety. Then Harris hurt his ankle. Then
Nolan Cromwell suffered a knee injury that required
offseason surgery.

Cornerbacks LeRoy Irvin and Green were relatively
healthy, but the Rams went into the April draft looking
for depth and drafted Texas All-American Jerry Gray.

"We spent the year just trying to stay consistent in the
secondary," Shurmur says. "I thank God we had Vinny
Newsome to step in and help out. But either by design

Jim Collins

Henry Ellard

Johnnie Johnson

or new personnel, we need a stronger pass rush to make our coverages work. We're never going to have the great statistics in pass defense because we play so much zone. But we can get better. We gotta be better at putting the heat on the passer. That's all there is to it."

SPECIAL TEAMS

If the Rams weren't the most potent offensive team in the NFL last year, they struck fear in opponent's hearts. And not just when Eric Dickerson came glaring out of the backfield cradling a football.

Special teams' coach Gil Haskell came armed with the best 1-2 punch in the NFC. Henry Ellard led the conference in punt returns with a 13.4 average. He returned two punts for touchdowns. The Rams also had the number-one kick returner in Redden, who has made the transition from top draft choice to special teams player without complaint. Redden averaged a conference-best 23.0 yards per kick return. Entering 1985, the Rams are deep in return men. Drew Hill ranked eighth in the conference with a 20.9 average.

While the Rams ranked second in the league in punt returns, they also had the third-best punt-coverage team. That helped make the season more acceptable for punter John Misko, who averaged just 38.7 yards. Misko will have more competition in training camp now that the Rams have signed former New Orleans Saints specialist Russell Erxleben.

Kicker Mike Lansford had an average first half in 1984. Strangely enough, his season improved dramatically when regular holder Nolan Cromwell was injured and replaced by quarterback Steve Dils. Lansford made 13 straight field goals and 18 of his last 20.

VETERAN ROSTER

No.	Name	Pos.	Ht.	Wt.	NFL Exp.	Birthdate	College	Games in 1984
52	Andrews, George	LB	6-3	225	7	11/28/55	Nebraska	11
62	Bain, Bill	T	6-4	290	11	8/9/52	Southern California	16
86	Barber, Mike	TE	6-3	237	10	6/4/53	Louisiana Tech	11
96	Barnett, Doug	LB	6-3	250	3	4/12/60	Azusa Pacific	0
73	Bolinger, Russ	G	6-5	255	9	9/10/54	Long Beach State	16
90	Brady, Ed	LB	6-2	228	2	6/17/60	Illinois	16
89	Brown, Ron	WR	5-11	181	2	3/31/61	Arizona State	16
50	Collins, Jim	LB	6-2	230	5	6/11/58	Syracuse	16
21	Cromwell, Nolan	S	6-1	200	9	1/30/55	Kansas	11
28	Croudip, David	CB	5-8	183	2	1/25/59	San Diego State	16
45	Crutchfield, Dwayne	RB	6-0	235	4	9/30/59	Iowa State	15
70	DeJurnett, Charles	NT	6-4	260	9	6/17/52	San Jose State	16
29	Dickerson, Eric	RB	6-3	220	3	9/2/60	Southern Methodist	16
8	Dils, Steve	QB	6-1	191	7	12/8/55	Stanford	10
71	Doss, Reggie	DE	6-4	263	8	12/7/56	Hampton Institute	16
55	Ekern, Carl	LB	6-3	222	9	5/27/54	San Jose State	16
80	Ellard, Henry	WR	5-11	170	3	7/21/61	Fresno State	16
	Erxleben, Russell	P	6-4	221	5	1/13/57	Texas	0
84	Farmer, George	WR	5-10	175	4	12/5/58	Southern	14
88	Faulkner, Chris	TE	6-4	260	2	4/13/60	Florida	8
15	Ferragamo, Vince	QB	6-3	212	8	4/24/54	Nebraska	3
82	Grant, Otis	WR	6-3	197	3	8/13/61	Michigan State	14
27	Green, Gary	CB	5-11	191	9	10/2/55	Baylor	16
44	Guman, Mike	RB	6-2	218	6	4/21/58	Penn State	16
60	Harrah, Dennis	G	6-5	265	11	3/9/53	Miami	16
26	Harris, Eric	CB	6-3	202	6	8/11/55	Memphis State	7
81	Hill, David	TE	6-2	228	10	1/1/54	Texas A&I	16
87	Hill, Drew	WR	5-9	170	7	10/5/56	Georgia Tech	16
72	Hill, Kent	G	6-5	260	7	3/7/57	Georgia Tech	16
47	Irvin, LeRoy	CB	5-11	184	6	9/15/57	Kansas	16
59	Jerue, Mark	LB	6-3	229	3	1/15/60	Washington	16
77	Jeter, Gary	DE	6-4	260	9	3/24/55	Southern California	5
20	Johnson, Johnnie	S	6-1	183	6	10/8/56	Texas	9
24	Jones, A. J.	RB	6-1	202	4	5/30/59	Texas	13
46	Kamana, John	RB	6-2	215	2	12/3/61	Southern California	3
9	Kemp, Jeff	QB	6-0	201	5	7/11/59	Dartmouth	14
76	Kowalski, Gary	T	6-5	275	2	7/2/60	Boston College	0
1	Lansford, Mike	K	6-0	183	4	7/20/58	Washington	16
57	Laughlin, Jim	LB	6-1	222	6	7/5/58	Ohio State	3
83	McDonald, James	TE	6-5	230	3	3/29/61	Southern California	16
63	McDonald, Mike	LB	6-1	235	2	6/22/58	Southern California	16
69	Meisner, Greg	NT	6-3	253	5	4/23/59	Pittsburgh	16
98	Miller, Shawn	NT	6-4	255	2	3/14/61	Utah State	8
6	Misko, John	P	6-5	207	4	10/1/54	Oregon State	16
22	Newsome, Vince	S	6-1	179	3	1/22/61	Washington	16
58	Owens, Mel	LB	6-2	224	5	12/7/58	Michigan	16
75	Pankey, Irv	T	6-4	267	5	12/15/58	Penn State	16
43	Pleasant, Mike	CB	6-1	195	2	8/16/58	Oklahoma	5
30	Redden, Barry	RB	5-10	205	4	7/21/60	Richmond	14
93	Reed, Doug	DE	6-3	250	2	7/16/60	San Diego State	9
66	Reese, Booker	DE	6-6	260	4	9/20/59	Bethune-Cookman	10
64	Shearin, Joe	G	6-4	250	3	4/16/60	Texas	15
78	Slater, Jackie	T	6-4	271	10	5/27/54	Jackson State	7
61	Slaton, Tony	C	6-3	269	2	4/12/61	Southern California	0
56	Smith, Doug	C	6-3	253	8	11/25/56	Bowling Green	16
37	Sully, Ivory	S	6-0	200	7	6/20/57	Delaware	16
51	Vann, Norwood	LB	6-2	225	2	2/18/62	East Carolina	16
54	Wilcher, Mike	LB	6-3	235	3	3/20/60	North Carolina	15
85	Youngblood, Jack	DE	6-4	242	15	1/26/50	Florida	15

Coaching Staff

John Robinson, head coach; **Lew Erber,** wide receivers; **Marv Goux,** defensive line; **Gil Haskell,** special teams; **Hudson Houck,** offensive line; **Steve Shafer,** defensive backs; **Fritz Shurmur,** defensive coordinator, inside linebackers; **Bruce Snyder,** running backs, running game coordinator; **Norval Turner,** tight ends, U-backs; **Fred Whittingham,** outside linebackers.

1985 Schedule

Preseason

Aug. 10	HOUSTON	7:00
Aug. 15	ST. LOUIS	7:00
Aug. 24	Philadelphia	TBA
Aug. 31	NEW ENGLAND	7:00

Regular Season

Sept. 8	DENVER	1:00
Sept. 15	at Philadelphia	1:00
Sept. 23	at Seattle (Mon.)	6:00
Sept. 29	ATLANTA	1:00
Oct. 6	MINNESOTA	1:00
Oct. 13	at Tampa Bay	1:00
Oct. 20	at Kansas City	12:00
Oct. 27	SAN FRANCISCO	1:00
Nov. 3	NEW ORLEANS	1:00
Nov. 10	at N.Y. Giants	1:00
Nov. 17	at Atlanta	1:00
Nov. 24	GREEN BAY	1:00
Dec. 1	at New Orleans	12:00
Dec. 9	at San Francisco (Mon.)	6:00
Dec. 15	ST. LOUIS	1:00
Dec. 23	L.A. RAIDERS (Mon.)	6:00

1984 Results

Sept. 3	DALLAS (Mon.)	13-20
Sept. 9	CLEVELAND	20-17
Sept. 16	at Pittsburgh	14-24
Sept. 23	at Cincinnati	24-14
Sept. 30	N.Y. GIANTS	33-12
Oct. 7	ATLANTA	28-30
Oct. 14	at New Orleans	28-10
Oct. 22	at Atlanta (Mon.)	24-10
Oct. 28	SAN FRANCISCO	0-33
Nov. 4	at St. Louis	16-13
Nov. 11	CHICAGO	29-13
Nov. 18	vs. Green Bay at Milw.	6-31
Nov. 25	at Tampa Bay	34-33
Dec. 2	NEW ORLEANS	34-21
Dec. 9	HOUSTON	27-16
Dec. 14	at San Francisco (Fri.)	16-19
Dec. 23	N.Y. GIANTS	13-16

1985 Draft Choices

1. Jerry Gray—21. DB, Texas
2. Chuck Scott—50. WR, Vanderbilt
3. Dale Hatcher—77. P, Clemson
4. Choice to Minnesota
5. Kevin Greene—113, LB, Auburn, from Buffalo
5. Choice to Houston, through Kansas City
6. Mike Young—161, WR, UCLA, from Chicago
6. Damone Johnson—162, TE, Cal Poly-SLO

7. Danny Bradley—189, RB, Oklahoma
8. Marlon McIntyre—218, RB, Pittsburgh
9. Gary Swanson—245, LB, Cal Poly-SLO
10. Duval Love—274, G, UCLA
11. Doug Flutie—285, QB, Boston College, from Indianapolis
11. Kevin Brown—301, DB, Northwestern
12. Choice to Tampa Bay

NEW ORLEANS SAINTS

One of these years, logic says the New Orleans Saints will break ground on a winning season. One of these years they'll kick down the door to the playoffs and the celebration will resemble the Mardi Gras.

If that sounds familiar, it's because 1984 was supposed to be one of those years. Instead, New Orleans stumbled to a 7-9 record—its eighteenth consecutive non-winning season.

There were high hopes for a team that barely missed the playoffs with an 8-8 record the year before. After only the second .500 season in franchise history, there was reason to feel good about being a Saints fan again. The new quarterback was Richard Todd, acquired from the New York Jets for a number-one draft choice. George Rogers was fresh from another 1,000-yard season. And the Saints' defense was living in the NFL's high-rent district.

But Todd sank to the bottom of the NFC quarterback ratings behind an offensive line that was battered by injury. Rogers fell short of 1,000 yards. A run defense that had been rock-hard in 1983 was the league's third-poorest in 1984.

Maybe the most telling statistic defensively was the Saints' minus-18 turnover ratio, last in the NFL. A team that finally was supposed to make its mark in the NFC West finished 1-5 against division opponents.

"There's not much mystery as to what happened [in the season]," said head coach Bum Phillips. "We lost our left tackle minutes into the first game and he missed fifteen weeks. We lost a starting guard for twelve more. We just had too many injuries on offense. That's all there is to it."

Linebacker Rickey Jackson puts punch into Saints' defense.

Bum Phillips

There was concern in New Orleans during the offseason while the Saints waited for their future as a franchise to be determined. They weren't assured of staying in New Orleans until businessman Tom Benson announced his bid to purchase the team in March.

At that point, the Saints hadn't signed any of the 15 veteran players who had become free agents. And they entered the April draft without a number-one draft choice for the second year in a row.

But now the new season that awaits the Saints is brimming with hope, the hope that 1985 doesn't become a rerun of 1984.

OFFENSE

With the trade of George Rogers to the Washington Redskins, Phillips has solved one of his biggest problems: What to do with two running backs the caliber of former Heisman Trophy winners, Rogers and Earl Campbell, whom Phillips brought from Houston last season. Now there is no problem.

Campbell takes over for Rogers, whose production fell off to 914 yards in 1984 after a 1,144-yard season in 1983. Neither he nor Campbell (50 carries, 190 yards) seemed very comfortable after the trade that brought Campbell to New Orleans.

"We never really got a chance to use Earl last year," Phillips said. "I couldn't just put a guy ahead of George during the season. We brought Earl in to play this year [1985] and to have him in case something happened."

So now the Saints will give Campbell the job of generating ground power. Hokie Gajan, whose 6-yards-per-carry average was best among NFC starting running backs, joins Wayne Wilson and the others in the battle for the other running position.

Is the Saints' backfield safe enough for quarterback Richard Todd, or whoever wins the starting job?

Yes, there still is open competition there, one year after the Saints acquired Todd. It's open because Todd threw 11 touchdown passes and 19 interceptions in 14 games last year and had the lowest quarterback rating of any active quarterback in the NFC (60.6)

"Richard walked into a tough situation," Phillips said. "He didn't get a chance to do all the playing in preseason. None of the quarterbacks got enough work. But Richard has a great attitude and he's a good worker. I think we're in good shape with the people we have there."

Ken Stabler no longer is there, having retired during the 1984 season. Dave Wilson, who had shoulder surgery in mid-January, is. Wilson threw seven touchdown passes in 11 quarters of play and started the final two games of the season.

"It's anybody's job," Phillips said. "That's just the way it is in pro football."

The Saints might have a profitable reclamation project in tight end Junior Miller, cast off by the Atlanta Falcons a year ago. Miller and John Tice at least add depth to a position owned by Hoby Brenner (28 receptions, 554 yards in 1984).

No receiver finished in the conference's top 20 either in receptions or yardage. Tyrone Young has size (6 feet 6 inches). Jeff Groth has good hands but lacks speed. Gajan led the team in receptions with 35.

The passing game may have been more vulnerable a year ago, because of injuries on the offensive line.

Starting tackle Dave Lafary missed the season with a knee injury suffered in the first week. Guard Brad Edelman, perhaps the Saints' best offensive lineman, missed six games with a knee injury and underwent surgery. A turf toe sidelined Louis Oubre for nine more.

Hoby Brenner

Bruce Clark

Hokie Gajan

Only guard Steve Korte and center John Hill survived the season in some semblance of health.

The Saints' offensive line allowed 20 sacks through Week 11. In the next four games, New Orleans's quarterbacks were sacked 25 times.

"I've never had a season where you lose so many people at one area," Phillips said. "I've seen 'em go out for a quarter, a half, or maybe a game. But not for ten or twelve games like we were losing people. What we need in 1985 is to get all our offensive linemen back healthy again.

"When you have injuries like we did you can't protect the quarterback and you can't run the ball well."

DEFENSE

In NFL locker rooms, where finger-pointing is considered rude behavior, the Saints' defense went quietly about the 1984 season. It was, under the circumstances, a good choice.

Even though the New Orleans offense sagged and sputtered on frequent occasion, the defense was not a group without problems. One of the league's best run defenses in 1983 allowed six 200-yard rushing days in 1984. It was rocked with 422 yards by Atlanta in the season opener, and 407 by San Francisco in a 35-3 loss.

At the end, the Saints were left holding a bundle of diverse statistics: number-one against the pass; twenty-sixth against the run; fourth in the league defensively overall.

"A lot of statistics can be misleading," said Saints' defensive coordinator Wade Phillips. "A lot depends on how well your offense is doing. If you're down by a lot of points early, a team is more likely to keep running the ball on you."

In the case of the 1984 Saints, running the ball equated with eating up yardage. If there was no real knockout punch, the Saints did open the season somewhat dazed by a Falcons team that would soon go into a tailspin offensively. Without William Andrews in the lineup for the season opener, Atlanta beat New Orleans 36-28. The kudos went to Gerald Riggs, who ran through the Saints for 202 yards. "That first game really hurt us," said Phillips. "That put a lot of pressure on us

Three Years at a Glance

Averages NFL Rank	OFFENSE			DEFENSE		
	1984	1983	1982	1984	1983	1982
Points	**18.6**	**19.9**	**14.3**	**22.6**	**21.1**	**17.8**
Rank	20	17	26	19	12	8
Yards	**313.0**	**308.6**	**295.0**	**307.1**	**293.2**	**289.7**
Rank	20	23	20	4	2	5
Rushing Yards	**135.7**	**153.8**	**139.7**	**153.8**	**125.0**	**108.2**
Rank	8	6	6	26	11T	10
Passing Yards	**177.3**	**154.8**	**155.3**	**153.3**	**168.2**	**181.4**
Rank	24	26	25	1	1	8
Sacks	**2.8**	**2.2**	**2.6**	**3.4**	**3.5**	**3.4**
Rank	11T	6T	12T	7T	5	6T
Turnovers	**2.6**	**2.9**	**2.7**	**1.4**	**2.4**	**2.4**
Rank	23T	20T	17T	26	13T	14T
Punt Returns	**8.1**	**7.1**	**6.9**	**11.7**	**11.2**	**8.2**
Rank	16	23	19	28	27	14
Kickoff Returns	**20.3**	**20.3**	**22.2**	**20.4**	**21.3**	**19.4**
Rank	8	9	2	16	25	11
Penalty Yards	**53.1**	**50.1**	**57.1**	**64.1**	**50.9**	**51.0**
Rank	14	10	18	5	15	13

	W-L Total	Home	Road	Playoffs
1982	4-5	2-3	2-2	None
1983	8-8	5-3	3-5	None
1984	7-9	3-5	4-4	None

to perform well. Atlanta really hurt us, knocked us down a notch."

The main problem for the Saints was the health of nose guard Derland Moore, a seasoned veteran. In 1984, Moore was routinely helped off on the field with recurring leg and foot injuries. Another problem was Tony Elliot, who left the Saints with personal problems. Thus, offenses had two pretty good reasons to stick with an infantry game plan. As Wade Phillips says, "One guy wasn't healthy and the other guy wasn't here."

No one ran too often or with considerable success at defensive end Bruce Clark or linebacker Rickey Jackson, who shared the same side of the field and later played in the Pro Bowl.

Jackson led the team in sacks for the second year in a row. Whitney Paul, the Saints' best linebacker in pass coverage, had a solid season.

The secondary was another good news, bad news story for the Saints. Its top ranking in pass defense was helped by the fact that offenses ran the ball 126 more times than they passed. And when they did pass, there was very little glue on the hands of Saints defenders.

Dave Waymer led the team with just four interceptions ("and he dropped a lot he picked off in 1983," Wade Phillips said). As a unit, the Saints intercepted only 13 passes—half their 1983 total. Waymer, Johnnie Poe, and strong safety Russell Gary would seem to have locks on their jobs in 1985.

The most competitive spot will be free safety, where second-year player Terry Hoage is expected to push veteran Frank Wattelet. By season's end, Hoage and Wattelet were sharing time and it wasn't because of any injuries to Wattelet.

"Defensively, we've been fairly successful," Wade Phillips says. "We were second in our conference, fourth in the league. When you've had that kind of success, you don't forsee too many changes."

SPECIAL TEAMS

Everybody knew about Reggie Roby, the bionic leg of the Miami Dolphins. As the AFC's Pro Bowl punter in 1984, Roby had such great hang time that only 17 punts were returned against the Dolphins.

Brian Hansen   *Steve Korte*   *Johnny Poe*

Outside New Orleans, nobody knew much about Brian Hansen, the Saints' rookie punter who had a great season in his own right. Hansen led the NFC with a 43.8 average and earned his first trip to the Pro Bowl. Yes, that was Brian Hansen right there along with Reggie Roby in Hawaii.

"He really had a heckuva year," says Saints special teams coach Harold Richardson. "He made a few mistakes here and there. But I was really pleased with him and he's only going to get better."

The Saints feel the same way about kicker Morten Anderson, who hit 20 of 27 field goals and beat Cleveland with a 53-yarder. Inside 40 yards, Anderson made good on 13 of 14.

"We feel like we're in pretty good shape with those guys," Richardson said. "If there's an area to improve on it's punt coverage. That was sort of the weak link last year."

New Orleans allowed 11.7 yards per punt return and 20.4 on kick returns. Punt coverage needs to be upgraded, especially when you consider that the NFC's top two punt returners play for Western Division rivals.

While Jitter Fields and Groth handled punt returns in 1984, the Saints were more unsettled at kick returner. Kenny Duckett went on injured reserve with a series of medical problems last year, but he should help in that area if he stays healthy in 1985. Tyrone Anthony had some success with kick returns.

"Last year, we were never able to keep the same people back there for any length of time," Richardson said. "That hurt us some. I hope we won't have those problems this season."

VETERAN ROSTER

No.	Name	Pos.	Ht.	Wt.	NFL Exp.	Birthdate	College	Games in 1984
7	Andersen, Morten	K	6-2	205	4	8/19/60	Michigan State	16
22	Anthony, Tyrone	RB	5-11	212	2	3/3/62	North Carolina	15
85	Brenner, Hoby	TE	6-4	245	5	6/2/59	Southern California	16
67	Brock, Stan	T	6-6	288	6	6/8/58	Colorado	14
35	Campbell, Earl	RB	5-11	233	8	3/29/55	Texas	14
65	Carter, David	C	6-2	275	9	11/27/53	Western Kentucky	14
75	Clark, Bruce	DE	6-3	281	4	3/31/58	Penn State	15
68	Clark, Kelvin	G	6-3	273	7	1/30/56	Nebraska	16
83	Duckett, Kenny	WR	6-0	179	4	10/1/59	Wake Forest	11
63	Edelman, Brad	G	6-6	262	4	9/3/60	Missouri	11
99	Elliott, Tony	NT	6-2	280	4	4/23/59	North Texas State	4
26	Fields, Jitter	CB	5-8	188	2	8/16/62	Texas	13
46	Gajan, Hokie	FB	5-11	226	4	9/6/59	Louisiana State	14
20	Gary, Russell	S	5-11	196	5	7/31/59	Nebraska	16
97	Geathers, James	DE	6-7	267	2	6/26/60	Wichita State	16
88	Goodlow, Eugene	WR	6-2	181	3	12/19/58	Kansas State	10
86	Groth, Jeff	WR	5-10	181	7	7/2/57	Bowling Green	16
10	Hansen, Brian	P	6-3	218	2	10/26/60	Sioux Falls	16
28	Harding, Greg	S	6-2	197	2	7/31/60	Nicholls State	3
87	Hardy, Larry	TE	6-3	246	8	7/9/56	Jackson State	6
92	Haynes, James	LB	6-2	227	2	8/9/60	Mississippi Valley St.	10
61	Hilgenberg, Joel	C-G	6-3	253	2	7/10/62	Iowa	10
24	Hoage, Terry	S	6-3	199	2	4/11/62	Georgia	14
57	Jackson, Rickey	LB	6-2	239	5	3/20/58	Pittsburgh	16
34	Johnson, Bobby	CB-S	6-0	187	3	9/1/60	Texas	16
60	Korte, Steve	C	6-2	271	3	1/15/60	Arkansas	15
52	Kovach, Jim	LB	6-2	239	7	5/1/56	Kentucky	15
64	Lafary, Dave	T	6-7	285	8	1/13/55	Purdue	1
93	Lewis, Gary	NT	6-3	261	2	1/14/61	Oklahoma State	0
98	Lewis, Reggie	DE	6-2	251	4	1/20/54	San Diego State	13
29	Lewis, Rodney	CB	5-11	186	3	4/2/59	Nebraska	16
19	Merkens, Guido	QB-WR	6-1	197	8	8/14/55	Sam Houston State	16
84	Miller, Junior	TE	6-4	244	6	11/26/57	Nebraska	15
74	Moore, Derland	NT	6-4	273	13	10/7/51	Oklahoma	12
66	Oubre, Louis	G	6-4	272	4	5/15/58	Oklahoma	12
51	Paul, Whitney	LB	6-3	218	10	10/8/55	Colorado	16
53	Pelluer, Scott	LB	6-2	227	5	4/28/59	Washington State	16
25	Poe, Johnnie	CB	6-1	194	5	8/29/59	Missouri	16
58	Redd, Glen	LB	6-1	231	4	6/17/58	Brigham Young	16
41	Rogers, Jimmy	RB	5-10	195	6	6/29/55	Oklahoma	16
80	Scott, Lindsay	WR	6-1	200	4	12/6/60	Georgia	16
96	Thorp, Don	NT	6-4	260	2	7/10/62	Illinois	5
82	Tice, John	TE	6-5	243	3	6/22/60	Maryland	10
11	Todd, Richard	QB	6-2	212	10	11/19/53	Alabama	15
72	Ward, Chris	T	6-3	269	8	12/16/55	Ohio State	13
73	Warren, Frank	DE	6-4	278	5	9/14/59	Auburn	16
49	Wattelet, Frank	S	6-0	185	5	10/25/58	Kansas	16
44	Waymer, Dave	CB	6-1	188	6	7/1/58	Notre Dame	16
94	Wilks, Jim	DE	6-5	265	5	3/12/58	San Diego State	16
18	Wilson, Dave	QB	6-3	211	4	4/27/59	Illinois	5
45	Wilson, Tim	FB	6-3	237	9	1/14/55	Maryland	12
30	Wilson, Wayne	RB	6-3	220	7	9/4/57	Shepherd	14
56	Winston, Dennis	LB	6-0	244	9	10/25/55	Arkansas	16
89	Young, Tyrone	WR	6-6	192	3	4/29/60	Florida	16

Coaching Staff

O.A. (Bum) Phillips, head coach; **Andy Everest,** tight ends; **King Hill,** offensive coordinator; **John Levra,** offensive backfield; **Carl Mauck,** offensive line; **Russell Paternostro,** strength and conditioning; **Wade Phillips,** defensive coordinator; **Harold Richardson,** special teams; **Joe Spencer,** quality control; **John Paul Young,** linebackers; **Willie Zapalac,** defensive line.

1985 Schedule

Preseason

Aug. 10	at New England	3:30
Aug. 17	HOUSTON	7:00
Aug. 24	TAMPA BAY	7:00
Aug. 30	at San Diego	7:00

Regular Season

Sept. 8	KANSAS CITY	12:00
Sept. 15	at Denver	2:00
Sept. 22	TAMPA BAY	12:00
Sept. 29	at San Francisco	1:00
Oct. 6	PHILADELPHIA	12:00
Oct. 13	at L.A. Raiders	1:00
Oct. 20	at Atlanta	1:00
Oct. 27	N.Y. GIANTS	3:00
Nov. 3	at L.A. Rams	1:00
Nov. 10	SEATTLE	12:00
Nov. 17	Green Bay at Milw.	12:00
Nov. 24	at Minnesota	12:00
Dec. 1	L.A. RAMS	12:00
Dec. 8	at St. Louis	12:00
Dec. 15	SAN FRANCISCO	12:00
Dec. 22	ATLANTA	12:00

1984 Results

Sept. 2	ATLANTA	28-36
Sept. 9	TAMPA BAY	17-13
Sept. 16	at San Francisco	20-30
Sept. 23	ST. LOUIS	34-24
Sept. 30	at Houston	27-10
Oct. 7	at Chicago	7-20
Oct. 14	L.A. RAMS	10-28
Oct. 21	at Dallas*	27-30
Oct. 28	at Cleveland	16-14
Nov. 4	GREEN BAY	13-23
Nov. 11	at Atlanta	17-13
Nov. 19	PITTSBURGH (Mon.)	27-24
Nov. 25	SAN FRANCISCO	3-35
Dec. 2	at L.A. Rams	21-34
Dec. 9	CINCINNATI	21-24
Dec. 15	at N.Y. Giants (Sat.)	10-3

1985 Draft Choices

1. Choice to Houston
1. Alvin Toles—24, LB, Tennessee, from Washington
2. Daren Gilbert—38, T, Cal State-Fullerton
3. Jack Del Rio—68, LB, Southern California
4. Billy Allen—95, DB, Florida State
5. Choice to Washington
6. Choice To Atlanta
7. Eric Martin—179, WR, Louisiana State
8. Joe Kohlbrand—206, DE, Miami
9. Earl Johnson—236, DB, South Carolina
10. Choice to Washington
11. Choice to Washington
12. Treg Songy—320, DB, Tulane

SAN FRANCISCO 49ERS

Go back to January and the afterglow of Super Bowl XIX. San Francisco has just dismantled the Miami Dolphins' Marino Corps 38-16. The nation's media has descended on the new world champions with microphones and tape recorders. The theme is staying power, more specifically the dominance of a team that has won two of the past four Super Bowls and barely missed getting into a third. The questions concern the future. Will the 49ers someday be wearing more rings than Sammy Davis, Jr.? Will this be pro football's next dynasty?

"Dynasty?" said San Francisco wide receiver Dwight Clark. "That's a TV show."

Dynasty?

"I think," said 49ers Pro Bowl guard Randy Cross, "that our better years might be ahead of us."

What the 49ers accomplished in 1984 was a record 15 victories in the regular season, a perfect record on the road, and a clean sweep of their NFC West opponents. It's hard to believe they could be better. The nagging memory of having lost in the NFC Championship Game the year before became 1984's rallying point. The 49ers set team records for points scored, touchdowns, first downs, net yards offense, and total yards passing. San Francisco's offense set a Super Bowl record with 537 total yards. A defense that appeared mortal early on didn't allow a touchdown in its first two playoff games.

A loss to Pittsburgh in week 7 was the only smudge on San Francisco's season. So unnerved were the 49ers that they began a new streak the next week, one that ultimately stretched to the Super Bowl.

Wendell Tyler set a 49ers rushing record with 1,262 yards.

Bill Walsh

So, what now? The new rallying cry in San Francisco is: "Remember 1982." That was the denouement to San Francisco's first Super Bowl victory of the 1980s. The 49ers ended that season with a 3-6 record.

"I really don't have to mention 1982 to our players," head coach Bill Walsh said. "I think the veterans are aware of what happened and the young guys will follow their lead.

"In a way, though, we might have overreacted to 1982. It was the strike year. We lost some key people early. I spent considerable time talking to players and coaches who had been to a Super Bowl and tried to come back the next year. We might have given it too much time. It's probably better to go routinely about your business."

"I'm not sure we even know now what happened to us in 1982," said offensive line coach Bobb McKittrick. "But just just having that experience should be helpful to us in 1985."

So should having Joe Montana, Clark, three Pro Bowl offensive linemen, a double-barrel running game, and a defense with a Pro Bowl secondary. If Walsh worked around the clock to sign key players and trade for some others prior to 1984, this past offseason was somewhat simpler. As team president *and* head coach, Walsh simply went to work on signing himself to a new contract with help from the DeBartolo family.

The message of 1982 has been received loud and clear. Already, there has been talk among the 49ers' players that under no circumstances should a repeat be allowed.

"We've had more players working out this offseason than ever before," McKittrick said. "You have to take that as a pretty good sign."

Not to mention a pretty bad omen for the rest of the NFC.

OFFENSE

The only new look Joe Montana will have in 1985 is at his side. His new wife is Jennifer Wallace, the actress he appeared with in television commercials.

Montana credited the courtship with helping him handle the pressures of the 1984 season. There was further assistance from some guys named Dwight, Freddie, Roger, and Wendell...not to mention the 49ers' offensive line.

While Montana passed for 28 touchdowns and 3,630 yards, the 49ers were better balanced than ever before. Part of the reason was Montana himself. He was the 49ers' second-leading rusher in the playoffs with 144 yards.

"It used to be a 150-yard rushing game was virgin to the 49ers," said Atlanta defensive coordinator John Marshall. "Now, it's their *average*."

And back-up quarterback Matt Cavanagh grew considerably in the championship season, even getting a victory over Philadelphia when Montana was hurt.

Wendell Tyler (a club record 1,262 yards rushing) and Roger Craig (71 receptions for 675 yards, plus 649 yards rushing) are problems enough for opposing defenses. Craig scored three touchdowns in Super Bowl XIX. The 49ers expect 1983 ninth-round draft choice Derrick Harmon to add even more depth as Tyler's back-up in 1985. If San Francisco has a legitimate need in the backfield, it's a true fullback. Finesse will do just fine on the offensive line. It's a group that still is a few years short of the bridge to old age. With an average age of 30, "mature" is a better word for them. Cross, center Fred Quillan, and tackle Keith Fahnhorst were on the NFC Pro Bowl squad in 1984. Tackle Bubba Paris has the tools to be the 49ers' best lineman in the future,

Dwaine Board

Dwight Clark

Ronnie Lott

providing his injured knee holds up. Guard John Ayers already is the best pass blocker. Finding a weakness on the line is tougher than finding Montana behind it. The bench provides strong support too—Guy McIntyre, Allan Kennedy, and Jesse Sapolu.

"Everybody's playing well," McKittrick said. "And nobody's ready for graduation."

Last year, the 49ers ranked second in the NFL in offense—third in rushing and fourth in passing. They're back in 1985 with the same starting receivers.

Clark and Freddie Solomon were able to get their share of rest in 1984 with the 49ers' strategy of alternating quarters. Mike Wilson and Renaldo Nehemiah return as back-ups. If there is a push to be made, it's for Solomon's spot. But despite his age (32), Solomon makes San Francisco a more productive team if only by speed alone.

The tight end spot is a jigsaw puzzle of sorts. Earl Cooper, a converted running back, is the best receiver among the tight ends. John Frank is young, but an excellent blocker. Blend them, and you have the team's *starting* tight end, Russ Francis.

DEFENSE

Even while San Francisco was starting the 1984 season with a 6-0 record, its defense supposedly was suspect. Ronnie Lott was limping on a sore ankle. Fred Dean was holding out for a new contract. Nose guard Pete Kugler and linebackers Willie Harper and Bobby Leopold were in the USFL.

San Francisco won a long-awaited rematch in week 2 against Washington, the team that had beaten the 49ers in the playoffs the year before. But wasn't that San Francisco's defense holding on for a 37-31 victory after holding a 27-0 lead? Wasn't that reason to worry?

"What people don't remember about our defense," Walsh said, "is that we lost both corners in the very first game. We also were playing without Fred Dean, and we didn't have Gary Johnson with us yet.

"We had lost three guys to the USFL. We almost used overkill in replacing them, but we got the positions filled. It just took some time and it took some people getting healthy again.

Three Years at a Glance

Averages NFL Rank	OFFENSE			DEFENSE		
	1984	1983	1982	1984	1983	1982
Points Rank	**29.7** 2	**27.0** 4	**23.2** 7	**14.2** 1	**18.3** 4	**22.9** 22T
Yards Rank	**397.9** 2	**378.4** 4	**360.2** 3	**323.5** 10	**324.3** 10	**337.2** 21
Rushing Yards Rank	**154.1** 3	**141.1** 8	**82.2** 28	**112.2** 7	**121.0** 9	**133.2** 21
Passing Yards Rank	**243.8** 4	**237.3** 5	**278.0** 2	**211.3** 17	**203.3** 15	**204.0** 16
Sacks Rank	**1.7** 2	**2.1** 4T	**2.2** 9T	**3.2** 11	**3.6** 2T	**1.7** 25T
Turnovers Rank	**1.4** 1	**1.9** 4	**2.3** 11T	**2.4** 10	**2.6** 11	**1.4** 27
Punt Returns Rank	**11.6** 3	**10.1** 8	**11.1** 4	**6.3** 5	**7.3** 7	**11.2** 25
Kickoff Returns Rank	**22.1** 2	**18.4** 23	**20.6** 11	**19.2** 8	**21.5** 26	**21.4** 20
Penalty Yards Rank	**55.3** 17	**43.4** 4	**50.1** 13	**45.2** 24T	**49.6** 18	**60.2** 8

	W-L Total	**Home**	**Road**	**Playoffs**
1982	3-6	0-5	3-1	None
1983	10-6	4-4	6-2	1-1, Lost NFC Championship Game
1984	15-1	7-1	8-0	3-0, Won Super Bowl XIX

"That's still the thing people don't realize about the '82 season. At one point we had six of our eleven defensive starters out with injuries. That's difficult to deal with."

By the end of 1984, Ronnie Lott had lost his limp. Keena Turner was invited to his first Pro Bowl. With Turner, Riki Ellison, and Dan Bunz leading the linebackers, it became a team strength just one year after Harper and Leopold had left. Dean was signed, sealed, and delivering his pass rush, along with Dwaine Board, who led the team with 10 sacks and got another four in the playoffs. Three of Dean's seven sacks came with playoff money on the line.

Replacing Kugler at nose guard was easier than expected. Manu Tuiasosopo, acquired from Seattle before the season, probably had his best year as a pro. He did so well that McDonald's chose him for a commercial roundup of ex-employees who made good after leaving the fast-food chain. If Tuiasosopo keeps playing as he did in 1984, he'll never have to ask for his old job back.

"Kugler had a fine year in 1983," said Walsh. "But with Manu, Michael Carter, and Louie Kelcher, we basically upgraded ourselves. Manu ended up having a better year than Pete did in '83. Not to take anything away from Pete."

All four starting defensive backs were named to the NFC squad for the Pro Bowl. Safeties Dwight Hicks and Carlton Williamson joined Lott in the starting team chosen in NFC balloting. Cornerback Eric Wright, the team's best cover man, was selected as an alternate when the Giants' Mark Haynes came down with an injury.

The secondary is intact for 1985 and it still is young, even if it seems it has been together forever. With a healthy Lott, Walsh seems to sleep better.

"When Ronnie got back into playing shape last year," Walsh said, "that made us as good a defensive team as there was in football."

SPECIAL TEAMS

No team goes 15-1 in the regular season without doing some special things on special teams.

Fred Quillan   *Manu Tuiasosopo*   *Ray Wersching*

The 49ers ranked in the league's top 10 in the four special teams categories: second in kick returns, third in punt returns, fourth in punt coverage, and ninth in kick coverage.

Punt returner Dana McLemore finished second in the NFC behind the Rams' Henry Ellard with an 11.6 average. His returns in Super Bowl XIX were a key to beating Miami. Derrick Harmon also emerged to post a healthy 27.5 kick-return average.

"Dana isn't that big, isn't that flashy, and isn't that fast," said special teams coach Fred vonAppen. "He's just one of the best return guys in the league. He handles those knuckleball punts as well as anybody. What helped us, too, particularly in coverage, was that we found five or six rookies who weren't awestruck.

If not for Minnesota's Jan Stenerud, the NFC Pro Bowl kicker might have been Ray Wersching. A relative youngster among kickers at 35, Wersching led the NFL in scoring. He was perfect on 56 extra-point tries and made 25 of 35 field-goal attempts with a career long of 53 yards.

The 49ers expected that. But they weren't sure about punter Max Runager, who had to learn to kick in Candlestick Park. Runager's 41.8 average was his career best, and his punts were returned for only a 6.3 average.

"Max is one of those guys who his teammates take to right away," said vonAppen. "He's sort of like a cheerleader out there, a real team guy."

As in every other facet of the 49ers' game in 1984, special teams provided a *lot* to cheer about. And 1985 looks no different.

VETERAN ROSTER

No.	Name	Pos.	Ht.	Wt.	NFL Exp.	Birthdate	College	Games in 1984
68	Ayers, John	G	6-5	265	9	4/14/53	West Texas State	16
76	Board, Dwaine	DE	6-5	248	6	11/29/56	North Carolina A&T	16
57	Bunz, Dan	LB	6-4	225	7	10/7/55	Long Beach State	16
95	Carter, Michael	NT	6-2	281	2	10/29/60	Southern Methodist	16
6	Cavanaugh, Matt	QB	6-2	212	8	10/27/56	Pittsburgh	8
87	Clark, Dwight	WR	6-4	215	7	1/8/57	Clemson	16
29	Clark, Mario	CB	6-2	195	10	3/29/54	Oregon	11
47	Collier, Tim	CB	6-0	176	9	5/31/54	East Texas State	0
89	Cooper, Earl	TE	6-2	227	6	9/17/57	Rice	16
33	Craig, Roger	FB	6-0	222	3	7/10/60	Nebraska	16
51	Cross, Randy	G	6-3	265	10	4/25/54	UCLA	16
74	Dean, Fred	DE	6-2	232	11	2/24/52	Louisiana Tech	5
50	Ellison, Riki	LB	6-2	220	3	8/15/60	Southern California	16
55	Fahnhorst, Jim	LB	6-4	230	2	11/8/58	Minnesota	14
71	Fahnhorst, Keith	T	6-6	273	12	2/6/52	Minnesota	15
54	Ferrari, Ron	LB	6-0	212	4	7/30/59	Illinois	11
81	Francis, Russ	TE	6-6	242	10	4/3/53	Oregon	10
86	Frank, John	TE	6-3	225	2	4/17/62	Ohio State	15
49	Fuller, Jeff	S	6-2	216	2	8/8/62	Texas A&M	13
24	Harmon, Derrick	RB	5-10	202	2	4/26/63	Cornell	16
75	Harty, John	NT	6-4	263	4	12/17/58	Iowa	0
22	Hicks, Dwight	S	6-1	192	7	4/5/56	Michigan	16
28	Holmoe, Tom	CB-S	6-2	180	3	3/7/60	Brigham Young	16
97	Johnson, Gary	NT	6-2	261	11	8/31/53	Grambling	16
94	Kelcher, Louie	NT	6-5	310	11	8/23/53	Southern Methodist	16
66	Kennedy, Allan	T	6-7	275	4	1/8/58	Washington State	15
42	Lott, Ronnie	S-CB	6-0	199	5	5/8/59	Southern California	12
53	McColl, Milt	LB	6-6	230	5	8/28/59	Stanford	16
62	McIntyre, Guy	G	6-3	271	2	2/17/61	Georgia	16
43	McLemore, Dana	KR-CB	5-10	183	4	7/1/60	Hawaii	16
32	Monroe, Carl	RB-KR	5-8	166	3	2/20/60	Utah	16
16	Montana, Joe	QB	6-2	195	7	6/11/56	Notre Dame	16
52	Montgomery, Blanchard	LB	6-2	236	3	2/17/61	UCLA	16
83	Nehemiah, Renaldo	WR	6-1	183	4	3/24/59	Maryland	16
77	Paris, William (Bubba)	T	6-6	295	3	10/6/60	Michigan	16
65	Pillers, Lawrence	NT-DE	6-4	250	10	11/4/52	Alcorn A&M	16
56	Quillan, Fred	C	6-5	266	8	1/27/56	Oregon	16
64	Reynolds, Jack	LB	6-1	232	16	11/22/47	Tennessee	15
30	Ring, Bill	RB	5-10	205	5	12/13/56	Brigham Young	16
4	Runager, Max	P	6-1	189	7	3/24/56	South Carolina	14
61	Sapolu, Jesse	G	6-4	260	2	3/10/61	Hawaii	1
90	Shell, Todd	LB	6-4	225	2	6/24/62	Brigham Young	16
67	Shields, Billy	T	6-8	279	11	8/23/53	Georgia Tech	11
88	Solomon, Freddie	WR	5-11	188	11	1/11/53	Tampa	14
72	Stover, Jeff	NT	6-5	275	4	5/22/58	Oregon	6
79	Stuckey, Jim	DE	6-4	253	6	6/21/58	Clemson	16
78	Tuiasosopo, Manu	NT	6-3	252	7	8/30/57	UCLA	16
58	Turner, Keena	LB	6-2	219	6	10/22/58	Purdue	16
26	Tyler, Wendell	RB	5-10	200	8	5/20/55	UCLA	16
99	Walter, Michael	LB	6-3	238	3	11/30/60	Oregon	16
14	Wersching, Ray	K	5-11	210	13	8/21/50	California	16
27	Williamson, Carlton	S	6-0	204	5	6/12/58	Pittsburgh	15
85	Wilson, Mike	WR	6-3	210	5	12/19/58	Washington State	13
21	Wright, Eric	CB	6-1	180	5	4/18/59	Missouri	16

Coaching Staff

Bill Walsh, head coach; **Jerry Attaway,** conditioning; **Paul Hackett,** quarterbacks, receivers; **Norb Hecker,** linebackers; **Sherman Lewis,** running backs; **Bobb McKittrick,** offensive line; **Bill McPherson,** defensive line; **Ray Rhodes,** defensive backfield; **George Siefert,** defensive coordinator; **Fred von Appen,** special teams.

1985 Schedule

Preseason

Aug. 10	at L.A. Raiders	6:00
Aug. 19	DENVER	6:00
Aug. 24	SAN DIEGO	Noon
Aug. 30	at Seattle	6:00

Regular Season

Sept. 8	at Minnesota	12:00
Sept. 15	ATLANTA	1:00
Sept. 22	at L.A. Raiders	1:00
Sept. 29	NEW ORLEANS	1:00
Oct. 6	at Atlanta	1:00
Oct. 13	CHICAGO	1:00
Oct. 20	at Detroit	1:00
Oct. 27	at L.A. Rams	1:00
Nov. 3	PHILADELPHIA	1:00
Nov. 11	at Denver (Mon.)	7:00
Nov. 17	KANSAS CITY	1:00
Nov. 25	SEATTLE (Mon.)	6:00
Dec. 1	at Washington	4:00
Dec. 9	L.A. RAMS (Mon.)	6:00
Dec. 15	at New Orleans	12:00
Dec. 22	DALLAS	1:00

1984 Results

Sept. 2	at Detroit	30-27
Sept. 10	WASHINGTON (Mon.)	37-31
Sept. 16	NEW ORLEANS	30-20
Sept. 23	at Philadelphia	21-9
Sept. 30	ATLANTA	14-5
Oct. 8	at N.Y. Giants (Mon.)	31-10
Oct. 14	PITTSBURGH	17-20
Oct. 21	at Houston	34-21
Oct. 28	at L.A. Rams	33-0
Nov. 4	CINCINNATI	23-17
Nov. 11	at Cleveland	41-7
Nov. 18	TAMPA BAY	24-17
Nov. 25	at New Orleans	35-3
Dec. 2	at Atlanta	35-17
Dec. 8	MINNESOTA (Sat.)	51-7
Dec. 14	L.A. RAMS (Fri.)	19-16
Dec. 29	N.Y. GIANTS	21-10
Jan. 6	CHICAGO	23-0
Jan. 20	Miami	38-16

1985 Draft Choices

1. Jerry Rice—16, WR, Mississippi Valley, from New England
1. Choice to New England
2. Choice to New England
3. Ricky Moore—75, RB, Alabama, from New England
3. Choice to New England
4. Choice to Buffalo
5. Bruce Collie—140, T, Texas-Arlington
6. Scott Barry—168, QB, Cal-Davis
7. Choice to San Diego
8. Choice to New England
9. Choice to San Diego
10. Choice to Seattle
11. David Wood—308, DE, Arizona
12. Donald Chumley—336, DT, Georgia

FOR THE RECORD
STATISTICAL LEADERS OF THE NFL

AFC RUSHING LEADERS, 1984

Player, Team	Att.	Yards	Avg.	Long	TD
Earnest Jackson, San Diego	296	1179	4.0	32t	8
Marcus Allen, L.A. Raiders	275	1168	4.2	52t	13
Sammy Winder, Denver	296	1153	3.9	24	4
Greg Bell, Buffalo	262	1100	4.2	85t	7
Freeman McNeil, N.Y. Jets	229	1070	4.7	53	5
Frank Pollard, Pittsburgh	213	851	4.0	52	6
Craig James, New England	160	790	4.9	73	1
Larry Moriarty, Houston	189	785	4.2	51t	6
Randy McMillan, Indianapolis	163	705	4.3	31t	5
Herman Heard, Kansas City	165	684	4.1	69t	4

NFC RUSHING LEADERS, 1984

Player, Team	Att.	Yards	Avg.	Long	TD
Eric Dickerson, L.A. Rams	379	2105	5.6	66	14
Walter Payton, Chicago	381	1684	4.4	72t	11
James Wilder, Tampa Bay	407	1544	3.8	37	13
Gerald Riggs, Atlanta	353	1486	4.2	57	13
Wendell Tyler, San Francisco	246	1262	5.1	40	7
John Riggins, Washington	327	1239	3.8	24	14
Tony Dorsett, Dallas	302	1189	3.9	31t	6
Ottis Anderson, St. Louis	289	1174	4.1	24	6
George Rogers, New Orleans	239	914	3.8	28	2
Rob Carpenter, N.Y. Giants	250	795	3.2	22	7

TOP 10 RUSHERS IN NFL HISTORY

Player	Years	Att.	Yards	Avg.	Long	TD
Walter Payton	10	3,047	13,309	4.4	76	89
Jim Brown	9	2,359	12,312	5.2	80	106
Franco Harris	13	2,949	12,120	4.1	75	91
O.J. Simpson	11	2,404	11,236	4.7	94	61
John Riggins	13	2,740	10,675	3.9	66	96
Tony Dorsett	8	2,136	9,525	4.5	99	59
Earl Campbell	7	2,029	8,764	4.3	81	73
Jim Taylor	10	1,941	8,597	4.4	84	83
Joe Perry	14	1,737	8,378	4.8	78	53
Larry Csonka	11	1,891	8,081	4.3	54	64

AFC PASSING LEADERS, 1984

Player, Team	Att.	Comp.	Pct. Comp.	Yards	TD	Pct. TD	Had Int.	Rating Points
Dan Marino, Miami	564	362	64.2	5084	48	8.5	17	108.9
Tony Eason, New England	431	259	60.1	3228	23	5.3	8	93.4
Dan Fouts, San Diego	507	317	62.5	3740	19	3.7	17	83.4
Dave Krieg, Seattle	480	276	57.5	3671	32	6.7	24	83.3
Ken Anderson, Cincinnati	275	175	63.6	2107	10	3.6	12	81.0
Bill Kenney, Kansas City	282	151	53.5	2098	15	5.3	10	80.7

	Att.	Comp.	Pct. Comp.	Yards	TD	Pct. TD	Had Int.	Rating Points
Warren Moon, Houston	450	259	57.6	3338	12	2.7	14	76.9
John Elway, Denver	380	214	56.3	2598	18	4.7	15	76.8
Mark Malone, Pittsburgh	272	147	54.0	2137	16	5.9	17	73.4
Pat Ryan, N.Y. Jets	285	156	54.7	1939	14	4.9	14	72.0

NFC PASSING LEADERS, 1984

Player, Team	Att.	Comp.	Pct. Comp.	Yards	TD	Pct. TD	Had Int.	Rating Points
Joe Montana, San Fran.	432	279	64.6	3630	28	6.5	10	102.9
Neil Lomax, St. Louis	560	345	61.6	4614	28	5.0	16	92.5
Steve Bartkowski, Atlanta	269	181	67.3	2158	11	4.1	10	89.7
Joe Theismann, Wash.	477	283	59.3	3991	24	5.0	13	86.6
Lynn Dickey, Green Bay	401	237	59.1	3195	25	6.2	19	85.6
Gary Danielson, Detroit	410	252	61.5	3076	17	4.1	15	83.1
Steve DeBerg, Tampa Bay	509	308	60.5	3554	19	3.7	18	79.3
Jeff Kemp, L.A. Rams	284	143	50.4	2021	13	4.6	7	78.7
Phil Simms, N.Y. Giants	533	286	53.7	4044	22	4.1	18	78.1
Ron Jaworski, Philadelphia	427	234	54.8	2754	16	3.7	14	73.5

TOP 10 PASSERS IN NFL HISTORY

Player	Years	Att.	Comp.	Pct. Comp.	Yards	TD	Had Int.	Rating
Joe Montana	6	2,077	1,324	63.7	15,609	106	54	92.7
Roger Staubach	11	2,958	1,685	57.0	22,700	153	109	83.4
Danny White	9	1,943	1,155	59.4	14,754	109	90	82.7
Sonny Jurgensen	18	4,262	2,433	57.1	32,224	255	189	82.6
Len Dawson	19	3,741	2,136	57.1	28,711	239	183	82.6
Ken Anderson	14	4,420	2,627	59.4	32,497	194	158	82.0
Dan Fouts	12	4,380	2,585	59.0	33,854	201	185	81.2
Bart Starr	16	3,149	1,808	57.4	24,718	152	138	80.5
Fran Tarkenton	18	6,467	3,686	57.0	47,003	342	266	80.4
Joe Theismann	11	3,301	1,877	56.9	23,432	152	122	79.0

AFC PASS RECEIVING LEADERS, 1984

Player, Team	No.	Yards	Avg.	Long	TD
Ozzie Newsome, Cleveland	89	1001	11.2	52	5
John Stallworth, Pittsburgh	80	1395	17.4	51	11
Todd Christensen, L.A. Raiders	80	1007	12.6	38	7
Steve Largent, Seattle	74	1164	15.7	65	12
Mark Clayton, Miami	73	1389	19.0	65t	18
Mark Duper, Miami	71	1306	18.4	80t	8
Steve Watson, Denver	69	1170	17.0	73	7
Tim Smith, Houston	69	1141	16.5	75t	4
Byron Franklin, Buffalo	69	862	12.5	64t	4
Mickey Shuler, New York Jets	68	782	11.5	49	6

NFC PASS RECEIVING LEADERS, 1984

Player, Team	No.	Yards	Avg.	Long	TD
Art Monk, Washington	106	1372	12.9	72	7
James Wilder, Tampa Bay	85	685	8.1	50	0
Roy Green, St. Louis	78	1555	19.9	83t	12
James Jones, Detroit	77	662	8.6	39	5
Kevin House, Tampa Bay	76	1005	13.2	55	5

Roger Craig, San Francisco	71	675	9.5	64t	3
Ottis Anderson, St. Louis	70	611	8.7	57	2
Stacey Bailey, Atlanta	67	1138	17.0	61	6
John Spagnola, Philadelphia	65	701	10.8	34	1
James Lofton, Green Bay	62	1361	22.0	79t	7

TOP 10 PASS RECEIVERS IN NFL HISTORY

Player	Years	No.	Yards	Avg.	Long	TD
Charlie Joiner	16	657	10,774	16.4	87	56
Charley Taylor	13	649	9,110	14.0	88	79
Don Maynard	15	633	11,834	18.7	87	88
Raymond Berry	13	631	9,275	14.7	70	68
Harold Carmichael	14	590	8,985	15.2	85	79
Fred Biletnikoff	14	589	8,974	15.2	82	76
Harold Jackson	16	579	10,372	17.9	79	76
Lionel Taylor	10	567	7,195	12.7	80	45
Steve Largent	9	545	8,772	16.1	74	60
Lance Alworth	11	542	10,266	18.9	85	85

AFC SCORING LEADERS, 1984

Player, Team	TD	PAT	PAT Att.	FG	FGA	TP
Gary Anderson, Pittsburgh	0	45	45	24	32	117
Norm Johnson, Seattle	0	50	51	20	24	110
Marcus Allen, L.A. Raiders	18	0	0	0	0	108
Mark Clayton, Miami	18	0	0	0	0	108
Tony Franklin, New England	0	42	42	22	28	108
Nick Lowery, Kansas City	0	35	35	23	33	104
Jim Breech, Cincinnati	0	37	37	22	31	103

NFC SCORING LEADERS, 1984

Player, Team	PAT	PAT Att.	FG	FGA	TP
Ray Wersching, San Francisco	56	56	25	35	131
Mark Moseley, Washington	48	51	24	31	120
Neil O'Donoghue, St. Louis	48	51	23	35	117
Paul McFadden, Philadelphia	26	27	30	37	116
Mike Lansford, L.A. Rams	37	38	25	33	112
Rafael Septien, Dallas	33	34	23	29	102

TOP 10 SCORERS IN NFL HISTORY

Player	Years	TD	FG	PAT	TP
George Blanda	26	9	335	943	2,002
Jan Stenerud	18	0	358	539	1,613
Jim Turner	16	1	304	521	1,439
Jim Bakken	17	0	282	534	1,380
Fred Cox	15	0	282	519	1,365
Lou Groza	17	1	234	641	1,349
Mark Moseley	14	0	266	426	1,224
Gino Cappelletti	11	42	176	350	1,130
Don Cockroft	13	0	216	432	1,080
Garo Yepremian	14	0	210	444	1,074

Cappelletti's total includes four two-point conversions.